DIVINE BABY NAMES

SELLERS
PUBLISHING

The Legendary Names of Greek and Roman Gods,
Goddesses, Demi-Gods, Demi-Goddesses,
Heroes, Heroines, Royal Personages, and
Fantastic Mythological Beings for Your Divine Baby

DIVINE BABY NAMES

ERIC GROVES

Sellers Publishing, Inc.
161 John Roberts Rd.
South Portland, Maine 04106
For ordering information:
(800) 625-3386 toll free
Visit our Web site: www.rsvp.com • E-mail: rsp@rsvp.com

President & Publisher: Ronnie Sellers
Publishing Director: Robin Haywood
Managing Editor: Mary Baldwin
Senior Editor: Megan Hiller
Assistant Production Editor: Charlotte Smith

ISBN: 13: 978-1-4162-0511-1
LOC: 2007907851

10 9 8 7 6 5 4 3 2 1

Printed and bound in China.

CONTENTS

Introduction 6

Girls' Names
Goddesses, Demi-Goddesses,
Heroines, Royal Personages, and
Fantastic Mythological Beings 9

Boys' Names
Gods, Demi-Gods, Heroes,
Royal Personages, and Fantastic
Mythological Beings 117

INTRODUCTION

*D*ivine Baby Names actually began with a boy named Mars.

First, he was quite tall for a boy of eleven, nearly six feet, much taller than the other boys in my sixth-grade class. Second, he was stocky and muscular, more like a teenager in appearance than a sixth grader, with a powerful stride and an athletic quickness that the other boys obviously envied. Third, his intense, twinkling black eyes, peering from beneath a mop of unruly black hair, alerted everyone that he was tough, savvy, and not to be trifled with.

But Mars had one little weakness.

His name. Mars.

Most of the kids at the inner-city public school in Los Angeles, where I'd worked for several years, seemed to admire Mars's unique name, especially the girls, who reminded him often that his name was "tight," a slang term meaning, excellent and beautiful.

But Mars took me aside one afternoon after class and confided that he wasn't sure he really liked his name.

"What does 'Mars' mean?" he asked. "Was it somebody famous?"

Remembering my classes in Greek and Roman literature at the California State University, Long Beach, where I'd earned my BA in English, I explained that Mars means "War," and was the Latin name for the mythic Roman god of war, a deity the Romans had adopted from the Greeks, who had named their fierce war-god Ares.

"God of war?" asked Mars, brightening. "Was he bad?"

Another slang term, meaning, fearsome. I replied, "He sure was. Mars rode a chariot pulled by meat-eating horses, and he was rarely defeated in battle because he was the father of all battles and the father of all warriors."

Mars grinned. "What did Mars do? Did people respect him?"

I nodded. "Ohhh, yes. When he rode onto the battlefield with his two generals, named Fear and Destruction, people usually ran in the opposite direction — not that I expect you to be like him!" I added. "I just want you to know that Mars was a mighty god, and you should be proud to carry such a noble name."

"Thanks, Mr. G!" Mars cried as he raced happily outside.

Our conversation, and Mars's gleeful reaction, got me to thinking: How many more kids with classic names might benefit from knowing about their namesakes — the historic pantheon of ancient Greek and Roman gods and goddesses? Furthermore, would new, prospective parents enjoy Greek and Roman names enough to name their babies after these fascinating deities of classic Western literature?

Thus was born *Divine Baby Names*. If you are a new parent, or hope to become one someday soon, *Divine Baby Names* will help you pick a timeless, sacred name for your divine baby.

As I began researching ancient source-materials for this book, I discovered that parents throughout history have named their babies after gods, goddesses, heroes, heroines, kings, queens, emperors, and empresses, for aesthetic, poetic, cultural, or spiritual reasons.

For example, consider that the ancient Romans used the name Mars, god of war, to create theophoric or godlike names such as:

> **Marcian** (A.D. 396-A.D. 457), an Emperor of the Byzantine Empire, or "Nova Roma," after Rome itself fell in A.D. 410;
>
> **Marcus Crassus** (c. 115 B.C.-53 B.C.), the Roman general who defeated the armies of the legendary rebel Spartacus; and
>
> **Martial** (A.D. 40 – c. A.D. 102), a Roman poet who wrote satirical poems questioning every aspect of Roman society.

If these divine names were good enough for Roman babies, does your divine baby deserve anything less? When it comes to the name your baby will carry for a lifetime, why not do what the Romans did, and aim for the stars? *Divine Baby Names* gives your Cupid or Minerva a name that can truly be called heavenly.

Moreover, the ancient Greeks also saw the virtue in naming their newborns after their immortal gods — for example, names based on Dio, or Zeus, King of the Olympian gods, names which included:

Diocles (2nd Century B.C.), the famed mathematician who discovered geometric principles still used today;

Diomedes (12th Century B.C.), the warrior-hero of the Trojan War, and King of Argos, a Greek city-state; and

Diores (12th Century B.C.), father of Automedon, the charioteer for Achilles, the greatest of all Greek heroes.

Your little Apollo or Athena or Perseus or Sophia needs a name worthy of his or her divine radiance, and *Divine Baby Names* will help you select a *praenomen* (first name) that properly honors your little idol.

Consider how even in modern times, mothers have continued to turn to Greek and Roman deities for inspiration in naming their godlings. For instance, the deeds of the hero Hercules (Heracles, in Greek) have inspired recent generations of mothers to name their newborns after this legendary demi-god. These herculean names include

Hercules Brabazon (1821-1906), the British artist admired by American impressionist painter John Singer Sargent;

Herculez Gomez (1982-), the Mexican-American soccer star who plays professionally for the Colorado Rapids; and

Hercules Kyvelos (1975-), the Greek-Canadian boxer who won the bronze medal at the 1995 Pan-American Games, Argentina.

If other parents have glorified their babies with the names of ancient gods and godesses, you can, too. *Divine Baby Names* will provide you with hundreds of epic names to help you worship your divine baby.

Recent studies show that today's parents are choosing baby names that distinguish their children from the rest of the crowd. Shouldn't you choose a name that just might guarantee your baby a bit of immortality? Choose the name of a classical Greek or Roman god, goddess, hero, heroine, royal personage, or mythological being for your divine baby. *Divine Baby Names* will point you in the right direction. Good luck — and may your divine baby's name live for all eternity.

Section One

An alphabetical listing of
Goddesses, Demi-Goddesses,
Heroines, Royal Personages,
and Fantastic Mythological Beings

Acantha *(uh-KAN-thuh)* The Thorny One

Acantha was a beautiful young nymph or nature goddess who lived in the woods of ancient Greece. She fell in love with Apollo, god of healing and the arts, whose golden chariot pulled the sun across the sky each day. The couple loved one another for ages, but when Acantha died — as even immortal nymphs must do when their sacred trees are cut down by mortals — Apollo transformed Acantha into the Acanthus plant, a sun-loving herb. Acantha's sister, Acanthis, grieved so terribly for her sister that the gods changed her into a flowering thistle.

Modern Example: Acantha Lang, New Orleans-born blues singer currently based in New York City.

Actaea *(AK-tee-uh, ak-TEE-uh)* The One Who Is The Seashore

Actaea was a Nereid, one of the fifty beautiful sea-nymphs who lived at the bottom of the Mediterranean Sea. Her parents were Doris, goddess of river deltas, and gentle Nereus, the fish-tailed "Old Man of the Sea," god of fishing. The Nereids often rode dolphins up to the water's surface, to help sea-farers.

Acte *(AK-tee)* The One Who Is The Meal-Hour

Acte was one of the twelve "golden-haired" Horai or Hours — the goddesses of the twelve hours of daytime. The Horai stood along the heavenly route that their father, Helios, the sun, traversed each day, with each goddess representing a different hour. The Horai helped Helios remove his shimmering crown at day's end, and turned his flaming horses out to pasture. Helios created the Horai with the help of Cronus, god of creation. The twelve Horai were Auge, The Hour of First Light; Anatolia, The Dawn; Musica, The Music Hour; Gymnastica, The Gym Hour; Nympha, The Bath Hour; Mesembria, Noon; Sponde, The Hour of Wine After Lunch; Elete, The Grinding Hour; Acte, the Meal Hour; Hesperia, The Evening; and Dysis, Sunset.

Adicia *(uh-DEE-shuh)* The Unjust One

Adicia was the goddess of universal unfairness. Her sole parent was Nyx, goddess of night. Adicia was shown on Greek vases as a savage hag with tattoos on every part of her body. Her counterpart was the beautiful Nike, goddess of victory and justice, who often choked Adicia with one hand, while using her other hand to beat Adicia down with a divine hammer.

Related Names: Adikia.

Aegina *(ee-JEEN-uh)* The One Having To Do With Goats

Aegina was a nymph or nature goddess who bore a son, Aeacus, to her lover Zeus, High King of the Greek gods. Aeacus ruled over the Greek island-kingdom of Aegina, named in his mother's honor.

Aello *(ah-YELL-oh)* The Windstorm, The Cyclone, The Whirlwind

Aello was one of the four Harpies, the monstrous winged goddesses of wind-storms. The other Harpies were Celaeno, the Black One; Ocypete, the Swift Flyer; and Podarke, the Quick-Footed. The Harpies' parents were Thaumas, god of the ocean's marvels, and Electra, a sea-nymph; and their sister was Iris, goddess of rainbows. The Harpies had women's heads, feathered bodies, and sharp talons. They were called Zeus's hounds because they seized people and carried them away forever. But the Harpies were also sometimes depicted as beautiful god-desses with soft wings.

Related Names: Aellopos, Aellopus, Nikothoe, Nicothoe.
Modern Example: Lucky Aello, a character in the computer role-playing game Baldur's Gate, cre-ated by BioWare Corporation and relesed in 1998 by Interplay Entertainment.

Aethra *(EETH-ruh)* The Clear Blue Sky

Aethra was one of the Titans, the original deities who ruled in Heaven before be-ing overthrown by Zeus and his Olympian gods. Aethra was the goddess of light and the brilliance of the sky. She was thought to be the source of all light, even of the light given off gold. Aethra's father was Uranus, the sky; and her mother was Gaia, the earth. Aethra married Hyperion, god of light, and produced several children: "Rosy-armed" Eos, goddess of the dawn; Helios, the sun; and Selene, the moon.

Related Names: Euryphaessa, Thea, Theia.

Aetna *(ET-nuh)* Mount Aetna

Aetna was the goddess of the snow-covered volcano Mount Aetna, on Sicily, an island near Italy's southern coast. Aetna's father was Uranus, god of the sky; and her mother was Gaia, goddess of the earth. When Zeus, High King of the Olympian gods, slept with Aetna, she produced the Palikoi, gods of steam geysers. Aetna occasionally hurled lava into the sky, because the giant Typhoeus struggled to free himself from his prison beneath Aetna's rocky slopes.

Related Names: Aitna.

Agatha *(AG-uh-thuh)* The One Who is Good

Agatha Tykhe was the goddess of prosperity and fortune, of individuals and of cities. Her father was Oceanus, god of the river that encircled the earth; and her mother was Tethys, a Titan goddess of the earth's sources of fresh water. Numerous ancient Greek cities erected temples to Agatha Tykhe, in hopes that she would grant protection and good luck.

Related Names: Fortuna, Tyche, Tykhe.

Modern Example: Agatha Christie (Agatha Mary Clarissa, Lady Mallowan) (1890-1976), British mystery-novel writer.

Names for Babies Destined to Become Heroes and Heroines to Kids, Teens, and the Young-at-Heart

Girls

Algeiros • Angela • Anthracia • Bia • Carya • Circe
Danae • Danais • Galatea • Larenta • Pherusa • Selene

Boys

Amor • Apollo • Aries • Arion • Balius • Centauri • Cupid
Enamerion • Icarus • Indicus • Jason • Xanthus

Agave *(ah-GAH-vay, ah-GAH-vee)* The Renowned One

Agave was a Nereid, one of the fifty beautiful sea-nymphs who lived at the bottom of the Mediterranean Sea. Her mother was Doris, goddess of river deltas, and her father was gentle Nereus, the fish-tailed "Old Man of the Sea," god of fishing. The Nereids often rode dolphins up to the water's surface, to help sea-farers.

Related Names: Agaue.
Modern Example: Agave Kruijssen (1959-), Dutch linguist and children's-book author.

Agnes *(AG-nus)* The Pure One; The Lamb

Agnes of France (1171-1204) was an empress in Byzantium. Byzantium, located on the Strait of Bosphorus in the Near East, was a Greek-speaking city-state which became the new seat of the Eastern Roman Empire, the "Nova Roma," after Rome itself was conquered and sacked in A.D. 410. Agnes was a French princess, the daughter of King Louis VII, who married Prince Alexio of Byzantium in 1180, eventually becoming Byzantine Empress after Alexio's death.

Modern Example: Agnes Gonxha Bokaxhiu (1910-1997), also known as Mother Theresa, a Catholic missionary and winner of the Nobel Peace Prize in 1979.

Aigle *(AY-glee, EE-glee)* The One Who Gleams With Sunlight

Aigle was one of the three Hesperides, the goddesses of sunsets. Their mother was Nyx, goddess of night, who created her daughters without the help of a father. The Hesperides' task was to protect the tree of golden apples, given by Hera, Queen of the Olympian gods, to Gaia, the earth. The golden apples provided the sunset's golden glow, and they were guarded by the Drakon Ladon, a dragon with a hundred heads. The demi-god Heracles killed the snake and took the apples, but Athena, goddess of wisdom, returned them. The three Hesperides were Aigle, The One Who Gleams with Radiant Sunlight; Hesperia, The Swift Evening; and Chrysothemis, The Earnest Golden One.

Related Names: Erytheia, Erytheis.
Modern Example: Aigle, the Mongolian female wrestler in the Rumble Roses video game, created by the Konami Corporation and released in 2004.

Alala *(uh-LA-luh)* The One Who Is the War-Cry

Alala, "to whom soldiers are sacrificed," personified the primal scream made by combatants during the heat of war. Alala's sole parent was Polemos, a fierce god of war.

Alcyone *(al-KEE-uh-nee)* The Kingfisher

Alcyone was one of the seven Pleiades, the nymphs (nature spirits) who shine as seven bright stars in the night sky. Their father was Atlas, one of the Titans or original deities who had once ruled in Heaven, before being overthrown by Zeus and his Olympians. The Pleiades' mother was Pleione, goddess of cattle and sheep. The gods transformed the seven nymphs into the Constellation Pleiades to protect them from a pursuing giant, Orion. The Pleiades' names are Alcyone, The Kingfisher; Celaeno, The Black One (not the same as the winged Harpy named Celaeno); Electra, The Amber One; Maia, The Nursing Mother; Merope, The One Whose Face Is Turned; Taygete, The One from Mount Taygete; and Sterope, The Brilliant Light.

Related Names: Alkyone.

Modern Example: Alcyone, the pseudonym of Indian writer and philosopher Jiddu Krishnamurti (1895-1986).

Alecto *(uh-LEK-tow)* The One Who Is Constantly Angry

Alecto was one of the three Erinyes or Furies, the fearsome goddesses who visited mortals to right wrongs and avenge deaths. The 8th Century B.C. Greek poet Hesiod called Alecto, "unceasing in anger," meaning she always stood ready to punish wrong-doers. Alecto's sister-Furies were Tisiphone and Megaera.

Related Names: Alekto, Furia.

Modern Example: Alecto Melantha Carrows, a character in the novel, Harry Potter and the Half-Blood Prince, written by British author J.K. Rowling (Joanne Rowling) (1965-).

Alethea *(uh-LEE-thee-uh)* Truthfulness; Integrity

Alethea was the goddess of truthfulness. Her parents were Zeus, High King of the gods on Mount Olympus, and Prometheus, the Titan god of craftiness, who sculpted Alethea at Zeus's command. Alethea's counterparts were Apate (Falsehood), Dolos (Untruthfulness), and Psuedologoi (Lies). Alethea lived in the forest, apart from human society, because she was saddened by the number of liars among humankind.

Related Names: Alathea, Aletheia.

Alexandra *(al-ix-AND-ruh)* She Who Fills Men with Love

Alexandra, or Cassandra, was the mortal daughter of Queen Hecuba and King Priam, rulers of the city-state of Troy, site of the Trojan War (12th Century B.C.). Apollo, god of poetry and prophecy, was so enchanted by Alexandra's beauty that he gave her the ability to foretell the future. But when Alexandra refused Apollo's love, he decreed that no one would ever believe her prophecies. Thus, near the Trojan War's conclusion, when the Greeks hid inside their gigantic Trojan Horse, Alexandra begged the Trojans not to pull the huge wooden horse into the city; but everyone thought she was insane, and wheeled the statue through the city gates. When night fell, the Greeks left the Trojan Horse, opened the gates of Troy for their waiting armies outside, and destroyed the city.

Related Names: Alexa, Cassandra.
Modern Example: Alexandra Maria Lara (Alexandra Platareanu) (1978-), Romanian-German actress.

Algeiros *(al-JEER-os)* The One Who Is a Beautiful Poplar Tree

Algeiros was one of the beautiful Dryad sisters, the nymphs or nature goddesses who danced in the forests of ancient Greece, filling the bushes and trees with beauty and life. The Dryads' mother was Oxylos, the forest-goddess whose name meant Thick Woods; and their father was Hamadryas, the personification of the oak tree. The lovely Dryads were quite numerous, and included Ampelo, Balanos, Carya, Cranea, Morea, and Ptelea.

Modern Example: Algeiros, a city in Spain.

Alice *(AL-iss)* The One Who Is Noble

Alice Parlato (1905-?) was a member of the Palaiologos family, the dynasty that had ruled the Byzantine Empire from 1259-1453. Byzantium, located on the Strait of Bosphorus in the Near East, was a Greek-speaking city-state which became the new seat of the Eastern Roman Empire, the "Nova Roma," after Rome itself was conquered and sacked in A.D. 410.

Related Names: Allison.

Althea *(al-THEE-uh)* The One Who is a Healer

Althea was a beautiful maiden destined for a tragic end. Althea's father was the god Thestius, son of Ares, god of war. Althea married King Oeneus, ruler of the Greek city-state of Calydon. The marriage produced two daughters, Deianeira and Melanippe, and a son, Meleager. Before Meleager's birth, the three goddesses called The Moirae, or Fates, foretold that Meleager would die when a hot iron was placed in Althea's fireplace. Althea kept all irons away from her fireplaces, but when Meleager murdered his uncles, Althea immediately put a hot iron in the hearth, causing Meleager to fall dead.

Related Names: Althaea.
Modern Example: Althea Gibson (1927-2003), tennis champion.

Ambrosia *(am-BRO-zhuh)* Gift of the Gods; Food of the Gods

Ambroisia was one of the Hyades, the nymphs (nature spirits) who shine as bright stars in the night sky. Their father was Atlas, one of the Titans or Elder Deities, who had once ruled Heaven, but were overthrown by Zeus and his Olympians. The Hyades' mother was Pleione, goddess of cattle and sheep. The gods transformed the Hyades into stars after their brother, Hyas, a rain-spirit, was killed by a lion. Zeus changed Hyas into the Constellation Aquarius, then changed his grieving sisters — Ambrosia, Clea, Eudora, Koronis, Phaio, Phaisyle, and Thyone — into the Constellation Hyades. The Greeks believed that the Hyades' tears brought life-giving rain to earth.

Modern Example: Ambrosia Anderson (1984-), American basketball player for the Women's National Basketball Association (WNBA).

Amelie *(ah-mel-EE)* The One Who Works Extremely Hard

Princess Amelie (Anne Louise) d'Arenberg (1789-1823) was a member of the Palaiologos family, the dynasty that had ruled the Byzantine Empire from 1259-1453. Byzantium, located on the Strait of Bosphorus in the Near East, was a

Greek-speaking city-state which became the new seat of the Eastern Roman Empire, the "Nova Roma," after Rome itself was conquered and sacked in A.D. 410.

Related Names: Emily.
Modern Example: Amelie Chabannes (1974-), French Surrealist artist based in New York City, New York.

Ampelo *(am-PAY-lo)* The One Who Is a Beautiful Grapevine

Ampelo was one of the beautiful Dryad sisters, the nymphs or nature goddesses who danced in the forests of ancient Greece, filling the bushes and trees with beauty and life. The Dryads' mother was Oxylos, the forest-goddess whose name meant Thick Woods; and their father was Hamadryas, the personification of the oak tree. The lovely Dryads were quite numerous, and included Algeiros, Balanos, Carya, Cranea, Morea, and Ptelea.

Related Names: Ampelos.
Modern Example: Ampelo Roble, a variety of red wine produced by the Bodegas J. Ramirez S.L. vintner's group.

Amphitrite *(am-FIT-truh-tee)* The Cave of the Sea

Amphitrite was a Nereid, one of the fifty beautiful sea-nymphs who lived at the bottom of the Mediterranean Sea. Her parents were Doris, goddess of river deltas, and gentle Nereus, the fish-tailed "Old Man of the Sea," god of fishing. The Nereids often rode dolphins up to the water's surface, to help sea-farers. Amphitrite is often depicted sitting in a chariot beside Poseidon, god of the sea.

Anatolia *(an-uh-TOLL-yuh)* The One Who Is The Dawn; The Rising

Anatolia was one of the twelve "golden-haired" Horai or Hours — the goddesses of the twelve hours of daytime. The Horai stood along the heavenly route that their father, Helios, the sun, traversed each day, and each goddess represented a different hour. The Horai helped Helios remove his shimmering crown at day's end, and turned his flaming horses out to pasture. Helios created the Horai with the help of Cronus, god of creation. The twelve Horai were Auge, The Hour of First Light; Anatolia, The Dawn; Musica, The Music Hour; Gymnastica, The Gym Hour; Nympha, The Bath Hour; Mesembria, Noon; Sponde, The Hour of

Wine After Lunch; Elete, The Grinding Hour; Acte, the Meal Hour; Hesperia, The Evening; and Dysis, Sunset.

Related Names: Anatole.

Andromeda *(an-DROM-uh-duh)* The Ruler of Men

Andromeda was a mortal princess of Ethiopia, Africa. Her mother was Queen Cassiopeia of Ethiopia, and her father was King Cepheus. Queen Cassiopeia once bragged that she was as beautiful as the immortal Nereids, the sea-nymph daughters of Nereus, the Titan sea-god. (The Titans had once ruled in Heaven, but were overthrown by Zeus, High King of the new Olympian gods.) Poseidon, god of the sea, was furious when he heard Cassiopeia's bragging, and attacked Ethiopia with a murderous sea-monster. A few Ethiopians managed to flee to the oracle (prophetess) in Cyrene, Greece, where they learned they would have to feed Princess Andromeda to the sea-monster. The Ethiopians promptly chained Andromeda to the coastal rocks, but the demi-god hero Perseus — who had killed the monster Medusa and cut off her head — slew the monster and married Andromeda, despite her betrothal to King Phineus of Thrace. When King Phineus confronted Perseus and demanded the return of Andromeda, Perseus showed him the hideous head of Medusa, which magically turned Phineus into stone. Andromeda and Perseus produced six sons, called the Perseides: Alcaeus, Electryon, Heleus, Mestor, Perses (patriarch of the Persians), and Sthenelus. They also had a daughter, Gorgophone. The Perseides's descendants ruled in Mycenea for centuries. When Andromeda died, Athena, goddess of wisdom, made her immortal by transforming her into the Constellation Andromeda.

Modern Example: Andromeda, the super-heroine name for Laurel Gand, a member of DC Comics' Legion of Super-Heroes.

Angela *(AN-juh-luh)* The Message; The Tidings; The Proclamation

Angela was the Greek goddess of communication, letters, and announcements. Her sole parent was Hermes, messenger of the gods. One of Angela's most important tasks was to tell the world of the glories of the divine gods who lived on Mount Olympus.

Related Names: Angelia.
Modern Example: Angela Bassett (Angela Evelyn Bassett)(1958-), actress and author.

Anna *(ANN-uh)* The Circle of the Year

Anna, or Anna Perenna, was the Roman goddess of the calendar year. Her annual celebration was held on March 15, where gifts were offered to her in hopes that she would provide humanity with a successful year. Anna was also described by the great Roman poet Virgil (70 B.C.-19 B.C.), in his epic poem *The Aeneid*, as the sister of Dido, queen of Carthage, a city-state in North Africa. When Carthage was destroyed by invaders, Anna sailed to Lavinium, where the hero Aeneas had landed after escaping the destruction of his own city of Troy. Sadly, Anna drowned in a nearby river, but was reborn as a nymph or nature goddess.

Related Names: Anna Perenna, Hannah.
Modern Example: Anna Paquin (Anna Helena Paquin) (1982-), Canadian-New Zealander actress.

Annia *(AHN-yuh, ANN-yuh)* The Supportive One

Annia (Annia Aurelia Galeria Faustina) (A.D. 147-A.D. 165) was the daughter of Faustina Minor, a Roman Empress; and Marcus Aurelius, a Roman Emperor and celebrated philosopher. Annia's sister was Lucilla, portrayed by actress Connie Nielsen in the 2000 film, *Gladiator*, directed by Ridley Scott. Annia's brother was Commodus, who became Emperor after Marcus Aurelius's death in A.D. 180. Commodus was portrayed by actor Joaquin Phoenix, in, *Gladiator*.

Modern Example: Annia Portuondo Hatch (1978-), Cuban-American gymnast.

Antheia *(an-THEE-uh, AN-thee-uh)* The Flower; The Flowery One

Antheia was one of the "fair-cheeked" Kharites, or Graces, a family of goddesses who personified joy, youth, grace, and beauty. The Kharites' father was Zeus, High King of the Olympian gods; and their mother was Eurynome, goddess of meadows and flowers. The Kharites served as ladies-in-waiting to Hera, Queen of the Olympian gods, and to Aphrodite, goddess of love. The three best-known Kharites were Charis, goddess of glory; Euphrosyne, goddess of happiness; and Thalia, goddess of celebrations.

Modern Example: Antheia, original name of the modern-day seaside resort town of Sozopol, in Bulgaria.

Antonia *(an-TONE-yuh, an-tow-NEE-uh)* From the Antonius Family

Antonia (Antonia Minor) (36 B.C.-37 A.D.) was the Greek-born niece of the Roman Emperor Augustus. Antonia's mother was Octavia Minor, and her father was the legendary Marc Antony, the Roman general. Antonia's moral purity, sense of honor, and grace were legendary, eventually earning her the title of Augusta, meaning, "The Majestic One."

Modern Example: Vice Admiral Antonia Coello Novello (1944-), American physician and the United States Surgeon General, 1990-1993.

Anthracia *(an-THRAY-shuh)* The One Who Is Burning Embers

Anthracia was was a nymph or nature goddess who personified Mount Lykaios in ancient Greece. Anthracia's parents are unknown; however, her sisters were known to be Glauce, Ide, Neda, and Theisoa. Anthracia was renowned for nursing the young god Zeus, who later became King Zeus of the Olympian gods. Anthracia was always seen with her burning torch, giving light to humankind.

Related Names: Anthrakia.

Aphrodite *(af-ro-DYE-tee)* Born of the Sea-Foam

Aphrodite, or Venus, was the goddess of love, beauty, and desire. The Greek poet Homer (8th Century B.C.) said Aphrodite's father was Zeus, High King of the gods, and her mother was Dione, a sea goddess. However, Hesiod, another 8th Century B.C. Greek poet, said that when the god Cronos hurled bits of divine flesh into the sea, the "quick-glancing" Aphrodite rose from the sea-foam. Aphrodite was married-off to a hideous husband — Hephaestus, the deformed god of volcanoes and blacksmiths, who received Aphrodite in exchange for releasing Hera, Queen of the gods, from an evil spell. Aphrodite promptly cheated on Hephaestus by sleeping with with his brother, Ares, god of war. But Helios, the sun, told Hephaestus of the tryst, and Hephaestus caught the lovers in his magic net. Sadly, Hephaestus learned that a god as ugly as he could never possess such a beautiful goddess as Aphrodite. Aphrodite's beauty actually helped start the Trojan War, in the 12th Century B.C., according to legends. When King Peleus of the Myrmidons married the nymph Thetis, he invited all the gods to his wedding except Eris, goddess of strife. Furious at being snubbed, Eris tossed a golden Apple of Discord into the party, engraved with, "Kallisti," or, "To the Most Beautiful." Aphrodite, her mother Hera, and Athena, goddess of wisdom, asked Zeus to award the apple to the most beautiful goddess among them, but Zeus wisely declined. When the goddesses asked Prince Paris of Troy to judge, he picked Aphrodite. In gratitude, Aphrodite gave Paris the most beautiful woman in the world — Helen, wife of King Menelaus of Sparta. Enraged, Menelaus and other Greek kings took their armies to Troy, and after ten years of war, destroyed the city. Aphrodite's most famous son was Eros, god of love, called Cupid by the Romans. Eros was often depicted as a winged naked baby who flew among gods and men firing his love-arrows into their hearts. Aphrodite's most famous daughter was Harmonia, goddess of harmony.

Related Names: Aphrodite Acidalia, Aphrodite Pandemos, Aphrodite Urania, Cyprogenes, Cytherea, Philommedes, Venus.

Modern Example: Aphrodite Jones, author of true-crime books.

Arai *(uh-RYE)* The Ones Who Curse and Utter Maledictions

The Arai were fierce demons in feminine form. Their sole parent may have been Nyx, the primeval goddess of night. The Arai personified curses, and they drifted up from Hades — the underworld of the dead — to condemn evildoers.

Related Names: Arae.

Modern Example: Arai Hakuseki (1657-1725), Japanese philosopher and writer.

Arce *(AR-see)* The One Who Arcs Very Swiftly

Arce was the swift, winged goddess who carried messages for the Titans, the early gods who preceded Zeus and his Olympian gods. Arce's father was Thaumas, god of the ocean's breath-taking marvels; and her mother was the sea-nymph Electra. When Zeus and his Olympians eventually overthrew the Titans, Zeus took away Arce's wings and banished her to Hades, the underworld of the dead.

Related Names: Arke.

Modern Example: Arce, a community in the Lazio area of Italy.

Aria *(AR-ee-uh)* The Air; The Melody

Aria was a beautiful mortal from Crete, an island nation in the Aegean Sea. Aria was loved by Apollo, god of prophecy and music, and produced a son, Miletos, who later ruled over a city bearing his name.

Related Names: Deione.

Modern Example: Aria Giovanni (Cindy Renee Volk) (1977-), American model and actress.

Ariadne *(air-ee-AD-nee)* The Most Holy, Sacred, Pure One

Ariadne was the beautiful princess of the Greek island of Crete. Ariadne's parents were the goddess Pasiphaë, and the mortal King Minos of Crete. Crete was infamous for its Labyrinth, a stone maze where victims from Athens and other city-states were sacrificed to the hideous Minotaur — a half human, half-bull imprisoned there. Once, while Ariadne observed some Athenian victims being hauled to the Labyrinth, she spotted the handsome hero Theseus and fell in love with him. She offered to rescue him in exchange for a promise that he would take her to Athens and marry her. He agreed, and she gave him a mystic sword to kill the Minotaur, and a ball of red wool to use in finding his way back through the Labyrinth. After Theseus killed the Minotaur and found his way out of the maze, he and Ariadne fled by sea. But when their ship put-in at the island of Naxos, Theseus and his crew abandoned Ariadne there. Dionysus, god of wine, took pity on Ariadne and married her.

Modern Example: Ariadne Daskalakis, American concert violinist.

Artemis *(AR-tuh-muss)* The High Source of Water

Artemis — also called Cynthia, and Diana — was the young, beautiful goddess of hunting. She loved to track game in the forests of ancient Greece, and delighted in her skill with her bow and arrows. An important goddess, Artemis was the daughter of Zeus, High King of the gods, and Leto, Zeus's immortal lover. Artemis's twin brother was Apollo, god of healing and the arts. Artemis was also known as the goddess of nature, harvests, and child-bearing, and she shared the title of goddess of the moon with the immortal Selene.

Artemis played a significant role in the Trojan War, a conflict between Greece and Troy that lasted ten years in the 12th Century B.C., and resulted in Troy's

Names for Babies Destined to Become Artistic Prodigies

Girls

Aria • Calliope • Clio • Dysis • Euterpe • Musica • Petra
Polyhymnia • Sophia • Terpsichore • Thalia • Urania

Boys

Apollo • Augustus • Basil • Daedalus • Horus • Leneus
Linus • Orpheus • Pan • Phaunos

destruction. According to legend, Prince Paris of Troy fell in love with Helen, queen of the Greek city-state of Sparta. When Helen escaped with Paris to Troy, Helen's husband King Menelaus and numerous other Greek kings declared war on Troy. But the Greeks could not launch their armada from the Bay of Aulis because Artemis — angry that the Greeks had killed one of her beloved wild animals — sent storms to trap the ships in the port. King Agamemnon of Mycenae solved the problem by sacrificing his own daughter Iphigenia on the altar of Artemis's temple. Artemis sent fair winds, and the Greek ships departed.

Related Names: Cynthia, Diana.

Asia *(AY-zhuh)* The One Who Is Eternal Fame

Asia, also known as Clymene, was one of the Titans, the original deities who ruled in Heaven before being overthrown by Zeus and his Olympian gods. Asia was the "light-stepping" goddess of eternal fame. Her father was Oceanus, god of the river that encircled the earth; and her mother was Tethys, goddess of springs and other water sources. Asia married the Titan god Iapetos, and produced the legendary Titan gods Atlas, Epimetheus, and Prometheus. The continent of Asia is named after this beautiful goddess.

Related Names: Clymene, Klymene.

Asteria *(uh-STARE-ee-uh)* The Fiery One; The Meteor

Asteria was a Titan, one of the original deities who ruled in Heaven before Zeus and his Olympian gods overthrew them. Asteria was the goddess of astrology, prophecy, and premonitions. Her father was Coeus, the Titan god of prophecy; and her mother was Phoebe, Titan goddess of prophecy and intelligence. Because of Asteria's beauty, Zeus, High King of the gods, desired her; but Asteria hurled herself down from the sky, to escape. She landed in the sea and transformed herself into Delos, a Greek island. There, Asteria's sister Leto, Titan goddess of maternity, gave birth to her legendary son, Apollo, Olympian god of medicine, music, and prophecy.

Related Names: Astris, Delos.

Astraea *(ASS-stree-uh, uh-STRAY-uh)* Bright Maiden of the Stars

Astraea was the "star-bright" goddess of universal fairness. Her father was Astraeus, god of astrology and the stars, and one of the Titans, the elder deities who ruled in Heaven before being overthrown by Zeus and his Olympian gods. Astraea's mother was Eurybia, a sea goddess. Astrea lived on earth during humanity's so-called Golden Age, when all men and women were virtuous. But later, when Bronze Age men conquered the earth, Astrea fled, leaving humanity in a state of injustice, chaos, and warfare. Zeus took pity on Astrea and transformed her into the Constellation Virgo.

Related Names: Astraia, Astrape, Justitia, Libra.

Athena *(uh-THEE-nuh)* Wisdom; Knowledge; Enlightenment; Virtue

Athena — also called Minerva, and Xenia — was a unique and powerful deity, the "bright-eyed" goddess of wisdom, agriculture, art, Greek cities, and women's crafts such as weaving. But when necessary, she transformed herself into a warrior goddess. For example, after the Trojan War — a ten-year conflict between the Greeks and Trojans that destroyed Troy — the Greeks defiled one of Athena's altars, angering her so deeply that she convinced Poseidon, god of the sea, to destroy most of the Greek ships as they returned home.

Athena's birth had been unique among the immortals, because she sprang fully-formed, with armor and weapons, from the forehead of her father Zeus, High King of the gods. Zeus, who loved Athena more than any of the other immortals, gave Athena a magnificent shield, decorated with the face of Medusa, a terrifying monster.

Athena's most devoted human worshippers were the Athenians, who named their city-state Athens in her honor, in gratitude for her bringing the olive tree to humankind. The Athenians built a temple to Athena called the Parthenon, which, though partially ruined, still stands in modern Athens.

Related Names: Athene, Athena Ergane, Minerva, Pallas Athena, Parthenos, Xenia.

Modern Example: Athena Chu (1971-), Chinese singer and actress.

Atlantea *(at-LAN-tee-uh)* The Shining One

Atlantea was one of the Hamadryad nymphs, the nature goddesses who lived in North Africa. Atlantea's sole parent was the Titan god Atlas, who supported the earth on his shoulders. Atlantea married King Danaus of Libya and bore him many daughters.

Related Names: Atlantia.

Atropos *(uh-TRO-pus)* The One Who Cannot Be Turned Away

Atropos, Clotho, and Lachesis were the Moirai, or Fates — the three avenging goddesses who decided what would happen in each human life. Atropos and her sister Fates gave every human, at birth, a portion of good and evil, then punished those sinners who chose evil. The Fates were depicted in Greek poetry either as hags, or as unsmiling maidens. They were described as weavers, who wove the threads of human destiny: Clotho, the Spinner, created the thread of human life; Lachesis, the Fortune Giver, determined how long each thread would be; and Atropos, the Inevitable, used her scissors to cut the thread of each life. No one could change the Fates' decisions, not even Zeus or the other immortal gods.

Auge *(AW-gee)* The One Who is the Dawn; The Hour of First Light

Auge was one of the twelve "golden-haired" Horai or Hours — the goddesses of the twelve hours of daytime. The Horai stood along the heavenly route that their father, Helios, the sun, traversed each day, and each goddess represented a different hour. The Horai helped Helios remove his shimmering crown at day's end, and turned his flaming horses out to pasture. Helios created the Horai with the help of Cronus, god of creation. The twelve Horai were Auge, The Hour of First Light; Anatolia, The Dawn; Musica, The Music Hour; Gymnastica, The Gym Hour; Nympha, The Bath Hour; Mesembria, Noon; Sponde, The Hour of Wine After Lunch; Elete, The Grinding Hour; Acte, the Meal Hour; Hesperia, The Evening; and Dysis, Sunset.

Modern Example: Auge-Saint-Médard, a municipality of the Charente region of France.

Aura *(OR-uh)* The Fresh Morning Air; The Breeze

The "swift-footed" Aura was one of the Titans, the orginal deities who ruled in Heaven before being overthrown by Zeus and his Olympian gods. Aura personified the morning breezes that follow a warm night. Aura's mother was Periboia, a nymph or nature spirit; and her father was Lelantos, god of stealth. Aura was so proud of her virginity that she rudely questioned the virginity of her friend Artemis, goddess of hunting. Artemis appealed to Nemesis, goddess of revenge, to make Aura suffer for her insults. Nemesis persuaded Dionysus, god of wine, to rape Aura. Aura, now driven insane, became a killer of gods and men.

Related Names: Aure.
Modern Example: Aura Figueiredo (Aura Da Conceicao Carvalho Figueiredo), Portuguese-Canadian actress and film producer.

Aurelia *(or-REEL-ee-uh)* The Golden One; The Lovely One

Aurelia (Aurelia Cotta) (120 B.C.-54 B.C.) was the mother of Julius Caesar, perhaps the most famous Roman Emperor in history. Aurelia's husband was the Roman Senator Gaius Julius Caesar, and together they produced two daughters, in addition to their son Julius Caesar: Julia Caesaris Major, and Julia Caesaris Minor. Aurelia was considered the model of what a Roman mother was supposed to be.

Modern Example: Aurelia Read Rogers (1834-1922), early American suffragette (an activist who demanded that women be given the right to vote).

Aurora *(uh-ROR-uh)* The Dawn

The winged, "rosy-fingered" Aurora, or Eos, was the goddess of the rising sun and the new day. Aurora's father Hyperion, god of light, was a Titan, one of the elder deities who ruled in Heaven before being overthrown by Jupiter and his Olympian gods. Aurora's mother was Terra, the earth. Aurora's home was Oceanus, the great river that encircled the earth. From Oceanus, she ascended each morning to light the world and bring the dawn. An energetic goddess, Aurora had many lovers, including the handsome giant Orion, and Tithonos, prince of the city-state of Troy. Aurora's children were the winds and breezes, named Aquilo, Favonius, Auster, and Zephyrus.

Related Names: Aurore, Eos.
Modern Example: Aurora Aragón de Quezon (1888-1949), a First Lady of the Philippines; wife of President Manuel L. Quezon.

Autonoe *(aw-TAH-no-ee)* The One Who Has Her Own Independent Mind

Autonoe was a Nereid, one of the fifty beautiful sea-nymphs who lived at the bottom of the Mediterranean Sea. Her parents were Doris, goddess of river deltas, and gentle Nereus, the fish-tailed "Old Man of the Sea," god of fish and fishing. The Nereids often rode dolphins up to the water's surface, to help sea-farers.

Modern Example: Autonoe, the sea-nymph in the 1966 opera, Die Bassarids, by German composer Hans Werner Henzel, libretto by W.H. Auden.

Autumnus *(aw-TUM-nus)* The One Who is the Autumn Season

Autumnus was the Roman name for one of the Horai, the goddesses of earth's four seasons — not to be confused with the Horai who were the goddesses of the twelve hours of daylight. The Horai were servants in the golden palace of Sol, the sun.

Related Names: Autumn.
Modern Example: Ymber Autumnus, title of a song by Norwegian band Burzum, founded in 1991 by singer-musician Varg Vikernes (1973-).

Averna *(uh-VER-nuh)* Queen of the Underworld

In ancient Roman mythology, Averna, or Persephone, was the beautiful daughter of Ceres, goddess of the harvest, and Jupiter, High King of the gods. Averna eventually became goddess of spring and Queen of Tartarus, the underworld of the dead. One day, as Averna gathered flowers, Pluto, brother to Jupiter, emerged from the underworld and — filled with lust for Averna — seized her and dragged her below. Ceres searched the earth for kidnapped Averna, then retreated to her temple in Eleusis, grief-stricken. She laid waste to the earth. No crops grew, and humanity starved.

In desperation, Jupiter sent the gods to talk to Ceres, pleading with her to spare humanity. But Ceres vowed that no crops would grow until she could see Averna again. Finally, Jupiter sent Mercury, messenger of the gods, to Tartarus with a royal command: Let Averna go. Pluto obeyed, but convinced Averna to eat a few pomegranate seeds. Once she ate the food of the dead, she was condemned to return to Tartarus for part of each year. Now, when Averna rejoins Ceres, flowers bloom. When Averna returns to Tartarus, winter covers the earth.
Related Names: Core, Cura, Kore, Persephone, Proserpine, Proserpina, Regina Erebi.

Batia *(BAH-tee-uh)* The One Who Covers

Batia was a nymph, or nature goddess. She was one of the Naiad sisters, a family of nymphs who personified the sources of fresh water on earth. Batia's sole parent was Eurotas, a river god. Batia married the mortal King Oibalos of the Greek city-state of Sparta, and had three sons, named Hippokoon, Ikarios, and Tyndareos.

Related Names: Bateia.
Modern Example: Batia Lichansky (1901-1992), Israeli sculptress.

Bella *(BELL-uh)* The Warlike One

Bella — also called Bellona, or Enyo — "robed in saffron," was the Roman name for one of the Graeae, the grey-haired sea goddesses. The Graeae's parents were Ceto, goddess of sea-monsters, and Phorcys, god of the sea. The Graeae grew so old that they had to share one eye. When the demi-god Perseus stole the eye, they recovered it in return for information on how to slay the Gorgon, Medusa. Though often depicted as elderly, the Graeae were also shown with the heads of women and the bodies of swans. The other two Graeae were named Dino, The Terrible One; and Pemphredo, The Way-Shower.

Related Names: Bellona, Enyo.
Modern Example: Bella Abzug (Bella Savitsky Abzug) (1920-1998), American feminist, social activist, and United States Representative from Manhattan, New York City, New York, from 1971-1977.

Bia *(BEE-uh)* The One Who Is a Powerful, Mighty Force

Bia was the goddess of strength and power. Her mother was Pallas, a Lybian nature goddess; and her father was Styx, the god who personified the river running through Hades, the underworld. Bia was one of the powerful spirits who flanked the throne of Zeus, King of the Olympian gods.

Related Names: Vis.
Modern Example: Bia Figueiredo (1985-), Brazilian race-car driver, and one of the world's greatest female racers.

Cacia *(KAY-shuh)* The One Who Who Disdains Morality

Cacia was a goddess who personified the secret desire to ignore the moral codes of conduct imposed by society. Cacia's sole parent was the primeval goddess of night, Nyx. Cacia preferred to call herself Happiness, while her enemies called her Vice.

Related Names: Kakia.

Calliope *(kuh-LYE-uh-pee)* She Who Has an Excellent Voice

Calliope was one of the Muses, the goddess-daughters of Zeus, High King of the gods, and of Mnemosyne, goddess of memory. The Muses brought ideas and inspiration to all artists. Calliope, considered the chief Muse, inspired princes and others to write epic poetry; Clio inspired historians; Erato inspired romantic poetry; Euterpe inspired lyric poets; Melpomene inspired tragic playwrights; Polyhymnia inspired hymn-writers; Terpsichore inspired dancers and singers; Thalia inspired comedic playwrights; and Urania inspired astronomers. Together, the Muses sang with Apollo, god of healing and the arts, about the glorious accomplishments of gods and men.

Related Names: Caliope, Callyope.

Callisto *(kuh-LIS-tow)* The Beautiful Lady of Calliste Island

Callisto was a sea nymph, or goddess of the sea, who personified the spirit of the Greek island of Calliste. Callisto's father was Triton, a merman and a powerful sea-god. Triton created his daughter Callisto by first presenting a clump of earth to the Greek hero Euphemos, who fell asleep and dreamed that the clump transformed itself into a beautiful virgin. In the dream, Euphemos made love to the virgin, and she revealed herself to be a goddess, who promised to nurture Euphemos's descendants. When Euphemos awoke, he threw the clump of earth into the sea, creating the lovely island of Calliste. Euphemos's descendants called Calliste their home for generations thereafter.

Related Names: Calliste, Kalliste.
Modern Example: Princess Callisto, a charcter in the novel, On the Seas to Troy, *by American author Caroline B. Cooney (1947-).*

Callithyia *(ku-LITH-ee-uh)* The Offering to the Gods

Callithyia, or Io, was a nymph or nature goddess, one of the Naiad sisters who personified the Argive River in Greece. Callithyia's father was Inachus, a river god; and her mother was Argia, a river nymph. Callithyia caught the eye of Zeus, High King of the gods, who made love to her. But when Zeus's wife, Hera, discovered her husband's treachery, Zeus quickly changed Callithyia into a white cow. Furious, Hera ordered the monster Argus to keep Zeus away from the cow, Callithyia, at all costs. Zeus sent the messenger of the gods, Hermes, to kill Argus, but Hera sent Callithyia on a journey across the earth. When Callithyia arrived in Egypt, Zeus changed her back into a nymph, and she bore a son, Epaphus. Callithyia's offspring eventually became the rulers of the city-states of Argos and Thebes.

Related Names: Io, Kallithyia.
Modern Example: The Villa Callithyia, a resort villa in Prines, Rethymon, Crete.

Calypso *(kuh-LIP-so)* The One Who Conceals

Calypso was a beautiful sea-nymph, or goddess of the sea, whose father was the Titan, Atlas. Calypso lived with her servants on the island of Ogygia in the Mediterranean Sea. One day, the Greek hero King Odysseus, returning home from the Trojan War, was shipwrecked on Ogygia. Calypso fell in love with Odysseus and kept him prisoner for seven years, until Zeus ordered her to release him. Odysseus made a raft and sailed home to his wife Penelope, while Calypso, deprived of her mortal lover, died — as even goddesses can do when their hearts are broken.

Related Names: Calipsa.

Modern Example: Calypso, a character in the 2007 film, Pirates of the Carribbean: At World's End, *portrayed by British actress Naomi Harris.*

Camarina *(kam-uh-REE-nuh)* From the Town of Camarina

Camarina was one of the nymphs or nature goddesses called the Oceanides, who controlled much of the world's fresh water, including all underground springs and life-giving rain. Camarina's father was Oceanos, the river that encircled the world; and her mother was Tethys, goddess of fresh-water springs. Camarina's special province was the Greek town of Camarina on the island of Sicily, off the Southern coast of Italy; specifically, she protected and replenished the town's supply of fresh water.

Related Names: Kamarina.

Camilla *(kuh-MILL-uh)* The Perfect One; The Pure One

In ancient Roman mythology, the demigoddess Queen Camilla ascended to the throne of the Volsci, an Italian tribe who intermarried with Romans and were an integral part of Roman history. Camilla's mother was Queen Casmilla, and her father was King Metabus. When Metabus was overthrown, he fled with the newborn Camilla to the Amasenus River, chased by Volscan armies. Halting at

Names for Babies Destined to Be Astronomers and Star-Gazers

Girls

Andromeda • Asteria • Astraea • Clea • Dia • Electra
Elete • Luna • Maia • Phaio • Phaisyle • Selene

Boys

Astraeas • Castor • Hesperus • Hyperion • Jupiter • Kyon • Luciferus
Olympios • Orion • Philomelus • Polydeuces • Saturn

the river, he tied Camilla to a spear, prayed to Diana, goddess of hunting, then successfully hurled the spear across the river, saving Camilla. When Camilla grew to womanhood, Diana granted her super-speed, enabling her to race across the world in moments. Camilla became one of the greatest heroines in Roman history.

Modern Example: Camilla Marie Beeput (1986-), African-British actress and singer.

Carme *(KAR-may)* The One Who Slices and Cuts

Carme was a demi-goddess — half human and half divine — who personified the bounty of the harvest, and who lived on the island of Crete. Carme's mother was the goddess Cassiopeia, and her father was Euboulos, a demi-god of farming. Carme was said to have invented the traditional Greek nets which were used in hunting.

Related Names: Karme.
Modern Example: Carme Chacón Piqueras (1971-), Spanish political leader.

Carmenta *(kar-MEN-tuh)* The One Who Is a Poem and a Song

In ancient Roman mythology, Carmenta was one of the Camenea, the goddess-protectors of earth's sources of fresh water. Carmenta's sisters were Antevorta, Egeria, and Postvorta. Carmenta was the guardian of pregnant mothers, midwives, and newborns. Carmen also created the Latin letters used by the Romans and by other cultures, including our own. Carmenta's son, the god Evander, created a code of laws for the Romans.

Modern Example: Carmenta Mitchell, American track and field star.

Carya *(KARE-ee-uh)* The One Who Is a Beautiful Nut-Bush

Carya was one of the beautiful Dryad sisters, the nymphs or nature goddesses who danced in the forests of ancient Greece, filling the bushes and trees with beauty and life. The Dryads' mother was Oxylos, the forest-goddess whose name meant Thick Woods; and their father was Hamadryas, the personification of the oak tree. The lovely Dryads were quite numerous, and included Algeiros, Ampelo, Balanos, Carya, Cranea, Morea, and Ptelea.

Related Names: Karua, Karya.

Cassandra *(kuh-SAND-ruh)* She Who Fills Men with Love

Cassandra, or Alexandra, was the mortal daughter of Queen Hecuba and King Priam, rulers of the city-state of Troy, site of the Trojan War (c. 1300 B.C.-1200 B.C.). Apollo, god of poetry and prophecy, was so enchanted by Cassandra's beauty that he gave her the ability to foretell the future. But when Cassandra refused Apollo's love, he decreed that no one would ever believe her prophecies. Thus, near the Trojan War's conclusion, when the Greeks hid inside their gigantic Trojan Horse, Cassandra begged the Trojans not to pull the huge statue into the city; but everyone thought she was insane, and wheeled the statue through the city gates. When night fell, the Greeks left the Trojan Horse, opened the gates of Troy for their waiting armies outside, and destroyed the city.

Related Names: Alexandra.

Modern Example: Cassandra Peterson (1949-), American actress and television personality best known as, "Elvira, Mistress of the Dark."

Castalia *(kuh-STAY-lee-uh)* The One Who Is Sewn Together

Castalia was the nymph or nature goddess of two springs which flowed from Greece's Mount Parnassus to the temple of Apollo in Delphi. Castalia's father was Archelous, a river god; and her mother was Cephisus, a river goddess. Castalia's springs seemed to intertwine, thus the name Castalia, meaning Sewn Together. These springs were said to flow "with waters of silver," and to give the oracle, or priestess, at Delphi her ability to foretell the future.

Related Names: Cassotis, Kastalia, Kassotis.
Modern Example: Castalia Rosalinde Campbell, British Countess, wife of Granville Leveson-Gower, 2nd Earl Granville.

Caterina *(kat-ur-EEN-uh)* The One Who Is Pure

Princess Caterina Paleologo (1760-?) of Italy was a member of the Palaiologos family, the dynasty that had ruled the Byzantine Empire from 1259-1453. Byzantium, located on the Strait of Bosphorus in the Near East, was a Greek-speaking city-state which became the new seat of the Eastern Roman Empire, the "Nova Roma," after Rome itself was conquered and sacked in A.D. 410.

Related Names: Katherine.
Modern Example: Caterina Jarboro (1903-1986), opera singer.

Celaeno *(kel-LEE-no, suh-LEE-no, kel-LAY-no)* The Black One

Celaeno was one of the Harpies, the winged goddesses of windstorms. The other Harpies were Aello, the Whirlwind; Ocypete, the Swift Flyer, and Podarke, the Quick-Footed. The Harpies' parents were Thaumas, god of the ocean's marvels, and Electra, the sea-nymph; and their sister was Iris, goddess of rainbows. The Harpies had female heads, feathered bodies, sharp claws, and were called Zeus's hounds because they seized people and carried them away forever. But the Harpies were also sometimes shown as beautiful goddesses with soft wings.

Celaeno was also the name of one of the seven Pleiades, the nymphs (nature spirits) who shine as seven bright stars in the night sky. Their father was Atlas, one of the Titans or Elder Deities, who had once ruled in Heaven, but was overthrown by Zeus and his Olympians. The Pleiades' mother was Pleione, goddess of cattle and sheep. The gods transformed the seven nymphs into the constellation Pleiades to protect them from a pursuing giant, Orion. The Pleiades' names are Alcyone, The Kingfisher; Celaeno, The Black One; Electra, The Amber One; Maia, The Nursing Mother; Merope, The One Whose Face Is Turned; Taygete, The One from Mount Taygete; and Sterope, The Brilliant Light.

Related Names: Kelaino.
Modern Example: Celeano, a village in Gagliole, Italy.

Ceto *(KEE-tow)* The Sea-Monster; The Whale; The Leviathan

The "fair-cheeked" Ceto was the Greek goddess of sea-monsters, which included whales. As the wife of the sea god Phorcys, she produced many children, notably the Graeae — three grey-haired sisters named Deino, Enyo, and Pemphredo, who all shared one eye. Ceto also had three daughters called the Gorgons — Euryale, Medusa, and Stheno. These scaly, winged horrors had sharp tusks, long tongues, and snakes for hair. Worse, they were so ugly that anyone glimpsing their faces would instantly turn to stone.

Related Names: Crataeis, Cratais, Keto, Krataiis, Lamia, Trienos.
Modern Example: Ceto Özel, Kurdish author and educator.

Chloe *(KLO-ee)* The Green One; The Blooming One; The Earth Mother; The Mother of Grain; The Lady of Giving

Chloe was the Roman name for the Greek goddess Demeter, goddess of bread, wheat, agriculture, and the harvest. (Note: Chloe was not the goddess of Indian corn or maize. Corn was completely unknown to the ancient Greeks.) Chloe's parents were Saturn and Opis, the Titans who had ruled in Heaven before being overthrown by Jupiter and his Olympian gods.

Chloe's daughter Averna was fated to become the goddess of the underworld of the dead. One day, as Averna gathered flowers, Jupiter's brother Pluto, god of the dead, emerged from the underworld, and — filled with lust for Averna — seized her, dragging her underground. Chloe searched the earth for Averna, then retreated to her temple in Eleusis, grief-stricken. She made the earth barren and unfruitful. No crops grew, and humanity began to starve to death.

In desperation, Jupiter sent the gods to Chloe, pleading with her to spare humanity. But Chloe vowed that no crops would grow until she could see Averna again. Finally, Jupiter sent Mercury, messenger of the gods, to Pluto with a royal command: Let Persephone go. Hades vowed to obey, but he first persuaded Averna to eat some pomegranate seeds. Once she ate the food of the dead, she was condemned to return to Pluto for a portion of each year. Now, when Averna rejoins Chloe, flowers bloom. When Averna returns to Pluto, winter covers the earth.

Related Names: Ceres, Demeter, Eukomos Demeter, Eustephanos Demeter, Xanthe Demeter. *Modern Example: Chloe Aridjis (1971-), Mexican-American writer and social activist.*

Chloris *(KLOR-us)* The Flower; The One Who Is Green Plants

Chloris, or Flora, was a nymph or nature goddess who nurtured the world's flowers, and was known as the "mother of flowers." Chloris's father was Oceanus, god of the river that encircled the earth; and her husband was Zephyrus, god of the west wind. He blew the seeds of countless colorful flowers across the world, filling Chloris's gardens with beautiful blooms, some of which could cure diseases or even induce pregnancy. Chloris also gave honey to humankind, by calling her honeybees to pollinate violets, clover, thyme, and other flowers and herbs. Wherever Chloris went, people could sense her presence, because of the scent of flowers in the air.

Related Names: Flora, Khloris.
Modern Example: Cloris Leachman (1926-), American actress.

Circe *(SUR-see)* The Circle; The Ring; The Falcon

The "fair-locked" Circe was a powerful enchantress who shared the magical island of Aiaia with numerous nature goddesses. Circe's father was Helios, the sun; and her mother was Perseis, a nature goddess. Circe was the mistress of witchcraft, particularly turning men into beasts. When the hero King Odysseus of Ithaca stopped at Aiaia on his way home from victory in the Trojan War, Circe changed his men into pigs. Luckily, Hemes, the messenger of the gods, helped Odysseus to break the enchantement and restore his men. Odysseus reconciled with Circe and made love to her, producing one son, Telegonos.

Related Names: Kirke.
Modern Example: Circe Luna, Mexican voice-over actress who does Spanish dubbing for films and television.

Claire *(KLAIR)* The One Who Is Bright and Clear

Claire Chapelle, a descendant of Dr. Giovanni Chapelle Paleologo (1835-1901), was a member of the Palaiologos family, the dynasty that had ruled the Byzantine Empire from 1259-1453. Byzantium, located on the Strait of Bosphorus in the Near East, was a Greek-speaking city-state which became the new seat of the Eastern Roman Empire, the "Nova Roma," after Rome itself was conquered and sacked in A.D. 410.

Modern Example: Claire Danes (Claire Catherine Danes) (1979-), American actress.

Claudia *(CLAW-dee-uh)* The Lame One

Princess Claudia Augusta (A.D. 63-AD. 63) was the daughter of Nero Claudius Caesar Augustus Germanicus, Emperor of Rome. Claudia's mother was the Empress Poppaea Sabina. The infant Claudia was sickly, and died soon after she was born. In remembrance, Nero erected a temple to Claudia, who was officially proclaimed a goddess.

Modern Example: Claudia Hernández González (1975-), Salvadoran author.

Clea *(KLEE-uh)* The Famous One; The Renowned One

Clea was one of the Hyades, the nymphs or nature spirits who shine as bright stars in the night sky. Their father was Atlas, one of the Titans or original deities, who had once ruled in Heaven, but were overthrown by Zeus and his Olympians. The Hyades' mother was Pleione, goddess of cattle and sheep. The gods transformed the Hyades into stars after their brother, Hyas, a rain-spirit, was killed by a lion. Zeus changed Hyas into the Constellation Aquarius, then changed his grieving sisters — Ambrosia, Clea, Eudora, Koronis, Phaio, Phaisyle, and Thyone — into the Constellation Hyades. The Greeks believed that the Hyades' tears brought life-giving rain to earth.

Related Names: Kleeia.
Modern Example: Clea Simon, American author and journalist.

Clementia *(kluh-MEN-shuh)* Mercy; Forgiveness

Clementia was the Roman goddess of clemency and forgiveness. Clementia was said to be an attribute of the Emperor Julius Caesar, who was also worshipped as a deity upon his death in 44 B.C. That year, Rome dedicated two great statues, one of Clementia and one of Caesar, standing close together, to emphasize Caesar's compassion.

Related Names: Eleos, Eleus.

Cleone *(klee-OWN)* The One Who Is from the City of Cleone

The "bright-belted" Cleone was a nymph or nature goddess who personified the sparkling freshwater springs of the ancient Greek city of Cleone. Cleone's father was the river god Asopos; and her mother was Metope, daughter of Ladon. Cleone was blessed by the other gods with joy and good fortune, as was the city named after her.

Related Names: Kleone.
Modern Example: The Cleone Gardens Inn, a resort located in Fort Bragg, California, USA.

Cleopatra *(klee-oh-PAT-truh)* From a Renowned, Glorious Father

Princess Cleopatra of Macedonia (c. 356 B.C.-c. 308 B.C.) was the daughter of King Phillip II, and the sister to the legendary Macedonian conqueror, Alexander the Great. In 336 B.C., while Cleopatra was celebrating her marriage to King Alexander I of Epirus, her father was killed. She and Alexander retreated to Epirus, where she bore a daughter, Cadmeia, and a son, Neoptolemus II. At the end of her life, Cleopatra was killed, as her father had been. Her funeral rites were said to have been magnificent.

Modern Example: Cleopatra Borel-Brown (1979-), shot-put champion from the Caribbean island nation of Trinidad and Tobago.

Clio *(KLEE-oh)* The One Who Celebrates

Clio was one of the Muses, the goddess-daughters of Zeus, King of the gods, and of Mnemosyne, goddess of memory. The Muses brought ideas and inspiration to all artists. Calliope, considered the chief Muse, inspired princes and others to write grand poetry; Clio inspired historians; Erato inspired romantic poetry; Euterpe inspired lyric poets; Melpomene inspired tragic playwrights; Polyhymnia inspired hymn-writers; Terpsichore inspired dancers and singers; Thalia inspired comedic playwrights; and Urania inspired astronomers. Together, the Muses sang with Apollo, god of healing and the arts, about the glorious accomplishments of gods and men.

Related Names: Cleio, Cleo.
Modern Example: Clio Shand (formerly Clio Goldsmith), French actress, and sister-in-law to British royalite Camilla Parker-Bowles.

Clotho *(KLO-tho)* The Spinner

Clotho, Atropos, and Lachesis were called Moirai, or the Fates — the three avenging goddesses who decided what would happen in each human life. Clotho and her sister Fates gave every human, at birth, a portion of good and evil, then pursued those who chose evil with a terrible vengeance, punishing the sinners. The Fates were depicted in Greek poetry either as harsh old hags, or as unsmiling maidens. They were described as weavers, who wove the threads of human destiny: Clotho, the Spinner, created the thread of human life; Lachesis, the Fortune Giver, determined how long the thread would be; and Atropos, the Inevitable, used her scissors to cut the thread of each life. No one could change the Fates' decisions, not even Zeus or the other immortal gods.

Related Names: Nona.

Clymene *(KLIM-uh-nee)* The Famous One

Clymene was a sea-nymph or goddess of the sea, the "neat-ankled" daughter of Oceanus the Titan (the Titans were older gods than the immortals on Mount Olympus). Clymene's son was Atlas, who, with the other Titans, warred against the god-king Zeus, and lost. His punishment was to hold up the earth and the sky on his back, forever.

Concordia *(kun-KOR-dee-uh)* Harmony; Peace; Concord

Concordia was the goddess of brotherhood, sisterhood, happy marriages, and harmony. Her mother was Venus, goddess of love; and her father was Mars, god of war, Venu's lover. Because of Concordia's mixed heritage — born of war and of love — she was seen as uniquely qualified to end conflicts and bring people together. Unfortunately, Concordia's personal life was not very harmonious. Venu's husband Vulcan, god of volcanoes and blacksmiths, hated the illegitimate child Concordia. When Concordia married the mortal Cadmus, ruler of the Greek city-state of Thebes, Vulcan gave Concordia an enchanted necklace which doomed her and her children to lives of misery. After a series of misfortunes, Concordia and Cadmus fled to the island of Illyria, where they were changed into dragons, then transported to the legendary Islands of the Blessed.

Related Names: Harmonia.
Modern Example: Concordia Selander (1861-1935), Swedish actress and businesswoman.

Constantina *(kon-stun-TEEN-uh)* The Constant One; The Firm One

Constantina (c. A.D. 307-354) was a princess, the daughter of Constantine I, Emperor of Byzantium. Byzantium, located on the Strait of Bosphorus in the Near East, was a Greek-speaking city-state which became the new seat of the Eastern Roman Empire, the "Nova Roma," after Rome itself was conquered and sacked in A.D. 410.

Related Names: Constantia, Constantiana.

Modern Example: Constantina Tomescu (1970-), Romanian track and field star.

Coronis *(kuh-RO-nus)* The Curvy One

Coronis was one of the Hyades, the nymphs (nature spirits) who shine as bright stars in the night sky. Their father was Atlas, one of the Titans or original deities who had once ruled in Heaven, but were overthrown by Zeus and his Olympians. The Hyades' mother was Pleione, goddess of cattle and sheep. The gods transformed the Hyades into stars after their brother, Hyas, a rain-spirit, was killed by a lion. Zeus changed Hyas into the Constellation Aquarius, then changed his grieving sisters — Ambrosia, Clea, Eudora, Coronis, Phaio, Phaisyle, and Thyone — into the Constellation Hyades. The Greeks believed that the Hyades' tears brought life-giving rain to earth.

Related Names: Koronis.

Modern Example: Coronis, home planet of the character Sailor Coronis, in the Japanese anime television series, Sailor Moon, *created by Japanese artist Naoko Takeuchi.*

Cura *(KYOOR-uh)* The One Who Is Concerned

In Roman mythology, Cura was the beautiful daughter of Ceres, goddess of the harvest, and Jupiter, High King of the Olympian gods. Cura eventually became goddess of Spring and Queen of Tartarus, the underworld of the dead. One day, as Cura gathered flowers, Pluto, brother to Jupiter, emerged from the underworld and — filled with lust for Cura — seized her and dragged her below. Ceres searched the earth for kidnapped Cura, then retreated to her temple in Eleusis, grief-stricken. She laid waste to the earth. No crops grew, and humanity starved.

In desperation, Jupiter sent the gods to Ceres, pleading with her to spare humanity. But Ceres vowed that no crops would grow until she could see Cura again. Finally, Jupiter sent Mercury, messenger of the gods, to Pluto with a royal command: Let Cura go. Pluto obeyed, but convinced Cura to eat a few pomegranate seeds. Once she ate the food of the dead, she was condemned to return to Tartarus for part of each year. Now, when Cura rejoins Ceres, flowers bloom. When Cura returns to Tartarus, winter covers the earth.

Related Names: Averna, Core, Cura, Kore, Persephone, Proserpine, Proserpina, Regina Erebi.
Modern Example: Cura Carpignano, a town in the Pavia Province of Italy.

Cynthia *(SIN-thee-uh)* The High Source of Water

Cynthia — also called Diana — was the young, beautiful goddess of hunting and game-animals. She loved to track game in the forests of ancient Greece, and delighted in her skill with her bow and arrows. An important goddess, Cynthia was the daughter of Jupiter, King of the gods, and Leto, Jupiter's immortal lover. Cynthia's twin brother was Apollo, god of healing and the arts. Cynthia was also known as the goddess of nature, harvests, and child-bearing, and she shared the title of goddess of the moon with the immortal Luna.

Cynthia played a significant role in the bloody Trojan War, a conflict between Greece and Troy that lasted ten years in the 12th Century B.C., and resulted in Troy's destruction. According to legend, Prince Paris of Troy fell in love with Helen, queen of the Greek city-state of Sparta. When Helen escaped with Paris to Troy, Helen's husband King Menelaus and numerous other Greek kings declared war on Troy. But the Greeks could not launch their huge navy from the Bay of Aulis because Cynthia — angry that the Greeks had killed one of her beloved wild animals — sent a wind to trap the ships in the port. King Agamemnon of Mycenae solved the problem by sacrificing his own daughter Iphigenia on the altar of Cynthia's temple. Cynthia sent fair winds, and the Greek ships departed.

Related Names: Artemis and Diana.
Modern Example: Cynthia McKinney (1955-), statewoman and congresswoman.

Daira *(DAIR-uh)* The Knowing One; The Teacher

Daira was a nymph or nature goddess who personified the Greek city-state of Eleusis, where a secret festival called the Eleusian Rites was held annually. Daira's sole parent was Oceanus, god of the river that encircled the earth. Daira married Hermes, messenger of the gods, and bore one son, the Greek hero Eleusis.

Related Names: Daeira.

Damona *(duh-MO-nuh)* The Sacred Calf

In the ancient Gallo-Roman religion — a meld of Greco-Roman beliefs with Gallic (French) deities — Damona was the wife of Apollo, god of prophecy. Damona was also the divine personification of the geothermal springs at Bourbonne-les-Bains in Gaul (France).

Related Names: Matuber Gini.

Danae *(duh-NAY)* The Bright Star; The Shower of Gold

The beautiful Princess Danae was descended from the legendary King Danaus of the Greek city-state of Argos. Danae's father was King Akrisios of Argos; and her mother was Queen Eurydice. After the oracle (prophetess) of the god Apollo told Akrisios that his offspring would one day slay him, Akrisios imprisoned his daughter Danae in an underground cell. But Zeus, High King of the gods of Mount Olympus, easily penetrated fair Danae's cell and seduced her by changing himself into an enchanted golden shower. Danae later bore a son, Perseus, destined to become one of Greece's greatest heroes. Akrisios, determined to get rid of Danae and Perseus, locked them in a strongbox and pushed them out to sea. They drifted to Seriphos Island, where Perseus grew to manhood, and

---

Names for Babies Destined to Become Avengers and Defenders

Girls

Alala • Alecto • Arai • Artemis • Camilla • Elissa • Halia
Helena • Lachesis • Maria • Myrina • Tisiphone

Boys

Achilles • Agamemnon • Alexander • Alexandros • Ares • Caanthus
Cadmus • Cerberus • Daemon • Granius • Mars • Tereus

Danae married Seriphos's ruler, King Polydectes. Perseus went on to perform many noble deeds, such as rescuing Princess Andromeda of Ethiopia from a vicious sea-monster. When Perseus and Danae eventually returned to Argos, Perseus assumed his rightful place as rule of Argos.

Danais *(duh-NAY-us)* The Long-Lived One

Danais was a Greek nymph or nature goddess who personified the springs of the town of Pisa in ancient Greece (different from the Pisa located in Italy). Her sole parent was the River Alpheus in the Greek province of Arcadia. The god Pelops, founder of the original Olympic Games, made love to Danais, and she bore one son, Chrysippos, whom Pelops loved more than any of his other sons.

Modern Example: Danais Wynnycko, Ukranian-Argentine vocalist in the Argentinian band, Arco Iris.

Daphne *(DAF-nee)* The Laurel Tree; The Bay Tree

Daphne was a nymph or nature goddess. Her father was Ladon, a river in the Greek province of Arcadia; and her mother was Creusa, a river-nymph. Daphne's beauty soon attracted Apollo, god of poetry and healing, who chased her constantly. In desperation, Daphne called to Gaia, the earth, for help. Gaia pitied her, and changed her into the world's first laurel tree.

Modern Example: Daphne du Maurier (1907-1989), British author.

Deino *(DAY-no, DEE-in-no, DEE-no)* The Terrible One

Deino was one of the Graeae, the grey-haired goddesses of sea-foam. The Graeae's parents were Ceto, goddess of sea-monsters, and Phorcys, god of the sea. The Graeae grew so old that they had to share one eye. The demi-god Perseus stole the eye, but returned it in exchange for information on how to slay the Gorgon, Medusa. Though often depicted as elderly, the Graeae were also shown with the heads of women and the bodies of swans. The other Graeae were named Enyo, The Warlike One; and Pemphredo, The Way-Shower.

Demeter *(DEM-it-ur, duh-MEE-tur)* The Green One; The Blooming One; The Earth Mother; The Mother of Grain; The Lady of Giving

Demeter was the goddess of bread, wheat, agriculture, and the harvest. (Note: Demeter was not the goddess of Indian corn or maize. Corn was completely unknown to the ancient Greeks.) Demeter's parents were Cronus and Rhea, the Titans who had ruled Heaven before being overthrown by Zeus and his Olympian gods.

Demeter's beautiful daughter, Persephone, was fated to become the Queen of Hades, the underworld of the dead. One day, as Persephone gathered flowers, Zeus's brother Hades, lord of the dead, emerged from the underworld, and — filled with lust for Persephone — seized her, dragging her underground. Demeter searched the earth for her kidnapped daughter Persephone, then retreated to her temple in Eleusis, grief-stricken. She made the earth barren and unfruitful. No crops grew, and humanity began to starve to death.

In desperation, Zeus sent many gods to Demeter, pleading with her to spare humanity. But Demeter vowed that no crops would grow until she could see Persephone again. Finally, Zeus sent Hermes, messenger of the gods, to Hades with a royal command: Let Persephone go. Hades vowed to obey, but he first persuaded Persephone to eat some pomegranate seeds. Once she ate the food of the dead, she was condemned to return to Hades for a portion of each year. Now, when Persephone rejoins Demeter, flowers bloom. When Persephone returns to Hades, winter covers the earth.

Related Names: Ceres, Chloe, Deo, Eukomos Demeter, Eustephanos Demeter, Xanthe Demeter.

Dia *(DEE-uh)* All Brightness

Dia, or Pandia, was the "exceedingly lovely" goddess of the Greek city-state of Nemea. Dia's father was Zeus, High King of the gods on Mount Olympus in Thessaly; and her mother was Selene, goddess of the moon. Dia's sacred grove of cypress trees, near Nemea, was a place where anyone could come seeking forgiveness for past sins; and the goddess forgave everyone.

Related Names: Pandea, Pandia.
Modern Example: Dia Frampton (1987-), American lead singer for the band Meg & Dia.

Diana *(dye-ANN-uh)* The High Source of Water

Diana — also called Artemis, and Cynthia — was the Roman name for the beautiful goddess of hunting. Diana loved to track game in the forests of ancient Greece, and delighted in her skill with her bow and arrows. An important goddess, Diana was the daughter of Jupiter, High King of the gods, and Leto, Jupiter's immortal lover. Diana's twin brother was Apollo, god of healing and the arts. Diana was also known as the goddess of nature, harvests, and child-bearing, and she shared the title of goddess of the moon with the immortal Luna.

Diana played a significant role in the bloody Trojan War, a conflict between Greece and Troy that lasted ten years in the 12th Century B.C., and resulted in Troy's destruction. According to legend, Prince Paris of Troy fell in love with Helen, queen of the Greek city-state of Sparta. When Helen escaped with Paris to Troy, Helen's husband King Menelaus and numerous other Greek kings declared war on Troy. But the Greeks could not launch their huge navy from the Bay of Aulis because Diana — angry that the Greeks had killed one of her beloved wild animals — sent a storm to trap the ships in the port. King Agamemnon of Mycenae solved the problem by sacrificing his own daughter Iphigenia on the altar of Diana's temple. Diana sent fair winds, and the Greek ships departed.

Related Names: Artemis, Cynthia.
Modern Example: Diana Vishneva (1976-), ballerina with the Russian Kirov Ballet, and the American Ballet Theatre.

Dione *(dee-ON, DYE-uh-nee)* Heavenly; Of Zeus

Dione was a Titan, one of the original deities who had ruled in Heaven before Zeus and his Olympians took power. Dione and her two sisters, Phoebe and Themis, were famous oracles, or prophetesses. Dione received worshippers in her temple in Dodona, served by her three ancient priestesses, the Peleiades (Doves). Dione's sister Phoebe held court in Delphi, and Themis presided in Dodona and Delphi. All three sisters answered questions and were renowned for predicting the future.

Dione's daughter was Aphrodite, goddess of love and beauty, fathered by Zeus himself. Dione, a loving mother, once had to console Aphrodite, who had tried to fight in the Trojan War (12th Century B.C) and had been wounded. Dione reminded Aphrodite that men and gods constantly inflict terrible injuries, which often must be borne with patience. Then she passed her hand over Aphrodite and healed her.

Related Names: Dodone.

Dirce *(DUR-see)* Of the Spring-Time

Dirce was a nymph or nature goddess who personified the springs beneath Mount Kithairon, in Greece. Dirce's sole parent was Ismenus, a river god. Dirce married King Lycos, ruler of the Greek city-state of Thebes; but the marriage ended abruptly when angry subjects tied Lycos to a raging bull, killing him. Dionysus, god of wine, took pity on Dirce and changed her into a mountain stream.

Related Names: Dirke.
Modern Example: Dirce Reis, a town in São Paulo state, Brazil.

Dolores *(duh-LOR-us)* Pain; Suffering; Distress

The Dolores — also known as the Algea by the Greeks — were the Roman enchantresses who brought destruction, misery, and pain to humanity. The sole parent of the Dolores was Eris, goddess of strife.

Related Names: Algea, Algos, Algus.
Modern Example: Dolores Hart (1938-), American actress who became a Catholic nun and eventually a Reverend Mother of the Benedictine Abbey of Regina Laudis in Bethlehem, Connecticut.

Doris *(DOR-iss)* The One Who Is a Pure Gift

Doris was a beautiful sea nymph, goddess of the river deltas where fish are plentiful. Doris's parents were Oceanus, god of the river encircling the earth; and Tethys, goddess of underground springs. Doris later married gentle Nereus, the fish-tailed "Old Man of the Sea," god of fishing. Together, Doris and Nereus had fifty beautiful daughters, the Nereids or sea-nymphs of the Mediterranean Sea. One of the Nereids was also named Doris, after her mother. The younger Doris and her forty-nine sisters lived on the sea-bottom, often riding dolphins up to the surface to help sea-farers.

Modern Example: Doris Kearns Goodwin (1943-), Pulitzer-Prize-winning American journalist, historian, and author.

Dynamene *(dye-NAM-uh-nee)* The Capable and Powerful One

Dynamene was a Nereid, one of the fifty beautiful sea nymphs who lived at the bottom of the Mediterranean Sea. Her parents were Doris, goddess of river deltas, and gentle Nereus, the fish-tailed "Old Man of the Sea," god of fish and fishing. The Nereids often rode dolphins up to the water's surface, to help sea-farers.

Dysis *(DYE-sus)* The One Who Is the Sunset

Dysis was one of the twelve "golden-haired" Horai (Hours) — the goddesses of the twelve hours of daytime. The Horai stood along the heavenly route that their father, Helios, the sun, traversed each day, and each goddess represented a different hour. The Horai helped Helios remove his shimmering crown at day's end, and turned his flaming horses out to pasture. Helios created the Horai with the help of Cronus, god of creation. The twelve Horai were Auge, The Hour of First Light; Anatolia, The Dawn; Musica, The Music Hour; Gymnastica, The Gym Hour; Nympha, The Bath Hour; Mesembria, Noon; Sponde, The Hour of Wine After Lunch; Elete, The Grinding Hour; Acte, the Meal Hour; Hesperia, The Evening; and Dysis, Sunset.

Egeria *(ee-ZHEER-ee-uh)* The One Who Sends

In ancient Roman mythology, Egeria was one of the Camenea, the goddess-protectors of earth's sources of fresh water. Egeria's sisters were Antevorta, Carmenta, and Postvorta.

Modern Example: Queen Egeria, a charcter in the 1997-2007 science-fiction television series, Stargate SG-1, created by American writers Jonathan Glassner and Brad Wright.

Eione *(ee-OWN-ee)* The Beach

Eione was a Nereid, one of the fifty beautiful sea-nymphs who lived at the bottom of the Mediterranean Sea. Her parents were Doris, goddess of river deltas, and gentle Nereus, the fish-tailed "Old Man of the Sea," god of fish and fishing. The Nereids often rode dolphins up to the water's surface, to help sea-farers.

Eirene *(eye-REEN)* Peace

Eirene was the "garland-wearing" goddess of peace. Together with Dike, goddess of justice, and Eunomia, goddess of order, Eirene formed a triad of sisters called the Horai — guardians of the gates to Heaven, and protectors of peace and justice. Eirene's father was Zeus, High King of the Greek gods on Mount Olympus; and her mother was Themis, goddess of divine law. Eirene was depicted on ancient coins as a beautiful girl, holding the cone-shaped fruit-basket called a cornucopia, as well as an olive branch, the symbol of peace. Eirene blessed those nations where justice reigned, ensuring that their fields produced abundant crops, and their women produced healthy children.

Related Names:. Irene, Pax

Modern Example: Eirene, a character portrayed by the Italian actress Chiara Mastalli (1984-), in the 2005-2007 Home Box Office (HBO) television series, Rome, *created by American writers John Milius, William J. MacDonald, and Bruno Heller.*

Electra *(uh-LEK-truh)* The Amber One

Electra was a sea nymph or goddess of the sea, daughter of Oceanus, god of the River Ocean that encircled the earth. She married Thaumas, god of the ocean's marvels, and produced Iris, goddess of rainbows. Her other children were the Harpies, the winged goddesses of windstorms. The Harpies were named Aello, The Whirlwind; Celeano, the Black One; Ocypete, the Swift Flyer; and Podarke, the Quick-Footed. The Harpies had women's heads, feathered bodies, sharp claws, and were called Zeus's hounds because they seized people and carried them off forever. But the Harpies were also sometimes shown as beautiful goddesses with soft wings.

Electra was also the name of one of the seven Pleiades, the nymphs (nature spirits) who shine as seven bright stars in the night sky. Their father was Atlas, one of the Titans, the original deities who had once ruled in Heaven but were overthrown by Zeus and his Olympians. The Pleiades' mother was Pleione, goddess of cattle and sheep. The gods transformed the seven nymphs into the constellation Pleiades to protect them from a pursuing giant, Orion. The Pleiades' names are Alcyone, The Kingfisher; Celaeno, The Black One (not the same as the winged Harpy named Celaeno); Electra, The Amber One; Maia, The Nursing Mother; Merope, The One Whose Face Is Turned; Taygete, The One from Mount Taygete; and Sterope, The Brilliant Light.

Related Names: Elektra.
Modern Example: Electra Isabel Avellan (1987-), Venuzuelan-American actress.

Elete *(ee-LEE-tee; ee-LEE-tay)* The One Who Is the Grinding-Hour

Elete was one of the twelve "golden-haired" Horai (Hours) — the goddesses of the twelve hours of daytime. The Horai stood along the heavenly route that their father, Helios, the sun, traversed each day, and each goddess represented a different hour. The Horai helped Helios remove his shimmering crown at day's end, and turned his flaming horses out to pasture. Helios created the Horai with the help of Cronus, god of creation. The twelve Horai were Auge, The Hour of First Light; Anatolia, The Dawn; Musica, The Music Hour; Gymnastica, The Gym Hour; Nympha, The Bath Hour; Mesembria, Noon; Sponde, The Hour of Wine After Lunch; Elete, The Grinding Hour; Acte, the Meal Hour; Hesperia, The Evening; and Dysis, Sunset.

Modern Example: Elete, a division of Mineral Resources International, a Utah manufacturer of electrolyte supplements for athletes.

Elisabeth *(el-EES-uh-beth)* My God Is a Sacred Promise

Empress Elisabeth of Austria (1837-1898) was a member of the Palaiologos family, the dynasty that had ruled the Byzantine Empire from 1259-1453. Byzantium, located on the Strait of Bosphorus in the Near East, was a Greek-speaking city-state which became the new seat of the Eastern Roman Empire, the "Nova Roma," after Rome itself was conquered and sacked in A.D. 410.

Related Names: Elizabeth.
Modern Example: Elisabeth Radó (1899-1986), Yugoslavian educator and vocalist.

Elissa *(uh-LISS-uh)* The Wanderer

Elissa, also called Dido, established the African city-state of Carthage (called Tunisia today) and was its original monarch. She also assisted the legendary Aeneas, who fled the destruction of Troy at the end of the Trojan War (12th Century B.C.), and eventually founded Rome. Elissa was immortalized as virtuous and honorable, in the epic poem, The Aeneid, written by the Roman poet Virgil around 29 B.C.

Modern Example: Elissa Khoury (1978-), Lebanese singer.

Enyo *(EN-yo)* The Warlike One

Enyo — also called Bella, or Bellona — "robed in saffron," was one of the Graeae, the three grey-haired goddesses of sea-foam. The Graeae's parents were Ceto, goddess of sea-monsters, and Phorcys, god of the sea. The Graeae grew so old that they had to share one eye. When the demi-god Perseus stole the eye, they recovered it in return for information on how to slay the Gorgon, Medusa. Though often depicted as elderly, the Graeae were also shown with the heads of women and the bodies of swans. The other two Graeae were named Deino, The Terrible One; and Pemphredo, The Way-Shower.

Related Names: Bella, Bellona.

Eos *(EE-ohss)* The Dawn

The winged, "rosy-fingered" Eos, or Aurora, was the goddess of the rising sun and the new day. Eos's father Hyperion, god of light, was a Titan, one of the elder deities who ruled in Heaven before being overthrown by Zeus and his Olympian gods. Aurora's mother was Gaia, the earth. Eos's home was Oceanus, the great river that encircled the earth. From Oceanus, she ascended skyward each morning to light the world and usher in the dawn. An energetic goddess, Eos had many lovers, including the handsome giant Orion, and Tithonos, prince of the city-state of Troy. Eos's children were the winds and breezes, named Boreas, Favonius, Notus, and Zephyrus.

Related Names: Aurora, Aurore.
Modern Example: Eos Chater (1976-), Welsh violinist for the Australian-British string quartet, Bond.

Erato *(air-ROT-oh)* The Beloved, Lovely One

Erato was one of the Muses, the goddess-daughters of Zeus, High King of the gods, and of Mnemosyne, goddess of memory. The Muses brought ideas and inspiration to all artists. Calliope, considered the chief Muse, inspired princes and others to write grand poetry; Clio inspired historians; Erato inspired romantic poetry; Euterpe inspired lyric poets; Melpomene inspired tragic playwrights; Polyhymnia inspired hymn-writers; Terpsichore inspired dancers and singers; Thalia inspired comedic playwrights; and Urania inspired astronomers. Together, the Muses sang with Apollo, god of healing and the arts, about the glorious accomplishments of gods and men.

In addition to the Erato who was a Muse or goddess of inspiration, another Erato was a Nereid, one of the fifty beautiful sea-nymphs who lived at the bottom of the Mediterranean Sea. Her parents were Doris, goddess of river deltas, and gentle Nereus, the fish-tailed "Old Man of the Sea," god of fishing. The Nereids often rode dolphins up to the water's surface, to help sea-farers.

Modern Example: Erato Tsouvala, modern Greek painter and art historian.

Eris *(AIR-us)* Strife; Discord

Two goddesses were named Eris: The first Eris, goddess of discord and strife, was a Titan, daughter of Cronus, the Titan god-king, and Nyx, the goddess of night. The second Eris was also a goddess of discord and strife, but was the daughter of Zeus, High King of the gods, who overthrew the old Titans and wrested control of heaven.

The first Eris encouraged healthy competition, according to Homer, the 8th Century B.C. Greek poet. But Hesiod, another 8th-Century Greek poet, spoke more harshly of Eris. Hesiod said that Eris produced a number of combative children: Algea, or agony; Amphillogiai, disputes; Androctasiai, murder; Ate, stupidity; Dysnomia, anarchy; Horkos, oaths; Hysminai, violence; Lethe, procrastination; Limos, starvation; Malchai, combat; Neikea, argumentation; Phonoi, killing; Ponos, drudgery; and Pseudea, lies.

The second Eris was cruel, fostering evil wars among men. Homer, the 8th-Century B.C. Greek poet, said that Eris always began small, then grew until she strode across the earth with her head touching the sky. Then she could hurl down bitterness on all sides, increasing men's agony.

Names for Babies Destined to Become Celebrities

Girls

Helen • Helene • Io • Isis • Justina • Lanassa • Leda
Libya • Martina • Meta • Niobe • Parea

Boys

Actor • Adonis • Bacchus • Bromios • Dionysus • Eros
Faunus • Leneus • Liber • Linus • Mark • Memnon

Eris's delight in provoking violence helped start the great Trojan War, in the 12th Century B.C. Legend says that when King Peleus of the Myrmidons married Thetis, a nymph, he invited all the gods to his wedding except Eris. Furious at being snubbed, Eris tossed a golden Apple of Discord into the party, engraved with, "Kallisti," or, "To the Most Beautiful." Aphrodite, goddess of love, her mother Hera, and Athena, goddess of wisdom, asked Zeus to award the apple to the most beautiful among them, but Zeus wisely declined. When the goddesses asked Prince Paris of Troy to judge, he picked Aphrodite. In gratitude, Aphrodite gave Paris the most beautiful woman in the world — Helen, wife of King Menelaus of Sparta. Enraged, Menelaus and other Greek kings took their armies to Troy, and after ten years of war, destroyed the city.

Ersa *(UR-suh)* The Morning Dew

Ersa was the Roman name for the goddess of the morning dew. Her father was Jupiter, King of the gods who ruled the universe from Mount Olympus in Thessaly, Greece; and her mother was Aurora, the "rosy-fingered" goddess of the dawn. Ersa's task was to nurture the plants of the world with life-giving dew.

Related Names: Herse, Pandeia.
Modern Example: Ersa, a French town in the Haute-Corse province of the island of Corsica, France.

Eucleia *(yoo-KLEE-uh)* The One Who Is Fame and Great Reputation

Eucleia was the joyful goddess of the warm glow of fame, good reputation, and renown. Eucleia's father was Hephaestus, god of volcanoes and blacksmiths; and her mother was Aglaia, the goddess of adoration. Eucleia served Aphrodite, goddess of love and beauty, as a virtuous handmaiden.

Related Names: Eukleia.

Eucrante *(yoo-KRON-tay)* Success

Eucrante was a Nereid, one of the fifty beautiful sea-nymphs who lived at the bottom of the Mediterranean Sea. Her parents were Doris, goddess of river deltas, and gentle Nereus, the fish-tailed "Old Man of the Sea," god of fishing. The Nereids often rode dolphins up to the water's surface, to help sea-farers.

Related Names: Eukrante.
Modern Example: Eucrante, the female warrior featured in Konami Toys' online game, Busou Shinki.

Eudora *(yoo-DOR-uh)* The One Who Is Well-Gifted; Good Giver

Eudora was one of the Hyades, the nymphs (nature spirits) who shine as bright stars in the night sky. Their father was Atlas, one of the Titans or original gods, who had ruled Heaven before being overthrown by Zeus and his Olympians. The Hyades' mother was Pleione, goddess of cattle and sheep. The gods transformed the Hyades into stars after their brother, Hyas, a rain-spirit, was killed by a lion. Zeus changed Hyas into the Constellation Aquarius, then changed his grieving sisters — Ambrosia, Clea, Eudora, Koronis, Phaio, Phaisyle, and Thyone — into the Constellation Hyades. The Greeks believed that the Hyades' tears brought life-giving rain to earth.

In addition, another Eudora was a Nereid, one of the fifty beautiful sea-nymphs who lived at the bottom of the Mediterranean Sea. Her parents were Doris, goddess of river deltas, and gentle Nereus, the fish-tailed "Old Man of the Sea," god of fish and fishing. The Nereids often rode dolphins up to the water's surface, to help sea-farers.

Related Names: Eudore.
Modern Example: Eudora Welty (1909-2001), American author, and winner of the 1973 Pulitzer Prize for fiction.

Eulimene *(yoo-LIM-uh-nee)* The Good Harbors

Eulimene was a Nereid, one of the fifty beautiful sea-nymphs who lived at the bottom of the Mediterranean Sea. Her parents were Doris, goddess of river deltas, and gentle Nereus, the fish-tailed "Old Man of the Sea," god of fish and fishing. The Nereids often rode dolphins up to the water's surface, to help sea-farers.

Modern Example: Eulimene, an academic journal of Greek archaeology and anthropology, published by the Mediterranean Archaeological Society, in Crete, Greece.

Eunice *(YOO-niss, YOO-nik-ee)* Great Victory

The "rosy-armed" Eunice was a Nereid, one of the fifty beautiful sea-nymphs who lived at the bottom of the Mediterranean Sea. Her parents were Doris, goddess of river deltas, and gentle Nereus, the fish-tailed "Old Man of the Sea," god of fishing. The Nereids often rode dolphins up to the water's surface, to help sea-farers.

Related Names: Eunike.

Eupheme *(yoo-FEEM-ee)* The One Who Is Extremely Well-Spoken

Eupheme was a nymph or nature goddess who personified Mount Helicon, with its clear, pure springs, in the ancient Greek province of Boiotia. Eupheme's sole parent was Termessos, god of the Termessos River. Eupheme's gleeful manner and great beauty caught the eye of the mischievous woodland god Pan, who loved her passionately. Eupheme bore a son, the forest-spirit Krotos.

Eupompe *(yoo-POM-pee)* The Good Journey

Eupompe was a Nereid, one of the fifty beautiful sea-nymphs who lived at the bottom of the Mediterranean Sea. Her parents were Doris, goddess of river deltas, and gentle Nereus, the fish-tailed "Old Man of the Sea," god of fishing. The Nereids often rode dolphins up to the water's surface, to help sea-farers.

Modern Example: Queen Eupompe, a character in the anthology, Aphrodite's Touch, *by writers Lannette Currington and Joanne Wylde.*

Eurybia *(yoo-RIB-ee-uh)* Widespread Violent Power

Eurybia was the Greek goddess of the sea's power, including hurricanes. The 8th Century B.C. Greek poet Hesiod said Eurybia had "a heart of flint," because her sea-winds caused death and destruction. Eurybia married Krios, who was a Titan — one of the original gods who ruled in Heaven before being overthrown by Zeus and his Olympians. The rising of Krios's star in the constellation Aries each December 21st marked the beginning of the New Year. Eurybia and Krios had three Titan sons: Astraeus, and god of astronomy and astrology; Pallas, god of war; and Perses, the dog-star Sirius, god of destruction. Eurybia's grandchildren were the Anemoi, gods of the winds; the Astra, gods of stars; Bia, goddess of force; Hecate, goddess of witchcraft; Kratos, god of strength; Nike, goddess of victory; Selene, goddess of the moon; and Zelos, god of rivalry.

Modern Example: Eurybia, a warlock in the role-playing game, World of Warcraft, *created by Blizzard Entertainment, first released in 1994.*

Euterpe *(yoo-TUR-pee)* The One Who Gives Pleasure and Enjoyment

Euterpe was one of the Muses, the goddess-daughters of Zeus, High King of the gods, and of Mnemosyne, goddess of memory. The Muses brought ideas and inspiration to all artists. Calliope, considered the chief Muse, inspired princes and others to write grand poetry; Clio inspired historians; Erato inspired romantic poetry; Euterpe inspired lyric poets; Melpomene inspired tragic playwrights; Polyhymnia inspired hymn-writers; Terpsichore inspired dancers and singers; Thalia inspired comedic playwrights; and Urania inspired astronomers. Together, the Muses sang with Apollo, god of healing and the arts, about the glorious accomplishments of gods and men.

Modern Example: Euterpe Boukis Dukakis, mother of former presidential candidate Michael Dukakis.

Evagora *(ay-vuh-GOR-uh)* The Great Gatherer

Evagora was a Nereid, one of the fifty beautiful sea-nymphs who lived at the bottom of the Mediterranean Sea. Her parents were Doris, goddess of river deltas, and gentle Nereus, the fish-tailed "Old Man of the Sea," god of fishing. The

Nereids often rode dolphins up to the water's surface, to help sea-farers.

Related Names: Euagore.
Modern Example: Evagora Karagiori, Cypriot jazz singer.

Evarne *(ee-VAR-nee)* Rich in Sheep

Evarne was the Roman name for Euarne, one of the fifty beautiful Greek Nereids or sea-nymphs who lived at the bottom of the Mediterranean Sea. Her parents were Doris, goddess of river deltas, and gentle Nereus, the fish-tailed "Old Man of the Sea," god of fish and fishing. The Nereids often rode dolphins up to the water's surface, to help sea-farers.

Related Names: Euarne.
Modern Example: Evarne Rees, Australian triathlete (cyclist, runner, and swimmer).

Evelyn *(EV-uh-lin)* The One Who is Desired

Evelyn Parlato, a descendant of Countess Maria Teodora Wizzini Paleologo (1696-1778), was a member of the Palaiologos family, the dynasty that had ruled the Byzantine Empire from 1259-1453. Byzantium, located on the Strait of Bosphorus in the Near East, was a Greek-speaking city-state which became the new seat of the Eastern Roman Empire, the "Nova Roma," after Rome itself was conquered and sacked in A.D. 410.

Related Names: Ava.
Modern Example: Evelyn Lau (1971-), Chinese-Canadian author and poet.

Fauna *(FAWN-uh)* All the World's Creatures

Fauna, or Bona Dea, was the Roman goddess of virgins, and female fertility. Her father was Faunus, the Greek god of shepherds. Fauna's compassion was legendary among the poor, because she healed diseases, cured infertility, and helped slaves gain their freedom.

Related Names: Bona Dea.
Modern Example: Fauna Valetta, Mexican-American singer.

Flora *(FLOR-uh)* The Flower; The One Who Is Green Plants

Flora was the Roman name for Chloris, the Greek nymph or nature goddess who nurtured the world's flowers, and was known as the "mother of flowers." Flora's sole parent was Oceanus, god of the river that encircled the earth; and her husband was Favonius, god of the west wind. He blew the seeds of countless colorful flowers across the world, filling Flora's gardens with beautiful blooms, some of which could cure diseases or even induce pregnancy. Flora also gave honey to humankind, by calling her honeybees to pollinate violets, clover, thyme, and other flowers and herbs. Wherever Flora went, people could sense her presence, because of the scent of flowers in the air.

Related Names: Chloris, Khloris.
Modern Example: Flora Disney (1868-1938), mother of Walt Disney, filmmaker and builder of the Disneyland theme parks.

Gaia *(gah-EE-uh, GEE-uh)* The Earth

The goddess Gaia, or Terra — The Earth — was "the mother of all," and one of the four original elements created when time began, the other elements being air, water, and fire. Gaia was a huge disk, encircled by the river Oceanus, covered by the dome of the sky, and supported below by the fiery underworld of Tartarus. Gaia's only parent was Chaos, the blackness that existed before time began. When Gaia slept with Uranus, The Sky, she created the original pantheon of gods called the Titans. Eventually, Gaia warred against Uranus, because he tried to prevent her from giving birth to new gods. She also fought her own son, Cronus, god of time, when he tried to prevent Gaia from creating new gods. Gaia helped Zeus — later to become High King of the new gods on Mount Olympus — in his successful war against Cronus and the Titans. But when Zeus condemned the Titans to the underworld prison of Tartarus, Gaia turned against Zeus by unleashing the Gigantes, a race of gargantuan warriors. Yet the Gigantes could not defeat Zeus and his Olympian gods, not even with the help of the fearsome monster Typheus, and Gaia lost her war against Heaven.

Related Names: Gaea, Ge, Terra, Tellus.
Modern Example: Gaia Predassi (1973-), Italian animator, artist, and director.

Galatea *(gal-uh-TEE-uh)* The One Who Is White as Milk

Galateia was a Nereid, one of the fifty beautiful sea-nymphs who lived at the bottom of the Mediterranean Sea. Her parents were Doris, goddess of river deltas, and gentle Nereus, the fish-tailed "Old Man of the Sea," god of fishing. The Nereids often rode dolphins up to the water's surface, to help sea-farers.

Related Names: Galateia.
Modern Example: Galatea Ranzi (1967-), Italian actress.

Gale *(GAIL, GAY-lee)* The One Who Is a Storm

Gale was the old witch whom Hecate, the Greek goddess of magic, changed into a weasel, because Gale had lustful appetites which she made no effort to control.

Related Names: Abigail.
Modern Example: Gale Sondergaard (1899-1985), American actress and winner of the Academy Award.

Galene *(gay-LEEN, gay-LEEN-ee)* The One Who Is Calmness Itself

Galene was a Nereid, one of the fifty beautiful sea-nymphs who lived at the bottom of the Mediterranean Sea. Her parents were Doris, goddess of river deltas, and gentle Nereus, the fish-tailed "Old Man of the Sea," god of fishing. The Nereids often rode dolphins up to the water's surface, to help sea-farers.

Related Names: Galenaie.

Glauce *(GLOSS, GLAW-kee)* The One Who Is a Mountain Spring

Glauce was a nymph or nature goddess who personified numerous mountain springs in ancient Greece. Glauce's parents are unknown; however, her sisters were known to be Anthracia, Ide, Neda, and Theisoa. Glauce was renowned for nursing the young god Zeus, who later became King Zeus of the Olympian gods.

Related Names: Glauke.
Modern Example: Glauce Cerveira, Brazilian-born painter.

Gratia *(GRAY-shuh)* The One Who Is Grace and Beauty

The Gratia were the Greek sister-goddesses who personified grace, beauty, and the love of life. They were often portrayed as lovely young ladies, dancing together in a ring. The mother of the Gratia was Eurynome, goddess of meadows; and their father was Zeus, High King of the gods of Mount Olympus.

Related Names: Charites, Grace, Graces, and Kharites.

Gymnastica *(gym-NASS — tik-uh)* The One Who Is the Gym-Hour

Gymnastica was one of the twelve "golden-haired" Horai, or Hours — the goddesses of the twelve hours of daytime. The Horai stood along the heavenly route that their father, Helios, the sun, traversed each day, and each goddess represented a different hour. The Horai helped Helios remove his shimmering crown at day's end, and turned his flaming horses out to pasture. Helios created the Horai with the help of Cronus, god of creation. The twelve Horai were Auge, The Hour of First Light; Anatolia, The Dawn; Musica, The Music Hour; Gymnastica, The Gym Hour; Nympha, The Bath Hour; Mesembria, Noon; Sponde, The Hour of Wine After Lunch; Elete, The Grinding Hour; Acte, the Meal Hour; Hesperia, The Evening; and Dysis, Sunset.

Related Names: Gymnastike.

Halia *(HAL-yuh, HAIL-yuh)* The White-Armed Goddess

Halia was a sea nymph, or goddess of the sea. She personified the island of Rhodes, in Greece. Halia's sole parent was Thalassa, a sea goddess. Halia's life initally seemed promising, because she was loved by the great Poseidon, god of the sea, and bore six sons, as well as a daughter, Rhodes. However, Halia's life ended tragically after she insulted Aphrodite, goddess of love. Aphrodite bewitched Halia's sons, and they assaulted their mother. In despair, Halia fell into the sea and vanished.

Related Names: Haley, Kapheira, Leucothea, Leukothea.

Halie *(HAY-lee, HAL-ee-uh)* Sea-Salt

The lovely Halie was a Nereid, one of the fifty beautiful sea-nymphs who lived at the bottom of the Mediterranean Sea. Her parents were Doris, goddess of river deltas, and gentle Nereus, the fish-tailed "Old Man of the Sea," god of fishing. The Nereids often rode dolphins up to the water's surface, to help sea-farers.

Related Names: Haley, Halia.

Harmonia *(har-MO-nee-uh)* Harmony

Harmonia was the goddess of brotherhood, sisterhood, happy marriages, and harmony. Her mother was Aphrodite, goddess of love; and her father was Ares, god of war, Aphrodite's lover. Because of Harmonia's mixed heritage — born of war, and of love — she was seen as uniquely qualified to end conflicts and bring people together. Unfortunately, Harmonia's personal life was not very harmonious. Aphrodite's husband Hephaestus, god of volcanoes and blacksmiths, hated the illegitimate child Harmonia. When Harmonia married the mortal Cadmus, ruler of the Greek city-state of Thebes, Hephaestus gave Harmonia an enchanted necklace which doomed her and her children to lives of misery. After a series of misfortunes, Harmonia and Cadmus fled to the island of Illyria, where they were changed into dragons, and transported to the legendary Islands of the Blessed.

Related Names: Concordia.

Harpina *(har-PEEN-uh)* The Curved Sword

Harpina was a nymph or nature goddess who personified the sources of fresh water for the Greek town of Pisa in the province of Elis. Harpina's sole parent was Asopus, a river god. Because Harpina's name means "curved sword," she was chosen by Ares, god of warfare, to be his wife. Harpina produced a son, the god Oinomaos, a cruel warrior who lined the hallways of his home with human heads.

Related Names: Harpinna.

Hecate *(heh-KAH-tee)* She Who Will Work Her Will

Hecate was the goddess of childbirth, fertility, wild places, highway crossroads, and witchcraft. She is often depicted as a three-part being — girl, woman, and elderly matron. Hecate's father was Perses, the Titan god of disorder; and her mother was Asteria, the Titan goddess of premonitions. Hesiod, the great 8th Century Greek poet, claimed that Zeus, High King of the gods, honored Hecate above all other Olympian gods. Hesiod also said that Hecate sat in judgment of kings and lawmakers, and granted or denied victory to athletes, and soldiers in battle.

Hecate was originally a mortal, a religious leader who committed suicide, and was resurrected as a goddess by Artemis, goddess of hunting. Hecate was then worshipped as the Queen of Ghosts, and statues of her were placed by city gates, in cemeteries, and over doorways, to persuade Hecate not to summon evil spirits. She was thought to protect mortals by roaming through the night carrying a flaming torch, a knife to cut umbilical cords, and keys to open mystic doors of knowledge. Two black ghost-dogs accompanied her on her nightly journeys. At highway intersections, where three roads crossed, masks of Hecate's faces were placed on poles, each facing a different way, to protect travelers.

Related Names: Antania, Chtonian, Crataeis, Enodia, Hecate, Hekate, Kaitlyn, Katherine, Kayla, Kaylee, Kleidouchos, Kurotrophos, Phosphoros, Propolos, Propylaia, Soteira, Tricephalus, Triceps, Trioditis, Trivia.

Modern Example: Hecate Taglietti, singer in the British band, Liquid Sky.

Helen *(HEL-un)* The Torch; The Light

Helen was a demi-goddess, half-human and half-divine. Her father was Zeus, High King of the Greek gods; and her mother was Leda, a beautiful Greek princess. When Helen was old enough to marry, many kings competed for Helen's hand, because of her beauty. Eventually, she married King Menelaus of Sparta. But when Prince Paris of the city-state of Troy visited Menelaus's royal court, Helen fell in love with him. Paris and Helen fled to the safety of Troy's impregnable walls. Menelaus and the Greek kings massed their navies and armies, attacking Troy and destroying it after ten years of bloody warfare. According to different legends, Helen was either killed during the siege of Troy, or returned with Menelaus to Sparta.

Related Names: Ella, Helena, Helene.
Modern Example: Helen Mirren (Ilyena Vasilevna Mironov) (1945-),British actress and Academy-Award-winner.

Helena *(HEL-uh-nuh)* The Torch; The Light

Helena of Constantinople (Flavia Iulia Helena) (c. A.D. 250-c. A.D. 330) was the mother of an Emperor, Constantine I of Byzantium. Byzantium, located on the Strait of Bosphorus in the Near East, was a Greek-speaking city-state which became the new seat of the Eastern Roman Empire, the "Nova Roma," after Rome itself was conquered and sacked in A.D. 410. Helena's husband was Constantius Chlorus, an Emperor in the old Western Roman Empire before Rome was conquered. Later, Helena gave birth to Constantine, who moved the seat of the Roman Empire to Byzantium. Because Constantine became a Christian, he officially ended the Empire's discrimination against Christians.

Related Names: Ella, Helen, Helene.
Modern Example: Helena Meireles (1924-2005), Brazilian musician and singer-songwriter.

Helene *(hel-LEEN)* The Torch; The Light

Helene was a mortal woman, and a friend of Aphrodite, goddess of love. Helene's father was a mortal, Tityrus; and her mother was an Amazon warrior-woman. Helene helped Aphrodite seduce the handsome Prince Adonis, of the island of Cyprus. Aphrodite later bore Adonis's daughter, Beroe.

Related Names: Adrasteia, Ella, Helen, Helena.
Modern Example: Helene Deutsch (1884-1982), Austrian-American psychoanalyst, and contemporary of Sigmund Freud.

Hera *(HAIR-uh)* Beautiful Eyes; Beautiful Lady

Hera, or Juno, was the "white-armed" goddess of women and marriage, and the Queen of the gods on Mount Olympus. Her mother was Rhea, Queen of the Titans or Elder Deities, and her father was Cronos, King of the Titans. Hera's husband was Zeus, King of the gods, who seized control of heaven and over-threw the Titans, making Hera the new queen. Hera was often depicted wearing golden sandals, a golden polos or crown, and holding a pomegranate, symbol of love and death, while riding in her chariot pulled by peacocks. She was also revered as a goddess of cattle, and was affectionately called "cow-eyed" by Homer, the great 8th-Century B.C. Greek poet.

Hera was the goddess of marriage — but as a wife and mother she sometimes proved a bit harsh. For example, Hera was so jealous of her husband Zeus, who created Athena, goddess of wisdom, by himself, that Hera created Hephaestus, god of volcanoes and blacksmiths, without any male help. However, when she saw how ugly Hephaestus was, she threw him from Mount Olympus, where he fell for many days until he hit Ocean, the river circling the earth. Hephaestus later got revenge by making a golden throne which magically held Hera prisoner. She might have remained there forever, but when the other gods gave Aphrodite, goddess of love, to Hephaestus for his wife, he released Hera.

Hera's tantrums were legendary, especially against her cheating husband, Zeus. Zeus betrayed Hera often, and one such affair — between Zeus and Alcmene, a mortal — produced the demigod Heracles. Hera tried to kill the infant Heracles by sending two poisonous snakes to his crib, but Heracles choked each snake and played with their bodies. Years later, Hera gave Heracles a series of

Names for Babies Destined to Become Compassionate and Charitable

Girls
Ampelo • Carme • Clementia • Eirene • Fauna • Karya • Octavia
Pandora • Panopaea • Pherusa • Proto • Thetis

Boys
Aquarius • Enamerion • Evander • Letus • Maris • Matton
Neilos • Orpheus • Philomelus • Philemon

impossible tasks, the Twelve Labors, to perform for King Eurystheus of Mycenea. Heracles completed the tasks brilliantly and became Greece's greatest hero.

Often, when Zeus cheated on Hera, the nymph Echo helped him by distracting Hera with her nonstop chatter. But when Hera learned of Echo's treachery she cursed her, so that now Echo can only repeat other people's words.

Zeus again cheated on Hera with the Titan Leto, who bore twin deities — Apollo, god of poetry, and Artemis, goddess of hunting. Furious, Hera forbade Leto from giving birth anywhere on earth, but Leto found the floating island of Delos and delivered her babies there. Afterwards, the island grew four pillars which rooted it to the earth.

Another of Zeus's affairs was with Callisto, a mortal priestess of Artemis. Zeus changed himself into Apollo and seduced Callisto, who bore the demigod Arcas. Hera, enraged, changed Callisto into a bear, which Arcas almost killed during a hunt. To protect Arcas and Callisto, Zeus changed them into the constellations Ursa Major and Ursa Minor.

Another of Zeus's affairs produced Dionysus, god of wine and drunkenness. Zeus seduced Semele, the mortal daughter of Cadmus, prince of Thebes. Hera sent Titans to murder the infant Dionysus, and they ate his body but left behind his heart. They fled as Zeus scattered the assassins with his thunderbolts. Athena saved the god's heart, and Zeus placed it in Semele's womb, where Dionysus grew and was born a second time.

Zeus almost covered-up his affair with Io, daughter of Inachus, the river-god. Zeus changed Io into a white cow to hide her from jealous Hera, but Hera saw through the ruse and demanded the cow as a gift. Hera gave the cow to Argos, the hundred-eyed giant, ordering him to keep it away from Zeus. Zeus sent his son Hermes, messenger of the gods, to kill Argos and free Io. Hermes put Argos to sleep, and when the monster closed his hundred eyes, Hermes slew him.

Hera's rages extended to a mortal priest named Tiresias, who had been magically transformed from a man to a woman, then back again. When Zeus and Hera asked him which gender enjoyed lovemaking more, Tiresias agreed with Zeus that women enjoyed it more. Hera instantly blinded Tiresias. Zeus, pitying him, gave him the power to see the future.

Hera even vented her fury during the great Trojan War in the 12th Century B.C. When Hera saw her son Ares, god of war, fighting on the Trojan side against her beloved Greeks, she encouraged King Diomedes of Argos to attack Ares. Diomedes threw his spear, and Athena guided it into Ares's body, wounding him terribly. Ares retreated to Mount Olympus, allowing Hera's champions, the Greeks, to win the battle.

Related Names: Hera Argeia, Hero, Juno.

Modern Example: Hera McLeod, contestant on the CBS televion series, Amazing Race, *created by American producers Elise Doanierei and Bertram van Munster, and which premiered in 2001.*

Hermione *(hur-MY-uh-nee)*

Hermione was a lovely mortal girl, a princess of the Greek city-state of Sparta. Her father was King Menelaus; and her mother was the beautiful Queen Helen, who eventually ran away with Prince Paris of Troy, setting in motion the ten-year-long Trojan War. Hermione was engaged to Orestes, of the royal house of Atreus; but when Menelaus arranged for her to marry Neoptolemus, the son of the hero Achilles, instead. Hermione and the abusive Neoptolemus produced one child, whom Hermione tried to kill out of hatred for her husband. She ran away with Orestes, who later killed Neoptolemus in a duel. Hermione gave Orestes one son, Tisamenus.

Modern Example: Hermione Jane Granger (1979-), character in the Harry Potter series of books.

Hesperia *(HESS-pair-ee-uh)* The Swift Evening

Hesperia was one of the three Hesperides, the goddesses of sunsets. Their mother was Nyx, goddess of night, who created her daughters without the help of a father. The Hesperides' task was to protect the tree of golden apples, given by Hera, Queen of the Olympian gods, to Gaia, the earth. The golden apples provided the sunset's golden glow, and they were guarded by the Drakon Ladon, a dragon with a hundred heads. The demi-god Heracles killed the snake and took the apples, but Athena, goddess of wisdom, returned them. The three Hesperides were Aigle, The One Who Gleams with Radiant Sunlight; Hesperia, The Swift Evening; and Chrysothemis, The Earnest Golden One.

Related Names: Asterope, Hespera, Lipara.

Modern Example: Hesperia (incorporated 1988), a city in the high-desert region of Southern California.

Hesperis *(HESS-per-us)* The One Who Is the Evening

Hesperis was one of the twelve "golden-haired" Horai, or Hours — the god-desses of the twelve hours of daytime. The Horai stood along the heavenly route that their father, Helios, the sun, traversed each day, and each goddess repre-sented a different hour. The Horai helped Helios remove his shimmering crown at day's end, and turned his flaming horses out to pasture. Helios created the Horai with the help of Cronus, god of creation. The twelve Horai were Auge, The Hour of First Light; Anatole, The Dawn; Musica, The Music Hour; Gymnastica, The Gym Hour; Nympha, The Bath Hour; Mesembria, Noon; Sponde, The Hour of Wine After Lunch; Elete, The Grinding Hour; Acte, the Meal Hour; Hesperis, The Evening; and Dysis, Sunset.

Modern Example: Hesperis McGowan, lead character in the 1923 film, Tea — With a Kick! *by American director Victor Halperin (1895-1983).*

Hestia *(HESS-tee-uh)* The Hearth; The Home

Hestia, or Vesta, was the virgin-goddess of the home, family, and the hearth (fireplace), which was the center of cooking and warmth in ancient Greek homes. Hestia's mother was Rhea, Queen of the Titans or original deities, and her father

Names for Babies Destined to Become Clean-Living Health Fanatics

Girls

Aethra • Aigle • Anatolia • Aura • Camarina
Damona • Gymnastica • Nympha

Boys

Aether • Africus • Akesis • Arno • Boreas • Elisson
Enamerion • Euphrates • Hebros • Helias • Lovas

was Cronus, King of the Titans. Hestia was worshipped at public hearths and in private homes, where people prayed to her before eating.

Cronus, the Titan King, had long feared that one of his children would overthrow him, so he ate Hestia and all her brothers and sisters, except for young Zeus — who later deposed Cronos and seized control of Heaven. Zeus and his new gods ruled on Mount Olympus, and Hestia became part of the Olympian pantheon. She promised to safeguard her virginity forever, declining advances by Apollo, god of prophecy; Poseidon, god of the sea; and Priapus, god of fertility. Hestia was later worshipped as Vesta by the Romans. Hestia's public hearth-fire in the Forum in Rome was maintained by virginal priestesses called the Vestal Virgins.

Related Names: Vesta.

Honoria *(ah-NOR-ee-uh)* The One Who is Honor

Honoria, or Justa Grata Honoria, was a sibling of Valentinian III, an Emperor of Rome. When Honoria tried to murder her brother for his weakness and cowardice, she was arrested, and arrangements were made for her to marry Senator Flavius Herculanus, a minor politician. Honoria sent a letter, and her ring to the Mongol conqueror Attila the Hun, asking him to rescue her. Atilla interpreted the letter as a marriage proposal and plundered Italian cities in the 5th Century B.C.

Related Names: Justa Grata Honoria.

Ida *(EYE-duh)* The Lady of Mount Ida

Ida was a nymph or nature goddess who personified the spirit of Mount Ida on the island of Crete. Her father was Melisseus, the Titan god of honey and bees; and her mother was Amalthea. Ida, together with her sister-nymph Adrastea, nursed the young god Zeus in one of Ida's mountain caves. Zeus's father, Cronus, had tried to kill the young god to prevent him from becoming the new ruler in Heaven. To save Zeus's life, his mother Rhea entrusted him to Ida and Adrastea for safekeeping. The nymphs fed Zeus honey-comb and the milk of the goat Amalthea. Zeus and his Olympian gods later emerged to overthrow Cronus and the rest of the Titans, the original gods. Eventually, a grateful Zeus placed

Ida and Adrastea in Heaven, as the Constellations Ursa Major and Ursa Minor.

Related Names: Idothea.

Modern Example: Ida B. Wells (1862-1931), later Ida Wells-Barnett, feminist and civil rights leader.

Ide *(IDE, EYE-dee)* The One Who Is a Mountain Spring

Ide was a nymph or nature goddess who personified numerous mountain springs in ancient Greece. Ide's parents are unknown; however, her sisters were known to be Anthracia, Glauce, Neda, and Theisoa. Ide was renowned for nursing the young god Zeus, who later became King Zeus of the Olympian gods.

Modern Example: Ide Oumarou (1937-2002), Nigerian ambassador to the United Nations from 1979-1983.

Io *(EYE-oh)* The Moon; The Offering to the Gods

Io, or Callithyia, was a nymph or nature goddess, one of the Naiad sisters who personified the Argive River in Greece. Io's father was Inachus, a river god; and her mother was Argia, a river nymph. Io caught the eye of Zeus, High King of the gods, who made love to her. But when Zeus's wife, Hera, discovered her husband's treachery, Zeus changed Io into a white cow. Furious, Hera ordered the monster Argus to keep Zeus away from the cow, Io, at all costs. Zeus sent the messenger of the gods, Hermes, to kill Argus, but Hera quickly sent Io on a journey across the world. When Io arrived in Egypt, Zeus changed her back into a nymph, and she bore a son, Epaphus. Io's offspring eventually became the rulers of the city-states of Argos and Thebes.

Related Names: Callithyia, Isis, Kallithyia.

Irene *(eye-REEN)* Peace

Irene was the "garland-wearing" goddess of peace. Together with Dike, goddess of justice, and Eunomia, goddess of order, Irene formed a triad of sisters called the Horai — guardians of the gates of Heaven, and protectors of peace and justice. They are not to be confused with the twelve golden haired Horai (the Hours). Irene's father was Zeus, High King of the Greek gods on Mount

Olympus; and her mother was Themis, goddess of divine law. Irene was depicted on ancient coins as a beautiful girl, holding the cone-shaped fruit-basket called a cornucopia, and an olive branch, the symbol of peace. Irene blessed all nations where justice reigned, ensuring that their fields produced abundant crops, and their women produced healthy children.

Related Names: Eirene, Pax.

Modern Example: Irene Saez (1961-), crowned Miss Universe in 1981, and elected the mayor of Chacao, Caracas, Venezuela, in the 1990s.

Iris *(EYE-rus)* The One Who is the Rainbow

Iris was the colorful, "swift-footed" goddess of rainbows, as well as the messenger of the immortal gods and goddesses who lived on Mount Olympus. Iris's father was Thaumas, god of the ocean's mysteries; and her mother was Electra, a sea-goddess. Iris was later closely associated with Hera, queen of the gods, and Zeus, king of the gods, as their personal envoy to humanity. Iris married Zephyrus, god of the west winds, and bore Pothos, god of desire.

Related Names: Arcus, Eiris, Iris Thaumantias.

Modern Example: Iris Murdoch (Dame Jean Iris Murdoch) (1919-1999), Irish-British author.

Isabella *(iz-uh-BEL-uh)* My God Is a Sacred Promise

Isabella Paleologo (1365-?) was — although illegitimate — a member of the Palaiologos family, the dynasty that ruled the Byzantine Empire from 1259-1453. Byzantium, located on the Strait of Bosphorus in the Near East, was a Greek-speaking city-state which became the new seat of the Eastern Roman Empire, the "Nova Roma," after Rome itself was conquered and sacked in A.D. 410.

Related Names: Isabel, Isabelle.

Modern Example: Isabella Rossellini (1952-), Italian actress, filmmaker, and model.

Isis *(EYE-sus)* The Queen on Her Throne

Isis, or Io, was a nymph or nature goddess, one of the Naiad sisters who personified the Argive River in Greece. Isis's father was Inachus, a river god; and her mother was Argia, a river nymph. Isis caught the eye of Zeus, king of the gods, who made love to her. But when Zeus's wife, Hera, discovered her husband's treachery, Zeus changed Isis into a white cow. Furious, Hera ordered the monster Argus to keep Zeus away from the cow, Isis, at all costs. Zeus sent the messenger of the gods, Hermes, to kill Argus, but Hera quickly sent Isis on a journey across the world. When Isis arrived in Egypt, Zeus changed her back into a nymph, and she bore a son, Epaphus. Isis's offspring eventually became the rulers of the city-states of Argos and Thebes.

Related Names: Callithyia, Io, Kallithyia.

Julia *(JOO-lee-uh)* The Youthful One

Princess Julia (C. 5 A.D.-43 A.D.) was a member of the royal family of Rome, the daughter of Drusus Julius Caesar, a Roman Emperor. Julia married Nero Caesar in 20 A.D., but Nero was arrested and eventually took his own life. Julia married aqain, in 33 A.D., to Gaius Blandus, Proconsul of Africa, and bore him a son and a daughter.

Modern Example: Julia Boutros (1968-), Lebanese singer-songwriter.

Juno *(JOON-oh)* Beautiful Eyes; Beautiful Lady

Juno was the Roman name for Hera, the "white-armed" goddess of women and marriage, and the Queen of the gods on Mount Olympus. Her mother was Opis, Queen of the Titans or Elder Deities, and her father was Saturn, King of the Titans. Juno's husband was Jupiter, King of the gods, who seized control of heaven and overthrew the Titans, making Juno the new queen. Juno was often depicted wearing golden sandals, a golden polos or crown, and holding a pomegranate, symbol of love and death, while riding in her chariot pulled by peacocks. She was also revered as a goddess of cattle, and was affectionately called "cow-eyed" by Homer, the great 8th-Century B.C. Greek poet.

Juno was the goddess of marriage — but as a wife and mother she sometimes proved a bit harsh. For example, Juno was so jealous of her husband Jupiter, who created Minerva, goddess of wisdom, by himself, that Juno created Vulcan, god of volcanoes and blacksmiths, without any male help. However, when she saw how ugly Hephaestus was, she threw him from Mount Olympus, where he fell for many days until he hit Oceanus, the river circling the earth. Vulcan later got revenge by making a golden throne which magically held Juno prisoner. She might have remained there forever, but when the other gods gave Venus, goddess of love, to Vulcan for his wife, he released Juno.

Juno's tantrums were legendary, especially against her cheating husband, Jupiter. Jupiter betrayed Juno often, and one such affair — between Jupiter and Alcmene, a mortal — produced the demigod Heracles. Juno tried to kill the infant Heracles by sending two poisonous snakes to his crib, but Heracles choked each snake and played with their bodies. Years later, Juno gave Heracles a series of impossible tasks, the Twelve Labors, to perform for King Eurystheus of Mycenea. Heracles completed the tasks brilliantly and became Greece's greatest hero.

Often, when Jupiter cheated on Juno, the nymph Echo helped him by distracting Juno with her nonstop chatter. But when Juno learned of Echo's treachery she cursed her, so that now Echo can only repeat other people's words.

Jupiter again cheated on Juno with the Titan Latona, who bore twin deities — Apollo, god of poetry, and Diana, goddess of hunting. Furious, Juno forbade Latona from giving birth anywhere on earth, but Latona found the floating island of Delos and delivered her babies there. Afterward, the island grew four pillars which rooted it to the earth.

Another of Jupiter's affairs was with Callisto, a mortal priestess of Diana. Jupiter changed himself into Apollo and seduced Callisto, who bore the demigod Arcas. Juno, enraged, changed Callisto into a bear, which Arcas almost killed during a hunt. To protect Arcas and Callisto, Jupiter changed them into the constellations Ursa Major and Ursa Minor.

Another of Jupiter's affairs produced Bacchus, god of wine and drunkenness. Jupiter seduced Semele, the mortal daughter of Cadmus, prince of Thebes. Juno sent Titans to murder the infant Bacchus, and they ate his body but left behind his heart. They fled as Jupiter scattered the assassins with his thunderbolts. Minerva saved the god's heart, and Jupiter placed it in Semele's womb, where Bacchus grew and was born a second time.

Jupiter almost covered-up his affair with Io, daughter of Inachus, the river-god. Jupiter changed Io into a white cow to hide her from jealous Juno, but Juno saw through the ruse and demanded the cow as a gift. Juno gave the cow to Argus, the hundred-eyed giant, ordering him to keep it away from Jupiter. Jupiter sent his son Mercury, messenger of the gods, to kill Argos and free Io. Mercury put

Argos to sleep, and when the monster closed his hundred eyes, Mercury slew him.

Juno's rages extended to a mortal priest named Tiresias, who had been magically transformed from a man to a woman, then back again. When Jupiter and Juno asked him which gender enjoyed lovemaking more, Tiresias agreed with Jupiter that women enjoyed it more. Juno instantly blinded Tiresias. Jupiter, pitying him, gave him the power to see the future.

Juno even vented her fury during the great Trojan War, in the 12th Century B.C. When Juno saw her son Mars, god of war, fighting on the Trojan side against her beloved Greeks, she encouraged King Diomedes of Argos to attack Mars. Diomedes threw his spear, and Minerva guided it into Mars's body, wounding him terribly. Mars retreated to Mount Olympus, allowing Juno's champions, the Greeks, to win the battle.

Related Names: Hera, Hera Argeia, Hero.
Modern Example: Juno Mak (1984-), Hong Kong Chinese singer and songwriter.

Justina *(jus-TEEN-uh)* The Just One; The Fair One

Justina (?-A.D. 388) was a Roman Empress, the wife of Valentinian I, a Roman Emperor in the 4th Century A.D. Justina was a Roman-Sicilian who first married a pretender to the throne, Magnentius, but later divorced him to marry the Emperor Valentinian. She produced a son, who eventually became the Roman Emperor Valentinian II.

Karme *(KAR-may)* The One Who Slices and Cuts

Karme was a demi-goddess — half human and half divine — who personified the bounty of the harvest, and who lived on the island of Crete. Karme's mother was the goddess Cassiopeia, and her father was Euboulos, a demi-god of farming. Karme was said to have invented the traditional Greek nets which were used in hunting.

Related Names: Carme.

Names for Babies Destined to Be Doctors, Nurturers, and Healers

Girls

Althea • Chloris • Dione • Ersa • Fauna • Flora • Ida
Lucina • Macaria • Maria • Panacea

Boys

Akesis • Apollo • Asclepius • Enamerion • Horus
Jason • Nysus • Prometheus • Shai

Karya *(CARRY-uh, kuh-REE-uh)* The Walnut Tree

Karya was a young girl of Laconia, the ancient Greek province where the city-state of Sparta was located. Karya's beauty caught the eye of Dionysus, god of wine. But Karya's sisters were against the match and tried to keep Dionysus at bay. Furious, the god changed them into stones. Karya soon died of a broken heart, and the gods transformed her into the world's first walnut tree.

Kore *(KOR-ee)* The Maiden

Kore, or Persephone, was the beautiful daughter of Demeter, goddess of the harvest, and Zeus, king of the gods. Kore eventually became goddess of Spring and queen of the underworld of the dead. One day, as Kore gathered flowers, Hades, brother to Zeus, King of the gods, emerged from the underworld and — filled with lust for Kore — seized her and dragged her below. Demeter searched the earth for kidnapped Kore, then retreated to her temple in Eleusis, grief-stricken. She laid waste to the earth. No crops grew, and humanity starved.

In desperation, Zeus sent his gods to Demeter, pleading with her to spare humanity. But Demeter vowed that no crops would grow until she could see Kore again. Finally, Zeus sent Hermes, messenger of the gods, to Hades with a royal command: Let Kore go. Hades obeyed, but convinced Kore to eat a few pomegranate seeds. Once she ate the food of the dead, she was condemned to return to Hades for part of each year. Now, when Kore rejoins Demeter, flowers bloom. When Kore returns to Hades, winter covers the earth.

Related Names: Core, Cory, Cura, Persephone Proserpine, Proserpina, Regina Erebi. .

Koronis *(kuh-RO-nus)* The Curvy One

Koronis was one of the Hyades, the nymphs (nature spirits) who shine as bright stars in the night sky. Their father was Atlas, one of the Titans or original deities, who had once ruled Heaven, but were overthrown by Zeus and his Olympians. The Hyades' mother was Pleione, goddess of cattle and sheep. The gods transformed the Hyades into stars after their brother, Hyas, a rain-spirit, was killed by a lion. Zeus changed Hyas into the Constellation Aquarius, then changed his grieving sisters — Ambrosia, Clea, Eudora, Koronis, Phaio, Phaisyle, and Thyone — into the Constellation Hyades. The Greeks believed that the Hyades' tears brought life-giving rain to earth.

Related Names: Coronis.

Kymo *(KEE-mo, KIM-oh)* The Waves

Kymo was a Nereid, one of the fifty beautiful sea-nymphs who lived at the bottom of the Mediterranean Sea. Her parents were Doris, goddess of river deltas, and gentle Nereus, the fish-tailed "Old Man of the Sea," god of fishing. The Nereids often rode dolphins up to the water's surface, to help sea-farers.

Related Names: Cymo.

Lachesis *(luh-KEE-sus)* The One Who Measures the Thread

Lachesis, Clotho, and Atropos, were called Moirai, or The Fates — the three avenging goddesses who decided what would happen in each human life. Clotho and her sister Fates gave every human, at birth, a portion of good and evil, then pursued those who chose evil with a terrible vengeance, punishing the sinners.

The Fates were depicted in Greek poetry either as harsh old hags, or as unsmiling maidens. They were described as weavers, who wove the threads of human destiny: Clotho, the Spinner, created the thread of human life; Lachesis, the Fortune Giver, determined how long each thread would be; and Atropos, the Inevitable, used her scissors to cut the thread of each life. No one could change the Fates' decisions, not even Zeus or the other immortal gods.

Laetitia *(luh-TISH-uh)* The One Who Is a Delight

In Roman mythology, Laetitia was the goddess of delight and happiness. Laettita, along with the other Roman gods and goddesses, would gather at the world's center, an enormous room with a thousand doorways. There, she would trade rumors with the other immortals, and Fama, goddess of rumors, would listen, disseminating each rumor across the world.

Lampetia *(lam-PEE-shuh)* The Shining

The "lovely-haired" Lampetia and her sister Phaethousa were the Neaireides, two nymphs or nature goddesses who personified the island of Trinakria, or Sicily. Lampetia's father was Helios, the sun; and her mother was Neara, a nymph on Trinakria. Lampetia guarded her father's seven flocks of sheep on the island, while her sister guarded his seven herds of cattle.

Related Names: Lampetie.

Lanassa *(luh-NOSS-uh)* The One Who Is Wool

Lanassa was the daughter of Cleodaeus, a descendant of the legendary Greek hero Heracles (Hercules). Lanassa married Neoptolemus, son of the Greek hero Achilles, and bore him a son, Pyrrhus.

Lara *(LAR-uh)* The One Who Is a Laurel Tree

The Roman poet Ovid (Publius Ovidius Naso) (43 B.C.-A.D. 17), in his poem the *Fasti*, told the bittersweet story of the nymph or nature goddess Lara, sister of Juturna, goddess of fountains. When Lara heard the prnouncements of Jupiter,

High King of the gods on Mount Olympus, that Juturna should surrender to Jupiter's burning passion for her, Lara sped to Juturna and warned her to flee at once. Then Lara flew to Juno, Jupiter's wife, and told her that her husband was in love with Juturna. When Jupiter learned of Lara's tattling, her removed her tongue. Lara was thereafter known as Muta, "The Mute," and Dea Tacita, "The Silent Goddess." Jupiter orderd Mercury, messenger of the gods, to imprison Lara in Tartarus, the underworld of the dead. But before Mercury could complete his task, he fell under Lara's sway and slept with her. Later, Lara produced two sons, the Lares, the twin gods who guarded Rome's crossroads.

Related Names: Dea Tacita, Lala, Larentina, Muta.

Modern Example: Lara Dutta (1978-), United Nations Population Fund (UNPF) Goodwill Ambassador from India.

Larenta *(luh-REN-tuh)* The Earth Goddess

The Roman poet Ovid (Publius Ovidius Naso) (43 B.C.-A.D. 17), in his poem the *Fasti*, told of Larenta, wife of the shepherd Faustulus. Faustulus discovered the twin infants Romulus and Remus, the demi-god sons of Mars, god of war, in a nearby forest, being suckled by the she-wolf Lupa. The twins had been abandoned by Amulius, the vengeful father of Silvia, a virgin whom Mars had seduced against her will. Faustulus immediately brought the newborns home to his wife Larenta, who nursed them to young manhood. Romulus and Remus later founded the "Eternal City" of Rome, whose armies would one day conquer much of the world. To honor Larenta, the Romans celebrated the joyous festival of the Larentalia every December.

Related Names: Acca Larenta, Acca Larentia, Larentia, Laurentia.

Larentina *(lar-un-TEEN-uh)* The Little Earth Goddess

In ancient Roman mythology, Larentina was a nymph. Once, Larentina gossiped about Jupiter, High King of the immortals who ruled the universe from Mount Olympus in Thessaly, Greece. Enraged, Jupiter ripped out Larentina's tongue, and she became known thereafter as Muta, "The Quiet One," and Dea Tacita, "The Silent Goddess."

Related Names: Dea Tacita, Muta.

Larina *(luh-REEN-uh)* The Sea-Gull

Larina was the bodyguard of Princess Camilla, daughter of Queen Casmilla and King Metabus, rulers of the Italian tribe of the Volscians.

Modern Example: Larina Adamson, American film and television producer.

Larissa *(luh-RISS-uh)* The Cheerful One

Larissa was a mortal Princess of Argos, a Greek city-state. Larissa was loved by Poseidon, god of the sea, and gave him three sons: Akhaios, later to become King of Akhaia and Sikyonia; Pelasgos, who would become King of Arcadia; and Pythios, destined to become King of Phthiotis.

Modern Example: Larissa França (1982-), Brazilian beach-volleyball champion.

Laurine *(lor-EEN)* The Laurel Tree

Laurine was a Princess, the daughter of Latinus, King of the Latins, an ancient Italian tribe. Laurine married Locrus, Prince of the Greek city-state of Phaeacia.

Laverna *(luh-VERN-uh)* The One Who Is the Spring-Time

Laverna was the Roman goddess of the realm of the dead, inside the earth. She was also known as the goddess of petty criminals. Sacrifices were made to Laverna at the Porta Lavernalis, one of the gates of the huge Servian Wall surrounding the city of Rome in the 4th Century B.C.

Lavinia *(luh-VIN-ee-uh)* The Pure One; Purity

Princess Lavinia was the daughter of the demi-god King Latinus of the Latins, who was the son of King Odysseus of Ithaca and the enchantress Circe. Lavinia's mother was Queen Amata. Following the Trojan War (12th Century B.C.) and the sack of the city-state of Troy, King Latinus allowed the defeated Trojan army and their leader Aeneas to settle in Latium. Latinus was impressed with Aeneas, and broke-off his daughter Lavinia's engagement to King Turnus of the Rutuli, preferring Aeneas instead. Turnus attacked the Trojans and was defeated. Lavinia and Aeneas married, and produced a son, Silvius.

Modern Example: Lavinia Greenlaw (1962-), British poet and educator.

Leagora *(lee-uh-GOR-uh)* The Gatherer of Fish

Leagora was a Nereid, one of the fifty beautiful sea-nymphs who lived at the bottom of the Mediterranean Sea. Her parents were Doris, goddess of river deltas, and gentle Nereus, the fish-tailed "Old Man of the Sea," god of fishing. The Nereids often rode dolphins up to the water's surface, to help sea-farers.

Related Names: Leagore.

Leanira *(lee-uh-NEER-uh)* The Lioness

Leanira was the daughter of Queen Diomede and King Amyclas, rulers of the Greek city-state of Sparta. Leanira married the god Arcas, and produced two sons, Aphidas and Elatus, later to become rulers of the Greek city-state of Arcadia.

Modern Example: The Leanira Checkerspot, a large, beautiful, brown and white butterfly commonly found near rocky cliffs.

Leda *(LEE-duh, LAY-duh)* The Joyful One; The Merry One

Queen Leda was the wife of King Tyndareus of the Greek city-state of Sparta. Leda's mother was the maiden Eurythemis; and her father was Thestis, King of Aetolia, in Corinth. Leda had three children fathered by Zeus: sons Castor and Pollux and her famous daughter, Princess Helen. Helen, who later deserted her husband, King Menelaus of Sparta, and ran off with Prince Paris of the city-state of Troy (in present-day Turkey). Menelaus, enraged, appealed to the other kings of Greece, and a thousand ships were launched against Troy, beginning the bloody Trojan War. The war ended with Helen's capture, and the destruction of Troy.

Related Names: Leta.

Lelante *(luh-LON-tay, luh-LON-tee)* The Woodpecker

The Greek maiden Lelante married Munichus, the hero of the ancient Greek town of Munichus. Lelante produced four children: Alcander, the prophet; Hyperippe; Megaletor; and Philaeus. One night, when burglars entered Lelante's home and burned it to the ground, Zeus, High King of the gods, transformed

Lelante and her family into birds, saving their lives. Lelante became the world's first woodpecker.

Lena *(LEEN-uh)* From the High Tower

Princess Lena was the ruler of the Greek city-state of Messenia, whose father was King Leucippus of Messenia. Lena was one of the lovers of Poseidon, god of the seas, and produced a daughter, Euadne (evadne), a nymph or nature goddess, and eventually Princess of Messenia.

Related Names: Madeline, Pitane.
Modern Example: Lena Horne (Lena Mary Calhoun Horne) (1917-), singer, dancer, and actress.

Libra *(LEE-bruh)* The One Who Weighs and Balances

Libra was the "star-bright" goddess of universal fairness. Her father was Astraeus, god of astrology and astronomy, and one of the Titans, the elder deities who ruled in Heaven before being overthrown by Zeus and his Olympian gods. Libra's mother was Eurybia, a sea goddess. Libra lived on earth during humanity's so-called Golden Age, when all men and women were virtuous. But later, when Bronze Age men conquered the Earth, Libra fled, leaving humanity in a state of injustice, chaos, and warfare. Zeus took pity on Libra and transformed her into the Constellation Virgo.

Related Names: Astraea, Astraia, Astrape, Justitia.
Modern Example: Libra Dohko, a character in the Japanese anime television series, Saint Seya, *created by artist Masami Kurumada (1953-).*

Libya *(LIB-ee-uh)* The Heart of the Sea

Libya was a princess of Egypt, an ancient African civilization. Libya's father was King Epaphus of Egypt, son of Zeus, High King of the gods on Mount Olympus in Thessaly, Greece; and her mother was Memphis, a nature goddess who personified the fresh-water sources of Memphis, Egypt. When the sea god Poseidon saw Libya's beauty, he took her against her will. Three sons were born: Agenor, who later became King of Phoenicia, an African nation; Belus, who became King of Egypt; and Lelex, who became King of Laconia, a Greek city-state.

Modern Example: Libya, a Northern African nation on the Mediterranean Sea, bordering the nations of Chad, Egypt, Niger, and Sudan.

Licinia *(luh-SIN-yuh)* From the Licinius Family

Licinia (Licinia Eudoxia) (A.D. 422-A.D. 462) was an Empress of Rome. Her first husband was the Roman Emperor Petronius Maximus, and her second was the Roman Emperor Valentinian III. Licinia's mother was the Roman Empress Eudocia Augusta; and her father was the Emperor Theodocius III.

Lilaia *(lil-LAY-uh)* The One Who Is Desired

Lilaia was a nymph or nature goddess who personified the sources of "sweet-flowing" fresh water in the city of Lilaia, in ancient Greece. Lilaia's sole parent was Cephisus, a river god.

Related Names: Lilaea.

Livia *(LIV-ee-uh)* The Blue-Grey One

Livia (Livia Drusilla) (58 B.C.-A.D. 29) was an Empress of Rome, wife of the Roman Emperor Augustus. Augustus was Livia's second husband, after she divorced the Roman Emperor Tiberius. Livia was legendary for her political influence over Augustus.

Modern Example: Livia Turco (1955-), Italian Minister of Health in 2007.

Lotus *(LO-tus)* The Lotus Flower

Lotus was the "snow-white" nymph or nature goddess who personified the Sperkheios River in ancient Greece. Lotus's only parent was the Sperkheios River itself. When Lotus tried to hide from the lusty Priapus, god of vegetables, the gods changed her into the world's first lotus tree, which blooms with beautiful flowers and red berries.

Related Names: Lotis.

Lucina *(loo-SEEN-uh, loo-CHEEN-uh)* The Lamp; The Light

Lucina — also called Juno, or Hera — was the "white-armed" goddess of child-birth and marriage, and the queen of the gods on Mount Olympus. Her mother was Rhea, queen of the Titans or Elder Deities, and her father was Cronos, king of the Titans. Juno's husband was Zeus, king of the gods, who seized control of heaven and overthrew the Titans, making Lucina the new queen. Lucina was often depicted wearing golden sandals, a golden polos or crown, and holding a pomegranate, symbol of love and death, while riding in her chariot pulled by pea-cocks. She was also revered as a goddess of cattle, and was affectionately called "cow-eyed" by Homer, the great 8th-Century Greek poet.

Lucina was the goddess of marriage — but as a wife and mother she some-times proved a bit harsh. For example, Lucina was so jealous of her husband Zeus, who created Athena, goddess of wisdom, by himself, that Lucina created Hephaestus, god of volcanoes, without any male help. However, when she saw how ugly Hephaestus was, she threw him from Mount Olympus, where he fell for many days until he hit Ocean, the river circling the earth. Hephaestus later got revenge by making a golden throne which magically held Lucina prisoner. She might have remained there forever, but when the other gods gave Aphrodite, goddess of love, to Hephaestus for his wife, he released Lucina.

Lucina's tantrums were legendary, especially against her cheating husband, Zeus. Zeus betrayed Lucina often, and one such affair — between Zeus and Alcmene, a mortal — produced the demigod Heracles. Lucina tried to kill the infant Heracles by sending two poisonous snakes to his crib, but Heracles choked each snake and played with their bodies. Years later, Lucina gave Hera-cles a series of impossible tasks, the Twelve Labors, to perform for King Eurys-theus of Mycenea. Heracles completed the tasks brilliantly and became Greece's greatest legendary hero.

Often, when Zeus cheated on Lucina, the nymph Echo helped him by distract-ing Lucina with her nonstop chatter. But when Lucina learned of Echo's treachery she cursed her, so that now Echo can only repeat other people's words.

Zeus again cheated on Lucina with the Titan Leto, who bore twin deities — Apollo, god of poetry, and Artemis, goddess of hunting. Furious, Lucina forbade

Names for Babies Destined to be Explorers and Earth-Shakers

Girls

Bia • Callithyia • Elyssa • Eos • Eupompe • Gaia
Harpina • Hecate • Ida • Io • Isis • Lyssa

Boys

Actor • Aphros • Atlas • Castor • Dardanus • Jason • Montanus
Orontes • Perseus • Phineus • Pontus • Portunus • Poseidon

Leto from giving birth anywhere on earth, but Leto found the floating island of Delos and delivered her babies there. Afterwards, the island grew four pillars which rooted it to the earth.

Another of Zeus's affairs was with Callisto, a mortal priestess of Artemis. Zeus changed himself into Apollo and seduced Callisto, who bore the demigod Arcas. Lucina, enraged, changed Callisto into a bear, which Arcas almost killed during a hunt. To protect Arcas and Callisto, Zeus changed them into the constellations Ursa Major and Ursa Minor.

Another of Zeus's affairs produced Dionysus, god of wine and drunkenness. Zeus seduced Semele, the mortal daughter of Cadmus, prince of Thebes. Lucina sent Titans to murder the infant Dionysus, and they ate his body but left behind his heart, fleeing as Zeus scattered the assassins with his thunderbolts. Athena saved the god's heart, and Zeus placed it in Semele's womb, where Dionysus grew and was born a second time.

Zeus almost covered-up his affair with Io, daughter of Inachus, the river-god. Zeus changed Io into a white cow to hide her from jealous Lucina, but Lucina saw through the ruse and demanded the cow as a gift. Lucina gave the cow to Argos, the hundred-eyed giant, ordering him to keep it away from Zeus. Zeus sent his son

Hermes, messenger of the gods, to kill Argos and free Io. Hermes put Argos to sleep, and when the monster closed his hundred eyes, Hermes slew him.

Lucina's rages extended to a mortal priest named Tiresias, who had been magically transformed from a man to a woman, then back again. When Zeus and Lucina asked him which gender enjoyed lovemaking more, Tiresias agreed with Zeus that women enjoyed it more. Lucina instantly blinded Tiresias. Zeus, pitying him, gave him the power to see the future.

Lucina even vented her fury during the great Trojan War, in the 12th Century B.C. When Lucina saw her son Ares, god of war, fighting on the Trojan side against her beloved Greeks, she encouraged King Diomedes of Argos to attack Ares. Diomedes threw his spear, and Athena guided it into Ares's body, wounding him terribly. Ares retreated to Mount Olympus, allowing Lucina's champions, the Greeks, to eventually win the Trojan War.

Related Names: Hera, Hera Argeia, Hero, Juno.

Lucretia *(loo-KREE-shuh)* The Valuable One; The Profitable One

Lucretia (6th Century B.C.) was a respected Roman noblewoman who was cruelly assaulted by Sextus Tarquinius, son of the ancient Roman king Lucius Tarquinius Superbus. Lucretia reported the crime to her family, then took her own life, rather than live in dishonor. A Roman nobleman, Lucius Junius Brutus, arranged for her body to lie in state, fueling the anger and outrage of the Roman people. Brutus then spearheaded a successful revolt against the king and established a Roman Republic, or representative government. Lucretia became one of the great legendary heroines of Rome.

Modern Example: Lucretia Rudolph Garfield (1832-1918), American First Lady, and wife of President James Garfield.

Luna *(LOO-nuh)* The Moon

Luna was the Roman name for the "bright" Selene, one of the Titans, the original Greek deities who ruled in Heaven before being overthrown by Jupiter and his Olympian gods. Luna's father was Hyperion, the Titan god of light; and her mother was Thea, a Titan sky goddess. Luna was a goddess of the moon, one of several in Greek mythology. The moon was Luna's crown, which she wore nightly, while riding in her chariot pulled by winged horses, to visit her husband, the mortal Endymion. Together, Luna and Endymion had fifty daughters, called the Menai, or Months. They represented the fifty lunar months of the four-year Olympiad.

Related Names: Mene, Selene.
Modern Example: Luna Bergere Leopold (1915-2006), American scientist.

Lysianassa *(lis-ee-uh-NAH-suh)* The Royal Deliverer

Lysianassa was a Nereid, one of the fifty beautiful sea-nymphs who lived at the bottom of the Mediterranean Sea. Her mother was Doris, goddess of river deltas; and her father was gentle Nereus, the fish-tailed "Old Man of the Sea," god of fishing. The Nereids often rode dolphins up to the water's surface, to help seafarers.

Lyssa *(LISS-uh)* Frenzy; Fury; Rage; Raging Madness

Lyssa was the goddess of anger, panic, and insanity, the "queen of sorrow." She was often associated with the Mania, the raging spirits of uncontrollable frenzy. Lyssa's mother was Nyx, goddess of night; and her father was Uranus, god of the sky. Lyssa was charged by Hera, queen of the gods, to drive the mighty demi-god Heracles insane. Lyssa was also said to accompany Ares, god of war, during his many bloody battles. She was also said to derive satisfaction from the fire and smoke of cities burned in warfare.

Related Names: Furor, Irae, Lytta.

Macaria *(muh-KAR-ee-uh)* The Blessed One

Macaria was the goddess of the merciful release of death. Her mother was Persephone, Queen of Tartarus, the underworld of the dead; and her father was Hades, god of the dead. Macaria helped the dead pass on to the fabled Nesoi Macarioi, The Islands of the Blessed.

Related Names: Makaria.

Maia *(MY-uh)* The Good Nursing Mother

Maia was one of the seven Pleiades, the nymphs (nature spirits) who shine as seven bright stars in the night sky. Their father was Atlas, one of the Titans or Elder Deities, who had once ruled in Heaven, but was overthrown by Zeus and his Olympians. The Pleiades' mother was Pleione, goddess of cattle and sheep. The gods transformed the seven nymphs into the constellation Pleiades to protect them from a pursuing giant, Orion. The Pleiades' names are Alcyone, The Kingfisher; Celaeno, The Black One (not the same as the winged Harpy named Celaeno); Electra, The Amber One; Maia, The Nursing Mother; Merope, The One Whose Face Is Turned; Taygete, The One from Mount Taygete; and Sterope, The Brilliant Light.

Related Names: Maea, Maya.
Modern Example: Maia Chiburdanidze (1961-), Georgian chess grandmaster and Women's World Chess Champion.

Maira *(MEER-uh, MY-ruh)* The Sparkling One

Maira was a nymph or nature goddess who personified the star Sirius, also called the Dog Star. Maira's sole parent was Atlas, the Titan god who held up the earth on his shoulders. When Maira's star could be seen over the horizon, the ancient Greeks knew that Summer had officially arrived.

Modern Example: Maira Kalman (1949-), Israeli-American artist and author.

Marcia *(MAR-shuh)* The Warlike One

Marcia (Marcia Aurelia Ceionia Demetrias) (?-A.D. 193) was the concubine — the unofficial but beloved "wife" — of Marcus Aurelius Commodus Antoninus, Emperor of Rome. Marcia's mother was Marcia Aurelius Sabinianus, who had been a servant of Lucius Verus, another Roman Emperor; and her father is unknown. Marcia was an early Christian, and used her considerable influence with the Emperor to lessen Rome's persecution of Christians.

Modern Example: Marcia Anastasia Christoforides (1910-1994), British noblewoman and philanthropist.

Margaret *(MAR-grit, MAR-guh-rit)* The One Who Is on the Edge

Margaret of Hungary (1175-1223) was a Byzantine Empress. Byzantium, located on the Strait of Bosphorus in the Near East, was a Greek-speaking city-state which became the new seat of the Eastern Roman Empire, the "Nova Roma," after Rome itself was conquered and sacked in A.D. 410. Maragaret's father was King Bela III of Hungary; and her mother was Queen Agnes of Antioch. Margaret married Isaac II Angelus, Byzantine Emperor, in 1185. The marriage produced John Angelus, and Manuel Angelus.

Related Names: Margit.
Modern Example: Margaret Thatcher, British Prime Minister from 1979-1990.

Maria *(muh-REE-uh)* The Sacred Olive Tree

Maria was the Roman name for Moria, a Greek nymph or nature goddess, one of the Naiad sisters who personified the rivers of Lydia, a province in ancient Greece. Maria's sole parent was Hermos, a Lydian river god; and her only brother was Tylos, or Knot of the Tree. When Tylos was murdered by a dragon, Maria prayed to the woodland monster Damasen to kill the dragon, which Damasen happily did. But the dragon's wife squeezed magic flower-juice onto the dragon's corpse, restoring it to life. Maria used the same flower-juice on Tylos, bringing him back from the land of the dead.

Related Names: Mariah, Mary, Moria.
Modern Example: Maria Goeppert-Mayer (1906-1972), American scientist, and winner of the 1963 Nobel Prize in physics.

Marica *(muh-REE-kuh)* The Sacred Olive Tree

In Roman mythology, Marica was a nymph or nature goddess who personified the forests and the lake near the Italian town of Minturno. Marica married Faunus (Pan), god of shepherds, and produced Latinus, King of the Italian kingdom of Latium. (Note: Marica is also a Spanish-language term for "gay.")

Related Names: Marika.

Martina *(mar-TEEN-uh)* The One Who Is Loved

Martina (7th Century A.D.) was an empress in Byzantium. Byzantium, located on the Strait of Bosphorus in the Near East, was a Greek-speaking city-state which became the new seat of the Eastern Roman Empire, the "Nova Roma," after Rome itself was conquered and sacked in A.D. 410. Martina married the Emperor Heraclius in 613, and accompanied him during his military campaigns against Persia (modern-day Iran). Martina became the Empress of Byzantium after Herclius's death in A.D. 641.

Modern Example: Martina McBride (1966-), American country-western singer and songwriter.

Medea *(mih-DEE-uh)* The One Who Thinks Deeply

The Greek demi-goddess Medea was a powerful enchantress, and Princess of Kolchis, a kingdom near the Black Sea. Medea's mother was Hecate, goddess of childbirth; and her father was the mortal King Aeëtes of Colchis. Aeëtes guarded the Golden Fleece, taken from the immortal ram Chrysomallos — a prize known throughout the ancient world as a symbol of wealth and power. One day, Prince Jason of the Greek city-state of Iolcus came to Colchis with his Argonauts, searching for the Golden Fleece, but Aeëtes forced Jason to perform three mighty tasks in exchange for the Fleece. Medea, knowing Jason would fail, pledged to aid him with sorcery, if he would take her back to Iolcus. Jason agreed, accomplished the tasks, stole the fleece, and sailed back to Iolcus with Medea.

Modern Example: Medea Benjamin (Susie Benjamin) (1952-), American social activist and co-founder of the antiwar group Code Pink.

Melaina *(muh-LAY-nuh)* The One Who Is Black

Melaina was a nymph or nature goddess who personified the underground sources of fresh water in the Greek city-state of Delphi. Melaina's sole parent was the river god Cephisus. Apollo, god of prophecy, made love to Melaina, and she bore a son, Delphos, who gave his name to the city of Delphi.

Related Names: Melaine, Melaena, Melanie.

Modern Example: Melaina Barnes, British artist and writer.

Melia *(muh-LEE-uh, MEL-yuh)* Sweetness; Honey

Melia was a nymph or nature goddess, one of the Naiad sisters who personified the sources of fresh water on the island of Ceos or Hydrussa, in the Aegean Sea. Melia's sole parent was Cephisus, a river god. Because Melia represented fresh water, she was called Sweetness, or Honey, because fresh water often tastes sweet after briny water has been consumed. Melia was loved by Apollo, god of prophecy, and she bore a son, Ceos, who later became King of Ceos, his namesake island. (Note: The Naiad nymph Melia is not to be confused with the spirit Melia who was the mother of the Centauri, the race of half-human, half-horse creatures renowned for their prowess as warriors.)

Related Names: Melie.
Modern Example: Melia Watras, American concert violinist.

Melissa *(muh-LISS-uh)* The Honey-Bee

Queen Melissa was the wife of the cruel King Periander, ruler of the Greek city-state of Corinth (6th Century B.C.). After Periander secretly killed Melissa, Periander buried her, with piles of fine clothing — instead of burning all her clothing as required by local customs. Years later, when Periander sent emissaries to the Corinthian Oracle of the Dead, inquiring about some buried treasure, Melissa's spirit suddenly appeared — but swore she would reveal nothing, due to Periander's abuse of her. Periander ordered his servants to immediately burn mounds of clothes in the Corinthian Temple of Hera, while he humbly prayed to Melissa's spirit. Melissa relented, and gave Periander the information he desired.

Modern Example: Melissa Ng Mei Hang (1972-), Hong Kong actress.

Melita *(MEL-uh-tuh)* The One Who Is as Sweet as Honey

The gracious Melita was a Nereid, one of the fifty beautiful sea-nymphs who lived at the bottom of the Mediterranean Sea. Her parents were Doris, goddess of river deltas, and gentle Nereus, the fish-tailed "Old Man of the Sea," god of fishing. The Nereids often rode dolphins up to the water's surface, to help sea-farers.

Related Names: Melite.
Modern Example: Princess Melita (1951-), German princess who is 117th in line to assume the British throne.

Merope *(MAIR-uh-pee)* The One Whose Face Is Turned Away

Merope was one of the seven Pleiades, the nymphs (nature spirits) who shine as seven bright stars in the night sky. Their father was Atlas, one of the Titans or original gods who had once ruled in Heaven, before being overthrown by Zeus and his Olympians. The Pleiades' mother was Pleione, goddess of cattle and sheep. The gods transformed the seven nymphs into the Constellation Pleiades to protect them from a pursuing giant, Orion. The Pleiades' names are Alcyone, The Kingfisher; Celaeno, The Black One (not the same as the winged Harpy named Celaeno); Electra, The Amber One; Maia, The Nursing Mother; Merope, The One Whose Face Is Turned; Taygete, The One from Mount Taygete; and Sterope, The Brilliant Light.

Mesembria *(meh-SEM-bree-uh)* The One Who is the Noon Hour

Mesembria was one of the twelve "golden-haired" Horai, or Hours — the goddesses of the twelve hours of daytime. The Horai stood along the heavenly route that their father, Helios, the sun, traversed each day, and each goddess represented a different hour. The Horai helped Helios remove his shimmering crown at day's end, and turned his flaming horses out to pasture. Helios created the Horai with the help of Cronus, god of creation. The twelve Horai were Auge, The Hour of First Light; Anatolia, The Dawn; Musica, The Music Hour; Gymnastica, The Gym Hour; Nympha, The Bath Hour; Mesembria, Noon; Sponde, The Hour of Wine After Lunch; Elete, The Grinding Hour; Acte, the Meal Hour; Hesperia, The Evening; and Dysis, Sunset.

Modern Example: Mesembria, an ancient Greek colony; now the resort town of Nesebar in modern-day Bulgaria.

Meta *(MET-uh, MAY-tuh)* The One Who Is Beyond

Meta was the wife of the mortal King Aegeas of the Greek city-state of Athens. Meta's father was known only as Hoples; and her mother is unknown. Meta and Aegeas had high hopes for their marriage, but no children were produced. Aegeas therefore divorced Meta and married Chalciope, hoping to produce royal heirs; but this marriage proved barren, also.

Modern Example: Meta Ramsey (1936-), member of the House of Lords, in the British Parliament.

Minerva *(min-NUR-vuh)* Wisdom; Knowledge; Enlightenment; Virtue

Minerva was the Roman name for Athena, or Xenia, a unique and powerful deity, the "bright-eyed" goddess of wisdom, agriculture, art, Greek cities, and women's crafts such as weaving. But when necessary, she transformed herself into a warrior goddess. For example, after the Trojan War — a ten-year conflict between the Greeks and Trojans that destroyed Troy — the Greeks defiled one of Minerva's altars, angering her so deeply that she convinced Neptune, god of the sea, to destroy most of the Greek ships as they returned home.

Minerva's birth had been unique among the immortals, because she sprang fully-formed, with armor and weapons, from the forehead of her father Jupiter, High King of the gods. Jupiter, who loved Minerva more than any of the other immortals, gave Minerva a magnificent shield, decorated with the terrifying face of the Medusa.

Minerva's most devoted human worshippers were the Athenians, who named their city-state Athens in her honor, in gratitude for her bringing the olive tree to humankind. The Athenians built a magnificent temple to Minerva called the Parthenon, which, though partially ruined, still stands in modern Athens.

Related Names: Athena, Athene, Athena Ergane, Parthenos, Pallas Athena.
Modern Example: Minerva Chapman (1858-1947), American painter.

Moira *(MOY-ruh)* The Sparkling One

Moira was a nymph or nature goddess, one of the Naiad sisters who personified the rivers and other sources of earth's fresh water. Moira's sole parent was Erasinos, a river god. Moira also belonged to a small subset of nymphs called the Erasinides — Anchiroe, Byze, Melita, and Moira — who guarded the Erasinos River in Greece. One of the Erasinides' tasks was to escort the goddess Britomartis, a daughter of Zeus, whenever she visited from Crete.

Related Names: Maira, Maera.
Modern Example: Moira MacTaggart (Dr. Moira Kinross MacTaggart) (1975-?), scientist in the X-Men Marvel comic book universe.

Moneta *(mo-NEET-uh, mo-NET-uh)* Memory

Moneta was the Roman name for Mnemosyne, one of the Greek Titans, the original deities who ruled in Heaven before being overthrown by Jupiter and his Olympian gods. Moneta's father was Uranus, god of the sky; and her mother was Terra, the earth. Moneta was the "golden-robed" goddess of remembrance, who retold ancient stories and helped preserve oral histories. Later, when Jupiter, High King of the gods, made love to Moneta for nine nights, she produced nine "gold-crowned" daughters — the Musa or Muses, the goddesses of dancing and music, who inspired humanity to create art.

Related Names: Mnemosyne.

Morea *(mor-AY-uh)* The One Who Is a Beautiful Mulberry Bush

Morea was one of the beautiful Dryad sisters, the nymphs or nature goddesses who danced in the forests of ancient Greece, filling the bushes and trees with beauty and life. The Dryads' mother was Oxylos, the forest-goddess whose name meant Thick Woods; and their father was Hamadryas, the personification of the oak tree. The lovely Dryads were quite numerous, and included Algeiros, Ampelo, Balanos, Carya, Cranea, and Ptelea.

Modern Example: Morea, a tropical island in the Tahitian Islands group, currently a part of France.

Musica *(MUZE-ik-uh, MOO-zih-kuh)* The One Who Is the Music Hour

Musica was one of the twelve "golden-haired" Horai, or Hours — the goddesses of the twelve hours of daytime. The Horai stood along the heavenly route that their father, Sol, the sun, traversed each day, and each goddess represented a different hour. The Horai helped Sol remove his shimmering crown at day's end, and turned his flaming horses out to pasture. Sol created the Horai with the help of Saturn, god of creation. The twelve Horai were Auge, The Hour of First Light; Anatole, The Dawn; Musica, The Music Hour; Gymnastica, The Gym Hour; Nympha, The Bath Hour; Mesembria, Noon; Sponde, The Hour of Wine After Lunch; Elete, The Grinding Hour; Acte, the Meal Hour; Hesperia, The Evening; and Dysis, Sunset.

Related Names: Mousike.
Modern Example: Musica, a sword-smith in the Japanese anime cartoon, Rave Master, *the 1998-2005 Japanese manga (comic book) created by artist Hiro Mashima.*

Myrina *(muh-REEN-uh)* From the Land of Mysia

Myrina was the queen of the fierce Amazon warrior-women of ancient Greece, often called "The Killers of Men." Myrina's Amazons were so dedicated to war and conquest that each warrior had her right breast removed, to facilitate the use of bows and arrows. Queen Myrina married King Dardanus of the Greek city-state of Dardania, and produced a son, Priam, later to become the legendary King Priam of the city-state of Troy.

Related Names: Batea, Batieia, Myrine.

Myrrha *(MEER-uh, MUR-uh)* The Myrrh Tree

Princess Myrrha was the mortal daughter of King Theias of Assyria. Because Myrrha failed to pay proper respect to Aphrodite, the goddess of love wrecked Myrrha's relationship with her father Theias, so that he tried to kill her with a sword. As he was about to cut her down, the gods rescued her by transforming her into the world's first myrrh-bush. After nine months had passed, the tree opened to reveal Adonis, god of rebirth and reincarnation. The fragrant sap of the myrrh tree was said to be Myrrha's tears.

Related Names: Smyrna.
Modern Example: Myrrha Lokhvitskaya (1869-1905), Russian poet and author.

Mystis *(MISS-tus)* The One Who Is Taught the Mysteries

Mystis was a nymph or nature goddess who personified Euboia Island, in Greece. Mystis's parents are unknown — a mystery. Mystis was an initiate, or student, of Dionysus, god of wine. She had one son, Korymbos, The Ivy Plant. The ivy plant was revered by Greek initiates, who wore strands of it while pursuing their holy studies.

Related Names: Makris.

Nana *(NAN-uh, NON-uh)* The Illuminator

Nana was a nymph or nature goddess, one of the Naiad sisters who personified the earth's rivers and other sources of fresh water. Nana's only parent was Sangarius, a river god. One day, as Nana sat under an almond tree, she gathered the nuts to herself and magically became pregnant. Nana had not known that the gods had buried the phallus of the demon Agdistis and caused an enchanted almond tree to grow, which is how Nana became pregnant. Nana bore a son, Attis, a forest god.

Related Names: Gianna.
Modern Example: Nana Mouskouri (Ioanna Mouskouri) (1934-), Greek singer and United Nations Goodwill Ambassador.

Neda *(NEE-duh)* The One Who Is a Mountain Spring

Neda was a nymph or nature goddess who personified numerous mountain springs in ancient Greece. Neda's parents are unknown; however, her sisters were known to be Anthracia, Glauce, Ide, and Theisoa. Neda was renowned for nursing the young god Zeus, who later became King Zeus of the Olympian gods.

Modern Example: Neda Arneric (1953-), Serbian actress.

Names for Babies Destined to Become Fiery Hot-Blooded Leaders of Men and Women

Girls

Adicia • Aetna • Alecto • Atropos • Celaeno • Ceto
Clotho • Electra • Eurybia • Gale • Lachesis • Lyssa

Boys

Atlas • Axion • Bacchus • Brontes • Cerberus • Daemon
Dionysus • Draco • Griffin • Hades • Hector • Nero

Nemea *(nuh-ME-uh)* Of the Town of Nemea

Nemea was a nymph or nature goddess who personified the fresh water sources of the town of Nemea in ancient Greece. Her mother was Selene, goddess of the moon, and her father was Zeus, High King of the gods who ruled from Mount Olympus in Thessaly, Greece.

Related Names: Nemeia.

Nesaea *(NEH-see-uh, neh-SEE-uh)* The Island

Nesaea was a Nereid, one of the fifty beautiful sea-nymphs who lived at the bottom of the Mediterranean Sea. Her mother was Doris, goddess of river deltas; and her father was gentle Nereus, the fish-tailed "Old Man of the Sea," god of fishing. The Nereids often rode dolphins up to the water's surface, to help sea-farers.

Related Names: Nesaie.
Modern Example: Nesaea, the name of a genus of flowering plants of the family Lythraceae.

Nesi *(NEH-see)* The Islands

The Nesi or Nesoi were the goddesses who guarded every island in ancient Greece. The Nesi were Protogenoi, or primal deities who existed before all other gods. Their sole parent was Gaia, the earth. The Nesi had existed as mountains at first; then, Posedion, god of the sea, sliced these mountains off with his trident and hurled them into the ocean, to create the many islands that exist today.

Related Names: Nesoi.
Modern Example: Nesi Ismailova, Bulgarian sculptress and painter.

Niobe *(nye-OH-bee)* The Refreshing One

Queen Niobe ruled the Greek city-state of Thebes. Niobe's father was Tanatalus, a son of Zeus, High King of the Olympian gods; and her mother was Dione, a Titan goddess and prophetess. Niobe bore twelve children, whom she claimed were the most beautiful children on earth, even greater than the children of Leto, the Titan goddess of mothers. Leto's two offspring — Apollo, god of prophecy, and Artemis, goddess of hunting — attacked Niobe in order to uphold their mother's good name. They destroyed Thebes and killed all of Niobe's children.

Modern Example: Niobe Menéndez, British track and field champion.

Nona *(NO-nuh)* The One Who Is the Nine Months of Pregnancy

Nona (Clotho) was one of the Roman sister goddesses called the Parcae (Moirai), or The Fates. The Fates were the three avenging goddesses who decided what would occur in each human life. Nona's sisters were Decima (Lachesis) and Morta (Atropos). Nona and her sister Fates gave every human, at birth, a portion of good and evil, then pursued those who chose evil with a terrible vengence, punishing all sinners. The Fates were depicted in Roman and Greek poetry either as harsh old hags or as unsmiling maidens. They were described as weavers, who wove the threads of human destiny: Nona created the thread of human life; Decim determined how long each thread would be; and Morta used her scissors to cut the thread of each life. No one could change the Fates' decisions, not even Jupiter or the other immortal gods.

Related Names: Clotho, Klotho.
Modern Example: Nona Gaprindashvili (1941-), Georgian chess champion.

Nympha *(NIM-fuh)* The One Who Is the Bath-Hour

Nympha was one of the twelve "golden-haired" Horai, or Hours — the goddesses of the twelve hours of daytime. The Horai stood along the heavenly route that their father, Helios, the sun, traversed each day, and each goddess represented a different hour. The Horai helped Helios remove his shimmering crown at day's end, and turned his flaming horses out to pasture. Helios created the Horai with the help of Cronus, god of creation. The twelve Horai were Auge, The Hour of First Light; Anatolia, The Dawn; Musica, The Music Hour; Gymnastica, The Gym Hour; Nympha, The Bath Hour; Mesembria, Noon; Sponde, The Hour of Wine After Lunch; Elete, The Grinding Hour; Acte, the Meal Hour; Hesperia, The Evening; and Dysis, Sunset.

Related Names: Nymphe.

Nyssa *(NISS-uh)* The One from From Mount Nysa

The "rich-haired" Nyssa was one of the Nysiades, the nymphs or nature god-desses who personified Mount Nysa in ancient Greece. Nyssa's sole parent was Oceanus, god of the river that encircled the earth. Nyssa reared the young Diony-sus, god of wine, in the valleys and caves near Mount Nyssa, singing hymns with him daily as he grew to manhood.

Related Names: Nusa, Nysa.

Octavia *(ahk-TAY-vee-uh)* The Eighth One

Octavia (Octavia Thurina Minor) (69 B.C.-11 B.C.) was a sibling of Augustus, the legendary Roman Emperor. Octavia's mother was Atia Caesonia, the niece of Julius Caesar; and her father was Gaius Octavius, a Roman Senator. While many in the Roman royal family were known for their cruelty, Octavia's reputation was one of honor and compassion.

Modern Example: Octavia Estelle Butler (1947-2006), science-fiction writer.

Olympias *(oh-LIM-pee-us)* The Time of the Contests at Olympia

Olympias (376 B.C.-316 B.C.) was a queen of Macedonia, a Greek-influenced nation that eventually ruled an immense empire. Olympia's father was Neoptolemus, ruler of the Greek city-state of Epirus, and a descendant of the Greek hero Achil-les. Olympias married King Phillip II of Macedonia, and produced a son, Alexan-der the Great, whom many military scholars have called the greatest general in history. (Queen Olympias was portrayed by American actress Angelina Jolie in the 2004 film, *Alexander*, directed by Oliver Stone.)

Related Names: Myrtale.

Pallas *(PAL-us)* The One Who Wields a Spear

Pallas was a nymph or nature goddess who personified Lake Tritonis in Libya, North Africa. Pallas's father was Triton, a god of the sea; and her mother was Tri-tonis, a sea nymph. Pallas's sister was Libyan Athene, a war-loving goddess who played so many brutal war-games with Pallas that one day she mistakenly killed her. Grief-stricken, Libyan Athene carved a beautiful statue of Pallas, to honor her forever.

Panacea *(pan-uh-SEE-uh)* The Universal Cure for All Ailments

Panacea was the goddess of healing. Her father was Asclepius, god of doctors and medications; and her mother was Epione, goddess of the relief of distress. Panacea was the mistress of every medicine that could cure the diseases of mortals and immortals alike. Doctors in ancient Greece were required to swear an oath of integrity to Panacea.

Related Names: Panakeia.

Modern Example: Panacea, an American rap/hip-hop group based in Washington, D.C.

Pandea *(PAN-dee-uh)* The One Who Is All Brightness

Pandea, or Dia, was the "exceedingly lovely" goddess of the Greek city-state of Nemea. Pandea's father was Zeus, High King of the gods on Mount Olympus; and her mother was Selene, a goddess of the moon. Pandea's sacred grove of cypress trees, near Nemea, was a place where anyone could come seeking forgiveness for past sins; and the goddess pardoned everyone.

Related Names: Dia, Pandia.

Pandora *(pan-DOR-uh)* All the Gifts; The Giver of All

By the command of Zeus, High King of the Olympian gods, every god helped to create Pandora, earth's first mortal woman, made from water and clay. Zeus had been angry because he had created mortals with limited abilities, yet the Titan god Prometheus had given mortals the gift of fire — making them far too god-like for Zeus's taste. Therefore, Zeus ordered the gods to create the intelligent, beautiful Pandora to plague mankind. (Zeus was a hopeless chauvinist.) Pandora also received a jar from Zeus, with strict instructions never to open it. She was then given in marriage to the Titan god Epimetheus, Prometheus's brother. Pandora immediately opened the jar and allowed evil to escape into the world. But the spirit of Hope also escaped, to aid humankind forever.

Panopaea *(pan-OH-pee-uh)* The Vista; The Panorama

Panopaea was a Nereid, one of the fifty beautiful sea-nymphs who lived at the bottom of the Mediterranean Sea. Her parents were Doris, goddess of river deltas, and gentle Nereus, the fish-tailed "Old Man of the Sea," god of fishing. The Nereids often rode dolphins up to the water's surface, to help sea-farers.

Related Names: Panopea, Panopeia.

Parea *(pur-REE-uh, puh-RAY-uh)* The One from Paros Island

Pareia was a nymph or nature goddess of the fresh water sources of Paros Island, in ancient Greece. Parea's sole parent was an unknown river god. She married King Minos, ruler of Crete, and produced four princes: Eurymedon, Khryses, Nephalion, and Philolaus. These princes were infamous for having battled the demi-god Heracles (Hercules), son of Zeus, High King of the Olympian gods.

Related Names: Pareia, Paria.

Modern Example: The Parea, also called the Chatham Island Pigeon, a large bird found in the Chatham Islands of New Zealand.

Parthenia *(par-THEEN-ee-uh)* The Maiden of the Parthenius River

Parthenia was a nymph or nature goddess who personified the Parthenius River in ancient Anatolia (modern-day Turkey). Parthenia's sole parent was Parthenius, a river god. Parthenia married the mortal hero Agamestor, and produced a son, Kleitos, who became famous battling the Greeks in the Trojan War.

Paula *(PAUL-uh)* The Little One

Paula (A.D. 347-A.D. 404) was a Roman noblewoman who claimed she was a descendant of King Agamemnon, ruler of the ancient Greek city-state of Mycenae. After having lived in wealth and comfort, Paula's husband, the Roman nobleman Toxotius, died. In her grief, Paula sought the counsel of Jerome, a Catholic scholar. Paula converted to Christianity and was canonized after her death as the patron saint of widows.

Modern Example: Paula Abdul (Paul Julie Abdul) (1962-), Syrian-Jewish-American entertainer, and panelist on the American Idol *television series, created by Simon Fuller, and which premiered in 2002.*

Paulina *(paul-EE-nuh)* The Little One

Paulina the Elder (?-85) was the Queen Mother of the Roman Emperor Hadrian, one of the "Five Good Emperors" who brought prosperity and peace to the Roman Empire. Paulina, a Roman noblewoman, married Publius Aelius Hadrianus Afer, a Roman-Spanish nobleman. The marriage produced a daughter, Aelia Domita Paulina, and a son — the boy who would become the renowned Emperor Hadrian.

Related Names: Domitia Paulina, Paulina Major.
Modern Example: Paulina Gretzky (1988-), American singer and model, daughter of hockey player Wayne Gretzky and actress Janet Jones.

Penelope *(puh-NELL-up-pee)* The Needle and Thread

Penelope was a nymph or nature goddess, one of the Dryad sisters who personified Mount Cyllene in Arcadia, Greece. Penelope's sole parent was the mountain nymph Dryopos. Penelope married Hermes, messenger of the gods, and bore him a unique son, the half-human, half-goat Pan, who later became god of shepherds.

Related Names: Penelopeia.
Modern Example: Penelope Miller (Penelope Andrea Miller) (1964-), American actress.

Persephone *(per-SEF-uh-nee)* The Maiden

In ancient Greek mythology Persephone, or Averna, was the beautiful daughter of Demeter, goddess of the harvest, and Zeus, High King of the gods. Persephone eventually became Queen of Hades, the underworld of the dead. One day, as Persephone had been gathering flowers, Hades, the brother of Zeus, emerged from the underworld and — filled with lust for Persephone — seized her and dragged her below. Demeter searched the earth for kidnapped Persephone, then retreated to her temple in Eleusis, grief-stricken. She laid waste to the earth. No crops grew, and humanity starved.

In desperation, Zeus sent his gods to Demeter, pleading with her to spare humanity. But Demeter vowed that no crops would grow until she could see Persephone again. Finally, Zeus sent Hermes, messenger of the gods, to Hades with a royal command: Let Persephone go. Hades obeyed, but convinced Persephone to eat some pomegranate seeds. Once she ate the food of the dead, she was condemned to return to Hades for part of each year. Now, when Persephone rejoins Demeter, flowers bloom. When Persephone returns to Hades, winter covers the earth.

Related Names: Averna, Core, Cura, Kore, Proserpine, Proserpina, Regina Erebi.
Modern Example: Persephone Apostolou, American film and television actress.

Petra *(PET-truh)* The One Who Is Like the Rocks

Petra was a nymph or nature goddess, one of the Libethrides sisters who personified the sources of fresh water rushing from Mount Helicon in Greece. The sole parent of Petra and the other Libethrides was Termessos, a river god. The Libethrides would emerge from their sacred caves to judge music-competitions between the Muses and other deities, and declare the winners.

Modern Example: Petra Burka (1946-), Dutch figure-skating champion.

Phaedra *(FAY-druh)* The Beautiful, Bright One

Princess Phaedra was the demi-god daughter of King Minos of Crete. She married Prince Hippolytus, son of King Theseus and Queen Antiope of the city-state of Athens. But Hippolytus, always in search of new adventures, descended into Hades, the underworld of the dead, and did not return for many years. The love-sick Phaedra was left behind to die of abroken heart.

Modern Example: Phaedra Hoste (1971-), Belgian actress.

Phaio *(FAY-oh, FEE-oh)* The Shining One

Phaio was one of the Hyades, the nymphs (nature spirits) who shine as bright stars in the night sky. Their father was Atlas, one of the Titans or original deities who had once ruled Heaven, before being overthrown by Zeus and his Olympian gods. The Hyades' mother was Pleione, goddess of cattle and sheep. The gods transformed the Hyades into stars after their brother, Hyas, a rain-spirit, was killed by a lion. Zeus changed Hyas into the Constellation Aquarius, then changed his grieving sisters — Ambrosia, Clea, Eudora, Koronis, Phaio, Phaisyle, and Thyone — into the Constellation Hyades. The Greeks believed that the Hyades' tears brought life-giving rain to earth.

Related Names: Phaeo.

Phaisyle *(FAZE-lee)* The Shining One

Phaisyle was one of the Hyades, the nymphs (nature spirits) who shine as bright stars in the night sky. Their father was Atlas, one of the Titans or original deities who had once ruled Heaven before being overthrown by Zeus and his Olympian gods. The Hyades' mother was Pleione, goddess of cattle and sheep. The gods transformed the Hyades into stars after their brother, Hyas, a rain-spirit, was killed by a lion. Zeus changed Hyas into the Constellation Aquarius, then changed his grieving sisters — Ambrosia, Clea, Eudora, Koronis, Phaio, Phaisyle, and Thyone — into the constellation Hyades. The Greeks believed that the Hyades' tears brought life-giving rain to earth.

Related Names: Phaesyla.

Pherusa *(fuh-ROO-zuh)* The One Who Carries the Burdens

Pherusa was a Nereid, one of the fifty beautiful sea-nymphs who lived at the bottom of the Mediterranean Sea. Her parents were Doris, goddess of river deltas, and gentle Nereus, the fish-tailed "Old Man of the Sea," god of fishing. The Nereids often rode dolphins up to the water's surface, to help sea-farers.

Related Names: Pherousa.

Phoebe *(FEE-bee)* The Radiant One; The Prophetess

"Gold-crowned" Phoebe was a Titan, one of the original gods who had ruled in Heaven before being overthrown by Zeus and his Olympian gods. Phoebe's father was Uranus, the sky; and her mother was Gaia, the earth. Phoebe was the goddess of brilliant wisdom, and served as the Oracle or prophetess to her grandson Apollo, god of prophecy, at Delphi, Greece. In fact, Apollo was commonly called Phoebus Apollo — Bright Apollo — because of his grandmother's name.

Related Names: Phoibe.
Modern Example: Phoebe DiTommaso (1990-), Australian figure skater.

Phyllis *(FILL-us)* The Green Branches

The beautiful Princess Phyllis was the mortal daughter of King Lycurgus of Thrace. Phyllis married the warrior Demophoon when he returned from the legendary Trojan War, in the 12th Century B.C. Demophoon eventually sailed home to Greece, abandoning Phyllis. Grief-stricken, Phyllis took her own life. A beautiful green almond tree flourished over her tomb.

Modern Example: Phyllis Ayame Whitney (1903-), Japanese-born American mystery-book writer.

Polyhymnia *(pol-ee-HIM-nee-uh)*

Polyhymnia was one of the Muses, the goddess-daughters of Zeus, High King of the gods, and of Mnemosyne, goddess of memory. The Muses brought ideas and inspiration to all artists. Calliope, considered the chief Muse, inspired princes

Names for Babies Destined to Become Intellectual Giants

Girls
Athena • Autonoe • Carmenta • Cyrene • Eucleia
Livia • Pandora • Phoebe • Sophia

Boys
Amphion • Anax • Asclepius Daedalus • Hadrian • Mentor
Myson • Periander • Plato • Proteus • Solon • Thales

and others to write grand poetry; Clio inspired historians; Erato inspired romantic poetry; Euterpe inspired lyric poets; Melpomene inspired tragic playwrights; Polyhymnia inspired hymn-writers; Terpsichore inspired dancers and singers; Thalia inspired comedic playwrights; and Urania inspired astronomers. Together, the Muses sang with Apollo, god of healing and the arts, about the glorious accomplishments of gods and mortals.

Prima *(PREEM-uh)* The First One

Prima was the first Princess of the great city-state of Rome. Prima's mother was Hersilia, the first Queen of Rome; and her father was Romulus, one of the twin brothers who founded Rome, and — ultimately — the famed Roman Empire.

Modern Example: Prima Rusdi (1967-), Indonesian writer.

Proto *(PRO-tow)* The One Who is First

Proto was a Nereid, one of the fifty beautiful sea-nymphs who lived at the bottom of the Mediterranean Sea. Her parents were Doris, goddess of river deltas, and gentle Nereus, the fish-tailed "Old Man of the Sea," god of fishing. The Nereids often rode dolphins up to the water's surface, to help sea-farers.

Modern Example: Proto, a soldier in the Japanese anime cartoon series, Ghost in the Shell, *a Japanese manga (comic book) created by artist Masamune Shirow (1961-), and which debuted in 2002.*

Psamathe *(SAM-uh-thee, suh-MATH-uh)* The Goddess of Sand

The charming Psamathe was a Nereid, one of the fifty beautiful sea-nymphs who lived at the bottom of the Mediterranean Sea. Her parents were Doris, goddess of river deltas, and gentle Nereus, the fish-tailed "Old Man of the Sea," god of fishing. The Nereids often rode dolphins up to the water's surface, to help sea-farers. Psamathe married Aecus, who had been King of Aegina, a Greek island, and who was transformed after death into one of the three Judges of the Underworld. Together, Psamathe and Aecus produced Phocus, a powerful demi-god who became the hero of Aegina Island.

Regina *(ruh-JEEN-uh)* The One Who Is a Queen

Regina was a Roman title, meaning, The One Who Is a Queen, and was often used as an alternate name in the case of several Roman mythological personages appropriated from Greek mythology:

Title	English Meaning	Roman Name	Greek Name
Regina Deorum	*Queen of the Gods*	*Tethys*	*Tethys*
Regina Erebi	*Queen of Hell*	*Averna*	*Persephone*
Regina Nemorum	*Queen of Forests*	*Diana*	*Artemis*

Modern Example: Regina Spektor (1980-), Russian-American musician and singer.

Rhea *(RAY-uh, REE-uh)* The Flow; The Ease

The "illustrious" Rhea was one of the Titanides, the original goddesses of the earth. Rhea's father was Uranus, the sky; and her mother was Gaia, the earth. Rhea was the goddess of human reproduction. Rhea's husband, King Cronus, god of time, regulated the steady movement of the centuries; and Rhea regulated the steady movement of mother's milk, bringing ease to nursing mothers. Rhea was also the queen of the Titan gods, before they were overthrown by Zeus and his Olympian gods. Her husband Cronus, terrified of a prophecy that he would be overthrown by his own offspring, had eaten each god or goddess as it was born. But Rhea hid her son Zeus on an island, and gave Cronus a huge stone to eat, tricking him. When Zeus came of age, he led his Olympian gods against Cronus and the Titans, defeating them.

Related Names: Magna Mater, Ops, Rhee, Rheia.
Modern Example: Rhea Durham (1978-), American actress and fashion model.

Rita *(REET-uh)*

Rita of Armenia (c. 1278-?) was the daughter-in-law of a Byzantine Emperor. Byzantium, located on the Strait of Bosphorus in the Near East, was a Greek-speaking city-state which became the new seat of the Eastern Roman Empire, the "Nova Roma," after Rome itself was conquered and sacked in A.D. 410.
Rita's mother was Queen Keran of Armenia; and her father was King Leo III of

Armenia. In 1296, Rita married Michael IX Palaiologos, son of Andronikos II Palaiologos, Emperor of Byzantium. The marriage produced two sons — Andronikos Palaiologos, and Manuel Palaiologos — and two daughters, Anna Palaiologos, and Theodora Palaiologos.

Related Names: Megan.
Modern Example: Rita Donagh (1939-), Irish-British painter and professor.

Rosmerta *(rose-MUR-tuh, rose-MAIR-tuh)* The Great Provider

In the ancient Gallo-Roman religion — a blending of Roman deities with Gallic (French) deities — Rosmerta was the goddess of prosperity, and the wife of Mercury, messenger of the gods. Rosmerta was often depicted holding the cornucopia, the cone-shaped basket used to hold fruits and vegetables.

Modern Example: Madam Rosmerta, a character in the Harry Potter series of books by British author J.K. Rowling (Joanne Rowling) (1965-).

Samia *(SAM-ee-uh)* From the Island of Samos

Samia was a nymph or nature goddess who personified the fresh water sources of the Greek island of Samos. Samia's sole parent was Meander, a river god. Samia married King Ancaeus, Samos's first ruler, and produced a daughter, Parthenope, and four sons — Alitherses, Enudos, Perilaus, and Samos.

Modern Example: Samia Maxine Smith (1982-), Lebanese-French-British actress.

Selene *(suh-LEEN, suh-LEE-nee)* The Moon

"Bright" Selene, or Luna, was one of the Titans, the original deities who ruled in Heaven before being overthrown by Zeus and his Olympian gods. Selene's father was Hyperion, the Titan god of light; and her mother was Thea, a Titan sky goddess. Selene was a goddess of the moon, one of several in Greek mythology. The moon was Selene's crown, which she wore nightly, while riding in her chariot pulled by winged horses, to visit her husband, the mortal Endymion. Together, Selene and Endymion had fifty daughters, called the Menai, or Months. They represented the fifty lunar months of the four-year Olympiad.

Related Names: Luna, Mene.
Modern Example: Selene Yeager, American health and fitness writer.

Serena *(suh-REEN-uh)* The Serene One; The Peaceful One

Serena (?-A.D. 408) was the Christian niece of Theodsius I (Flavius Theodosius), Emperor of Rome. Because of her Christian faith, Serena decided one night to remove some jewelry from a heathen statue of Rhea, goddess of pregnancy. Serena was cursed for this act of impiety by the Vestal Virgins, pagan nuns who served Vesta, goddess of hearth and home. Serena was then plagued with nightmares, where she foresaw her death at a young age. In A.D. 408, she was executed, following false charges that she was a traitor to Rome.

Modern Example: Serena Williams (Serena Jameka Williams) (1981-), American tennis champion.

Sibyl *(SIB-ull)* The Prophetess

A renowned Sybil, or prophetess, was Herophile Sybil, also called Artemis, the oracle of the Greek city-state of Erythraea. Herophile's father was Zeus, High King of the gods who ruled the universe from Mount Olympus; and her mother was Lamia, a daughter of the sea-god Poseidon. Herophile reportedly predicted that the beautiful demi-goddess, Helen, would cause the destruction of the city-state of Troy. Herophile also foretold the rise of Alexander of Macedonia as a great conquering general.

Sophia *(so-FEE-uh)* Wisdom; Knowledge

Sophia (c. A.D. 535-c. A.D. 602) was an Empress of Byzantium. Byzantium, located on the Strait of Bosphorus in the Near East, was a Greek-speaking city-state that became the new seat of the Eastern Roman Empire, the "Nova Roma," after Rome itself was conquered and sacked in A.D. 410. When Sophia's husband, the Emporer Justin II (Flavius Iustinus Augustus) (A.D. 565-A.D. 578) began his historic descent into debilitating insanity, Sophia became co-ruler of the Empire, along with the legendary general Tiberius II Constantine (c. A.D. 520-A.D. 582). Upon Justine's death, Tiberius became the sole Emperor of Byzantium.

Related Names: Sofia, Sophie.
Modern Example: Sophia Ali, (1964-), Pakistani-American poet and author.

Sylvia *(SIL-vee-uh)* The Forest Nymph

The beautiful Sylvia, or Ilia, was a Vestal Virgin, a pagan nun devoted to the service of Vesta, goddess of the hearth and home. Sylvia's uncle, Amulius, had placed her with the Vestals because he feared she might get pregnant at young age. But when Sylvia went to a nearby river and fell asleep, Mars (Ares), god of war, found her and seduced her. Sylvia produced twin sons, Romulus and Remus, who would eventually found the great city-state of Rome.

Related Names: Ilia, Rhea Silvia, Silvia.
Modern Example: Sylvia Plath (1932-1963), American poet and author.

Tatia *(TOT-ee-yuh)* The Daughter of King Tatius

Tatia was a princess in Sabinium, an ancient Italian kingdom. Tatia's father was King Tatius, ruler of the Sabines, who conquered Rome after its soldiers had raped the women of Sabinium. Princess Tatia married Numa III, King of Rome, and produced one daughter, Pomilia.

Names for Babies Destined to Become Lawyers and Judges

Girls
Astraea • Carmenta • Clementia • Concordia • Eirene • Irene
Lara • Libra • Octavia • Petra • Themisto • Tisiphone

Boys
Aeacus • Claudius • Hadrian • Lucius • Solon

Tereine *(ter-REEN)* The One Who Stabs Like a Sword

Tereine was one of the Naiad sisters, a family of nymphs or nature goddesses. Tereine personified the Strymon River in Thrace, a region of Greece. Her sole parent was Strymon, a Thracian river god. Ares, god of war, made love to Tereine, and in time she produced a daughter, Thrassa (meaning, from Thrace).

Modern Example: Koudia Tereine, a mountainous region of Algeria, in North Africa.

Terpsichore *(TERP-suh-kor, terp-SIK-uh-ree)* Delights in Dancing

Terpsichore was one of the Muses, the goddess-daughters of Zeus, High King of the gods, and of Mnemosyne, goddess of memory. The Muses brought ideas and inspiration to all artists. Calliope, considered the chief Muse, inspired princes and others to write grand poetry; Clio inspired historians; Erato inspired romantic poetry; Euterpe inspired lyric poets; Melpomene inspired tragic playwrights; Polyhymnia inspired hymn-writers; Terpsichore inspired dancers and singers; Thalia inspired comedic playwrights; and Urania inspired astronomers. Together, the Muses sang with Apollo, god of healing and the arts, about the glorious accomplishments of gods and men.

Related Names: Cybele.
Modern Example: Terpsichore, character depicted by Rita Hayworth in the 1947 American film, Down to Earth, *directed by Alexander Hall (1894-1968).*

Terra *(TAIR-uh)* The Earth

The goddess Terra, or Gaia — The Earth — was "the mother of all," and one of the four original elements created when time began — the other elements being air, water, and fire. Terra was a huge disk, encircled by the river Oceanus, covered by the sky, and supported below by the fiery underworld of Hades. Terra's only parent was Chaos, the blackness that existed before time began. When Terra mated with Uranus, The Sky, she created the original pantheon of sky-dwelling gods called the Titans. Eventually, Terra warred against Uranus because he tried to prevent her from giving birth to new gods. She also fought her own son, Chronos, god of time, when he tried to prevent Terra from creating new gods. Terra helped Zeus later to become High King of the new gods on Mount

Olympus — in his successful war against Chronos and the Titans. But when Zeus condemned the Titans to the underworld prison of Hades, Terra turned against Zeus by unleashing the Gigantes, a race of gargantuan warriors. Yet the Gigantes could not defeat Zeus and his Olympian gods, not even with the help of the fearsome monster Typhoeus, and Terra lost her war against Heaven.

Related Names: Gaea, Gaia, Ge, Tellus.
Modern Example: Terra Naomi, American singer, musician, and songwriter.

Thalia *(THAL-ee-uh, thuh-LEE-a)* The One Who Flourishes in Joy, Celebration, and Festivity

Thalia was one of the Muses, the goddess-daughters of Zeus, High King of the gods, and of Mnemosyne, goddess of memory. The Muses brought ideas and inspiration to all artists. Calliope, considered the chief Muse, inspired princes and others to write grand poetry; Clio inspired historians; Erato inspired romantic poetry; Euterpe inspired lyric poets; Melpomene inspired tragic playwrights; Polyhymnia inspired hymn-writers; Terpsichore inspired dancers and singers; Thalia inspired comedic playwrights; and Urania inspired astronomers. Together, the Muses sang with Apollo, god of healing and the arts, about the glorious accomplishments of gods and men.

Related Names: Thaleia.
Modern Example: Thalia Pellegrini (1978-), British journalist and television personality.

Thea *(THEE-uh, TAY-uh)* Divine Inspiration; The Clear Blue Sky

Thea was one of the Titans, the original deities who ruled in Heaven before being overthrown by Zeus and his Olympian gods. Thea was the goddess of light, and the brilliance of the sky. She was thought to be the source of all light, even of the light given off by jewelry, silver, and gold. Thea's father was Uranus, the sky; and her mother was Gaia, the earth. Thea married Hyperion, god of light, and produced Eos, goddess of the dawn; Helios, the Sun; and Selene, the Moon.

Related Names: Aethra, Euryphaessa, Theia.
Modern Example: Thea Christiansen Foss (1857-1927), nicknamed "Tugboat Annie," founder of the Foss Maritime tugboat service.

Theisoa *(THEE-uh-SO-uh)* The One Who Is a Mountain Spring

Theisoa was a nymph or nature goddess who personified numerous mountain springs in ancient Greece. Theisoa's parents are unknown; however, her sisters were known to be Anthracia, Glauce, Ide, and Neda. Theisoa was renowned for nursing the young god Zeus, who later became King Zeus of the Olympian gods.

Modern Example: Theisoa, a hamlet in the Andritsaina region of modern-day Greece.

Themisto *(thuh-MISS-tow)* The Law

Themisto was a Nereid, one of the fifty beautiful sea-nymphs who lived at the bottom of the Mediterranean Sea. Her parents were Doris, goddess of river deltas, and gentle Nereus, the fish-tailed "Old Man of the Sea," god of fishing. The Nereids often rode dolphins up to the water's surface, to help sea-farers.

Theodora *(thee-uh-DOR-uh)* Gracious Gift from God

Theodora (A.D. 500-A.D. 548) was an Empress of Byzantium. Byzantium, located on the Strait of Bosphorus in the Near East, was a Greek-speaking city-state which became the new seat of the Eastern Roman Empire, the "Nova Roma," after Rome itself was conquered and sacked in A.D. 410. Theodora's father was a Greek Cypriot peasant named Acacius; and her mother was an actress, whose name is unknown. Theodora followed her mother into the theatre, becoming an actress, dancer, and eventually a courtesan for the nobility. In 523, Theodora married Justinian I, the Byzantine Emperor, and provided him with invaluable political counsel throughout his career, including advice on how to help the poor. Theodora died of cancer in 548, and was canonized as a Catholic saint.

Modern Example: Theodora Goss, Hungarian-American educator and science fiction/fantasy writer.

Thetis *(THEE-tus, THET-us)* The Genesis; The Creation

The "silver-footed" Thetis was the most renowned of the Nereids, the fifty beautiful sea-nymphs who lived at the bottom of the Mediterranean Sea. Her parents were Doris, goddess of river deltas, and gentle Nereus, the fish-tailed "Old Man of the Sea," god of fishing. The Nereids often rode dolphins up to the water's surface, to help sea-farers. Thetis was loved by Poseidon, the sea god, and Zeus, High King of the gods — but when these two gods heard a prophecy that Thetis's son would become a rebel, they gave her in marriage to Peleus, the human ruler of the Myrmidons on the island of Aegina. Peleus and Thetis produced Achilles, one of the greatest Greek heroes of all time.

Modern Example: Thetis Blacker (1927-2006), British singer and painter.

Thrassa *(THRASS-uh)* From Thrace

Thrassa was a nymph or nature goddess from Thrace. Her father was Ares, god of war; and her mother was Tereine, another Thracian nymph. Thrassa married the mortal King Hipponous of Thrace, and produced a daughter, Polyphonte.

Thornax *(THOR-nax)* The One Who Is Mount Thornax

Thornax the Arcadian was a nature goddess who personified Mount Thornax, the summit that divided the Greek city-states of Sparta and Sellasia. Thornax married Iapetus, a Titan — one of the original deities who ruled in Heaven before being overthrown by Zeus and his Olympian gods. The marriage produced the Greek hero Buphagus, who ended up being shot with an arrow by Artemis, goddess of hunting.

Modern Example: Thornax, title of a novel by science fiction writer Steve Burgauer.

Tiasa *(tee-AH-suh)* The Tiasa River

Tiasa was a nymph or nature goddess who personified the Tiasa River that flowed through Amyklai, a town in ancient Greece. Tiasa's sole parent was Europas, a river god.

Tisiphone *(ty-SIFF-uh-nee)* Divine Retribution for Murder

Tisiphone was one of the three Erinyes or Furies, the fearsome goddesses who visited mortals to right wrongs and avenge deaths. Tisiphone and the other Erinyes were born when the blood of Uranus, god of the sky, magically mixed with that of Nyx, the Night. Tisiphone's sister-Furies were Alecto and Megaera. Tisiphone guarded the gates of Hades, the underworld of the dead.

Modern Example: Tisiphone Edge, from the Game Boy Advance game, Golden Sun: The Lost Age, *created by Camelot Software Planning, published in 2002 by Nintendo.*

Urania *(yur-RAIN-yuh, yur-RON-yuh)* The Heavenly One

Urania was one of the Muses, the goddess-daughters of Zeus, High King of the gods, and of Mnemosyne, goddess of memory. The Muses brought ideas and inspiration to all artists. Calliope, considered the chief Muse, inspired princes and others to write grand poetry; Clio inspired historians; Erato inspired romantic poetry; Euterpe inspired lyric poets; Melpomene inspired tragic playwrights; Polyhymnia inspired hymn-writers; Terpsichore inspired dancers and singers; Thalia inspired comedic playwrights; and Urania inspired astronomers. Together, the Muses sang with Apollo, god of healing and the arts, about the glorious accomplishments of gods and men.

Valeria *(vuh-LAIR-ee-uh)* The Strong One

Valeria was a maiden of the Roman city of Tusculum. Valeria engaged in an unfortunate episode involving forbidden sexual intercourse, and as a result, gave birth to the god Aigipan, half-goat and half-human.

Modern Example: Saint Valeria of Milan (c. 1st Century B.C.), killed by the Romans for burying early Christian martyrs.

Verina *(vuh-REEN-uh)* The Truthful One

Verina (Aelia Verina) (?-A.D. 484) was an Empress in Byzantium. Byzantium, located on the Strait of Bosphorus in the Near East, was a Greek-speaking city-state which became the new seat of the Eastern Roman Empire, the "Nova Roma," after Rome itself was conquered and sacked in A.D. 410. Verina married Leo I, Byzantine Emperor, and produced one son, Marcian.

Modern Example: Verina Baxter, American sculptress.

Venus *(VEE-nus)* Born of the Sea-Foam

Venus, or Aphrodite, was the "golden" goddess of love, beauty, and desire. Some ancient writers said that Venus's father was Jupiter, High King of the gods, and her mother was Dione, an ocean nymph or sea-goddess; while others claimed that when the god Saturn hurled bits of divine flesh into the sea, the "quick-glancing" Venus rose from the sea-foam. The beautiful Venus was married-off to a hideous husband — Vulcan, the deformed god of volcanoes and black-smiths, who received Venus in exchange for releasing Juno, queen of the gods, from an evil spell. Venus promptly cheated on Vulcan by sleeping with with his brother, Mars, god of war. But Sol, the Sun-god, told Vulcan of the tryst, and Vulcan caught the lovers in his magic net and put them on display. Sadly, Vulcan learned that a god as ugly as he could never possess such a divinely beautiful goddess. Venus's beauty actually helped start the Trojan War, in the 12th Century B.C., according to legends. When King Peleus of the Myrmidons married Thetis, a nymph, he invited all the gods to his wedding except Eris, goddess of strife and discord. Furious at being snubbed, Eris tossed a golden Apple of Discord into the party, engraved with, "Kallisti," or, "To the Most Beautiful." Venus, her mother Juno, and Minera, goddess of wisdom, asked Jupiter to award the apple to the most beautiful goddess among them, but Jupiter wisely declined. When the goddesses asked Prince Paris of Troy to judge, he picked Venus. In gratitude, Venus gave Paris the most beautiful woman in the world — Helen, wife of King Menelaus of Sparta. Enraged, Menelaus and other Greek kings took their armies to Troy, and after ten years of war, destroyed the city. Venus's most famous son was Cupid, god of love. Cupid, whose father was Mars, was often depicted as a winged, naked baby, who flew among gods and men firing his love-arrows into their hearts. Venus's most famous daughter was the fair Concordia, goddess of harmony and peace.

Related Names: Aphrodite, Aphrodite Acidalia, Aphrodite Pandemos, Aphrodite Urania, Cyprogenes, Cytherea, Philommedes.
Modern Example: Venus Williams (Venus Ebone Starr Williams) (1980-), American tennis champion.

Vesta *(VESS-tuh)* The Hearth; The Home

Vesta was the Roman name for Hestia, the virginal goddess of the home, family, and the hearth (fireplace), which was the center of cooking and warmth in ancient Greek homes. Vesta's mother was Opis, Queen of the Titans or Elder Deities, and her father was Saturn, King of the Titans. Vesta was worshipped at public hearths, and in private homes, where families prayed to her before eating.

Saturn, the Titan king, had long feared that one of his children would overthrow him, so he ate Vesta and her brothers and sisters, except for young Jupiter — who later deposed Saturn and seized control of Heaven. Jupiter and his new gods ruled on Mount Olympus, and Vesta became part of the Olympian pantheon.

She promised to safeguard her virginity forever, declining advances by Apollo, god of prophecy; Neptune, god of the sea; and Priapus, god of fertility. Vesta's public hearth-fire in the Forum in ancient Rome was maintained by virginal priestesses called the Vestal Virgins.

Related Names: Hestia.

Modern Example: Vesta Tilley (1864-1952), stage name of British male-impersonator Matilda Alice Powles.

Victoria *(vik-TOR-ee-uh)* The Victorious One

Victoria was the Roman name for the "far-famed" Nike, the Greek goddess of triumph over one's opponents, whether in athletics, war, or any other pursuits. Victoria's father was Pallas, the Titan god of war; and her mother was Styx, the river that ran through Hades, the underworld of the dead. Victoria was depicted with golden bird-wings to carry her to victory, and grasping a palm frond, the symbol of victory. Victoria played a role in the war of the older gods, the Titans, against Jupiter and his new Olympian gods. Victoria drove Jupiter's chariot in battle, helping him emerge triumphant as the new High King of the gods. Victoria's battlefield allies were her siblings, Vis (Forcefulness), Potestas (Power), and Zelus (Zeal).

Related Names: Nicae, Nice, Nikai, Nike.

Virginia *(ver-JIN-yuh)* The Virgin; The Maiden

Virginia, or Verginia, was a beautiful maiden who lived in Rome in the 5th Century B.C. Virginia's father was Lucius Verginius, a well-known Roman military official. When the Roman Emperor Claudius decided he wanted to seduce Virginia, he had her kidnapped, under the pretext that she was the slave of his friend Marcus Claudius. Actually, she was a respected Roman citizen, engaged to be married to Lucius Icilius, a government official. When the Roman people learned of the Emperor Claudius's crime, a trial was held. Claudius stopped the trial by military force, and Virginia's father, in desperation, stabbed his daughter to death, rather than let her be abused and dishonored. Virginia became a legendary heroine of Rome.

Related Names: Verginia.
Modern Example: Virginia Woolf (1882-1941), British author, feminist, and pacifist.

Vittoria *(vih-TOR-ee-uh)* The Victorious One

Princess Vittoria di Capua (1587-1648) of Italy was a member of the Palaiologos family, the dynasty that had ruled the Byzantine Empire from 1259-1453. Byzantium, located on the Strait of Bosphorus in the Near East, was a Greek-speaking city-state which became the new seat of the Eastern Roman Empire, the "Nova Roma," after Rome itself was conquered and sacked in A.D. 410.

Modern Example: Vittoria Aganoor (1855-1910), Italian-Armenian poet.

Xenia *(ZEEN-yuh)* The One Who Is Hospitable

Xenia wa an epithet (a characterizing titile) for the powerful divinity Athena, the ancient Greek goddess of wisdom, agriculture, art, Greek cities, and women's crafts. And, although Athena could transform herself into a goddess of war when necessary, she was widely known for her gracious hospitality to strangers; hence her name Athena Xenia, meaning, Athena the Hospitable. In the Greek city-state of Sparta, a statue of Athena Xenia stood near a statue of her father, Zeus Xenios (Zeus the Hospitble), High King of the Olympian gods, to honor the legendary hospitality of both deities.
Related Names: Athena, Athene, Athena Ergane, Minerva, Pallas Athena, Parthenos.

Zoe *(ZO-ee)* The One Who Is Life Itself

Zoe Carbonopsina (10th Century A.D.) was an empress of Byzantium. Byzantium, located on the Strait of Bosphorus in the Near East, was a Greek-speaking city-state which became the new seat of the Eastern Roman Empire, the "Nova Roma," after Rome itself was conquered and sacked in A.D. 410. Queen Zoe's husband was the Byzantine Emperor Leo VI the Wise; and her son was Emperor Constantine VII. After her husband died, Zoe became the sole ruler in A.D. 914. But due to numerous military defeats, Zoe was forced to enter a convent and live as a nun.

Modern Example: Zoe Koplowitz (1948-), marathon runner, author, and motivational speaker.

Section Two

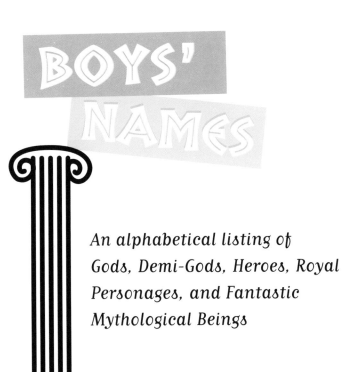

BOYS'

NAMES

An alphabetical listing of
Gods, Demi-Gods, Heroes, Royal
Personages, and Fantastic
Mythological Beings

Achilles *(uh-KIL-eez)* The One Who Is the Sadness of the Nation

Achilles was a demi-god, half human and half divine. His father was King Peleus, ruler of the Greek island of Aegina; and his mother was the "silver-footed" Thetis, the most renowned of the Nereids — the fifty beautiful sea-nymphs or nature goddesses who lived at the bottom of the Mediterranean Sea.

Achilles was destined to become "the best and bravest" of Greece's warriors, according to the legendary Greek poet Homer, in his epic, *The Iliad*. Other poets also wrote of Achilles's early life; for example, Statius (Publius Papinus Statius) (c. A.D. 45-A.D. 96), a Roman poet, said that Achilles's mother Thetis had dipped the infant Achilles into the Styx, the river running through Hades, the underworld of the dead. Achilles's body became invulnerable to harm — except for his left heel, where Thetis had gripped the child.

Achilles gained fame during the Trojan War, waged in the 12th Century B.C. Homer said the Trojan War began when Paris, Prince of the city-state of Troy (modern-day Turkey), ran off with the beautiful Queen Helen, wife of King Menelaus of Sparta. Menelaus allied with other Greek kings and their armies, and the Greeks sailed to Troy in a thousand ships, to wage bloody warfare for ten years. During the war, Hector, the Trojans' greatest soldier, and son of King Priam of Troy, killed Achilles's dear friend Patrocles in battle. Enraged, Achilles killed Hector, tied his body to a chariot, and dragged it around Troy's walls for nine days.

In the end, the Greeks won the war because of King Odysseus of Ithaca. He convinced the Greeks to build an immense wooden horse, the symbol of Troy — but leave the inside hollow. Greek soldiers hid in the horse, and the other Greek armies sailed away — but only to hide, out of sight of the Trojans. The Trojans thought they had won the war, but Cassandra, a Trojan prophetess, begged the Trojans not to pull the statue into the city. Everyone thought she was insane, and wheeled the statue through the gates. That night, the Greeks exited the Trojan Horse, opened the gates of Troy for their waiting armies outside, and destroyed the city. Achilles could not enjoy his triumph, though, because Prince Paris shot a poisoned arrow through his vulnerable heel, killing him. Nonetheless, Achilles is remembered as the greatest warrior of the Trojan War.

Related Names: Akhilleus.

Acmon *(AK-mun, AK-mahn)* The One Who Never Tires; The Anvil

The "ethereal" Acmon or Uranus was the sky, which the ancient Greeks believed was a blue hemisphere covering the earth. His sole parent was Gaia, the earth. Acmon ruled in heaven for countless eons, and was the father of the Titans, the original deities who governed the universe before being overthrown by Zeus and his Olympian gods. But before Zeus was born, Acmon's son, the Titan god Cronus, overthrew his father Acmon. Cronus then ruled the Titans before Zeus wrested control.

Related Names: Akmon, Acmonides, Akmonides, Caelum, Caelus, Ouranos, Uranus.

Actor *(AK-tur)* The One Who Is Light

Actor was one of the great Argonauts or legendary explorers who journeyed to the Greek city-state of Colchis, to retrieve the mystic Golden Fleece. Actor's mother was Queen Xuthus of Phocis; and his father was King Deion of Phocis. In time, Actor's son Menoetius fathered Patrocles, who became the dear friend of the Greek warrior-hero Achilles.

Adamas *(uh-DAHM-us)* The One Who is Steel

Adamas was the son of King Asius of the kingdom of Phrygia. Adamas fought on the side of the Trojans during the legendary Trojan War (12th Century B.C.). The famed Greek poet Homer recorded in his epic poem *The Iliad* that Adamas tried to kill the Greek warrior Antilochus, but Poseidon, Greek god of the sea, would not let Adamas's spear touch Antilochus. Immediately after attacking Antilochus, Adamas was killed by Meriones, a Greek warrior, son of King Molus of Crete.

Adonis *(uh-DON-us, uh-DOE-nus)* The One Who Is the Lord

Adonis was the handsome young god of reincarnation, resurrection, and the annual flowering of plants and trees. He was also the prince of Cyprus, an island in the Mediterranean Sea. Adonis was born this way: When the mortal Princess Myrrha, daughter of King Theias of Assyria, failed to worship Aphrodite, goddess of love, Aphrodite wrecked Myrrha's relationship with her father Theias, so that he tried to kill her. But the gods rescued her by transforming her into the world's first myrrh bush. After nine months passed, the tree opened to reveal Adonis. Aphrodite, enchanted by Adonis's beauty, hid him in a chest, and temporarily gave it to Persephone, goddess of death. But Persephone quickly fell in love with Adonis. Zeus, High King of the gods, decreed that Adonis would live four months with Aphrodite, four months with Persephone, and four months on his own. During his time with Aphrodite, they conceived a daughter, Beroe. Soon afterwards, Adonis was killed by a wild boar while hunting.

Modern Example: Adonis Adelecino Jordan (1970-), basketball player for the National Basketball Association (NBA), and for Australia's National Basketball League (NBL).

Aeacus *(EE-uh-kus)* The Shrieking; The Wailing; The Grieving

Aeacus was one of the Judges of the Dead, the avenging gods who lived in Hades, the underworld. The Judges sat at a fork in the road, one leading to Hades, the other to the Islands of the Blessed; and they passed sentence on all human beings in the afterlife. Aecus's brother Judges were Minos, "the ruler," and Rhadamanthys, "the blameless and strong." The Judges were the sons of Zeus, High King of the gods of Mount Olympus, in Greece; and their mother was Aegina, a nymph or nature goddess of the Greek island of Aegina. The Judges gained their positions in Hades in recognition of their integrity as earthly judges. Aecus was charged with sending souls to Hades; Rhadamanthys sent souls to The islands of the Blessed, the heavenly afterlife; and Minos had the "tie-breaking" vote," if one was needed.

Related Names: Aiacos, Aiakos.
Modern Example: Aeacus, a character in the Japanese anime television series, Saint Seya, *created by Japanese artist Masami Kurumada.*

Aeon *(Eon)* The One Who Is Time

Aeon, or Cronus, was the King of the Titans — the original deities who ruled in heaven, before being overthrown by Jupiter and his Olympian gods. Aeon was the god of the steady movement of time, as well as the decay caused by the time's passage. Aeon had gained heaven's throne by murdering his father Acmon, or Uranus, the sky. But Aeon secretly lived in terror of a well-known

---

Names for Babies Destined to Become Legends in Their Own Time

Girls

Agnes • Antonia • Ariadne • Asia • Bia • Clymene
Dirce • Dynamene • Helen • Persephone

Boys

Achilles • Adamas • Aeon • Ajax • Alexander • Antonius
Augustus • Cleon • Constantine • Galerius • Heracles • Jupiter

---

prediction, that one of his own offspring would eventually depose him. So, he ate each god and goddess as he or she was born. But his wife Rhea, goddess of motherhood, gave Aeon a huge stone wrapped in a diaper to eat, instead of her son Jupiter, tricking Aeon. When Jupiter came of age, he led his Olympian gods against Aeon and the Titans, defeating them, and imprisoning them in Hades, the underworld of the dead. However, centuries later, Jupiter granted the Titans their freedom, and made Aeon King of the Islands of the Blessed, a heavenly afterlife.

Related Names: Chronos, Cronus, Kronos, Saturn, Saturnus.

Modern Example: Aeon Flux, *animated television series that began in 1991, created by Korean-American filmmaker Peter Chung (1961-); and, a 2005 live-action film of the same title, starring American actress Charlize Theron.*

Aether *(EE-thur)* The Shimmering Upper Atmosphere

Aether was the god of the sky-high atmosphere, the air breathed by the gods. Aether's father was Erebus, god of darkness; and his mother was Nyx, goddess of night, who draped her veil across Aether every evening, to cover earth in darkness. Aether hovered high above the god Aer, who was an invisible cloud of gas that clung to earth, allowing humans to breathe.

Related Names: Aither.

Aethon *(EE-thun)* The One Who Blazes with Fire

Aethon was one of the immortal horses of Helios, the sun. Each day, Apollo, god of prophecy, escorted Helios across the sky in a gleaming chariot pulled by these magnificent steeds: Abraxas, Aethiops, Aethon, Bronte, Eous, Phlegon, Pyrois, Sterope, and Therbeeo. But one day, Apollo foolishly granted his demi-god son, Phaëthon, the chance to drive the horses of Helios. Phaëthon, being half mortal, could not control the steeds, and brought Helios too close to earth, burning cities to ashes. Zeus, High King of the gods, witnessed this disaster and killed Phaëthon with a thunderbolt.

Related Names: Ethan.

Africus *(AF-ruh-cus)* The One Who Is from Africa

Africus was the Roman name for Lips, the Greek god of the warm south-west wind that blew across Greece from Africa. He was one of the brother-gods called the Venti, spirits who personified the winds that blew from the north, south, east, and west. The father of the Venti was Astraeus, god of the stars; and his mother was Aurora, the "rosy-fingered" goddess of the dawn. The Venti were often de-picted with wings, to help them waft across the earth.

Related Names: Afer Ventus, Livos.

Agamemnon *(ag-uh-MEM-non)* The One Who is Extremely Determined

King Agamemnon, ruler of the Greek city-state of Mycenae, was a legendary figure in Greek history. Agamemnon's father was Atreus, King of Mycenae; and his mother was Queen Aerope. Agamemnon's brother was King Menelaus, ruler of the Greek city-state of Sparta. Menelaus pleaded for Agamemnon's help, after Prince Paris of the kingdom of Troy (modern-day Turkey) ran off with Menelaus's wife Helen. Agamemnon agreed to help, and — according to the Greek poet Homer, in his epic *The Iliad* — formed an alliance with the other kings of Greece. Under Agamemnon's command, the Greek armies prepared to sail to Troy in a thousand ships. However, Artemis, goddess of hunting, had been insulted by Agamemnon, who had boasted he was a greater hunter than Artemis. Artemis calmed the winds and would not allow the Greek armada to sail — and demanded that Agamemnon sacrifice his daughter Iphigeneia to her. Agamemnon obeyed, killing his daughter on a sacred altar. Satisfied, Artemis sent fair winds, and the Greek ships sailed to Troy, beginning the Trojan War (12th Century B.C.), a conflict that would last for ten bloody years and result in Troy's destruction.

In the end, the Greeks won the war because of King Odysseus of Ithaca. He convinced the Greeks to build an immense wooden horse, the symbol of Troy, and leave it hollow inside. Greek soldiers hid in the horse, and the other Greek armies sailed away — but only to hide, out of sight of the Trojans. The Trojans thought they had won the war, but Cassandra, a Trojan prophetess, begged the Trojans not to pull the statue into the city. Everyone thought she was insane and wheeled the statue through the gates. That night, the Greeks exited the Trojan Horse, opened the gates of Troy for their waiting armies outside, and destroyed the city. However, Agamemnon could not enjoy his triumph, for after he returned home, he was murdered by his vengeful wife Clytemnestra.

Modern Example: Agamemnon Busmalis, character portrayed by American actor Tom Mardrosian in the Home Box Office (HBO) television series, Oz.

Agrius *(AG-ree-us)* The One Who Is a Farmer

Agrius was the Roman name for Agrios, one of the Gigantes, the hundred giants whose mother was Terra, the earth, and whose father was Uranus, the sky. The armored Gigantes, whose legs were huge snakes, rebelled against Jupiter, High King of the immortal gods who lived on Mount Olympus, Greece. But when the demi-god Hercules entered the war on his father Jupiter's side, the Gigantes were annihilated. However, the Gigantes' blood magically transformed into the people of the nation of Thrace (present-day Bulgaria).

Modern Example: Agrius Shalandir the Assault Priest, a character in the universe of the fantasy role-laying game, Assault on Grayhawk.

Ajax *(AY-jax)* The Mighty Warrior

Ajax, the "great Telamonian," was a legendary warrior who gained fame during the Trojan War (12th Century B.C.). The seeds of the war were planted when Prince Paris of the city-state of Troy (modern-day Turkey) ran off with Helen, the wife of

King Menelaus of the Greek city-state of Sparta. Menelaus appealed for help to his brother, the powerful King Agamemnon of Mycenea, and together they allied themselves with the kings of Greece, launching a thousand ships against Troy. During the war, the tall, muscular Ajax killed numerous Trojan foes, according to the Greek poet Homer, in his epic tale *The Iliad*. Ajax cut down his enemies with his deadly war-hammer, and sought protection behind his shield of seven cowhides covered with bronze. In the end, dishonored because of bloodlust and madness, Ajax killed himself with a sword given to him by Hector, a Prince of Troy.

Modern Example: Ajax Keily, character in the 2001 novel, Cases, *by American author Joe Gores.*

Akesis *(uh-KEE-sus)* The One Who Is a Great Cure

Akesis was a demi-god, half human and half divine. His father was Ascelpius, the Greek god of healing; however, his mother's name is lost to history. Akesis, a child-god wearing a hooded cloak, was the god of healing and recovery from ill health.

Related Names: Enamerion, Eumerion, Telesphorus.

Alexander *(al-ix-AN-dur)* The Defender of Men

Alexander the Great (356 B.C.-323 B.C.) was the King of the Greek-influenced nation of Macedon, in the 4th Century B.C. Alexander's father was Philip II of Macedon; and his mother was Queen Olympias.

The Roman historian Pliny, in his book, *Natural History*, wrote that Alexander "roamed in the tracks of . . . Hercules and conquered India." The Greek historian Plutarch, in his book, *Concerning the Fortunes or Virtue of Alexander the Great*, called Alexander "sturdy, heavy-armed, terrific to the foe." And Plutarch added in his book, *Alexander*, that Alexander's father once told him, "My son, seek thee out a kingdom equal to thyself; Macedonia has not room for thee." From these and many other accounts, Alexander is considered one of the greatest military generals of all time, with an empire that stretched from Greece to North Africa to India.

But the empire was short-lived. After twelve years of military victories, Alexander got into a drunken argument with his dearest friend, Clitus the Black, and hurled a spear into his heart, killing him. Only five years later, Alexander was dead from excessive drinking and numerous fatal diseases.

Modern Example: Alexander A. Gurshtein (1937-), Russian astronomer and author.

Alexandros *(al-ix-AN-dur)* The Defender of Men

Alexandros, or Paris, was a Prince of Troy, the legendary walled city-state also known as Ilium (located in present-day Turkey). Alexandros's father was King Priam of Troy; and his mother was Queen Hecuba.

Alexandros bore much of the responsibility for starting the Trojan War, the ten-year-long conflict between the Trojans and the Greeks, during the 12th Century B.C. The Trojan War was chronicled in *The Iliad*, an epic poem written by the Greek poet Homer (c. 8th Century B.C.-?).

According to Homer, Alexandros ran off with Queen Helen of Sparta, wife of King Menelaus. Menelaus allied with other Greek kings and their armies, and the Greeks sailed to Troy in a thousand ships, to wage bloody warfare for ten years. In the end, the Greeks won the war because of King Odysseus of Ithaca. He convinced the Greeks to build an immense wooden horse, the symbol of Troy, and leave it hollow inside. Greek soldiers hid in the horse, and the other Greek armies sailed away — but only to hide, out of sight of the Trojans. The Trojans thought they had won the war, but Cassandra, a Trojan prophetess, begged the Trojans not to pull the statue into the city. Everyone thought she was insane, and wheeled the statue through the gates. That night, the Greeks exited the Trojan Horse, opened the gates of Troy for their waiting armies, and destroyed the city. Nonetheless, Alexandros, although not noted as a skillful warrior, shot a poisoned arrow through the heel of Achilles, Greece's greatest warrior, and killed him.

Related Names: Alexander, Paris.
Modern Example: Alexandros Koryzis (1885-1941), former Prime Minister of Greece.

Alopex *(AL-uh-pex)* The One Who Is a Fox

The Alopex Teumesios was a monstrous fox sent by Dionysus, the Greek god of wine, to invade and destroy the ancient city-state of Thebes. The hero Amphitry-on was dispatched along with the immortal hound Lailaps to subdue the Alopex, but Zeus, High King of the Olympian gods, turned both animals to stone.

Related Names: Alopekos Teumesios.

Alpheus *(AL-fee-us)* The One Who Is the Alpheus River

Alpheus was the Roman name for the Greek river god Alpheios, who personified the Alpheus River of the region of Arcadia, in ancient Greece. Alpheus's father was Oceanus, god of the river that encircled the earth; and his mother was Tethys, goddess of the earth's sources of fresh water. Alpheus was very amorous, and loved to startle beautiful nymphs (nature goddesses) while they were swimming in his waters, then pursue them.

Related Names: Alpheios.

Amnis *(AM-nus)* The Ones Who Are Many Rivers

The Amnis were the ancient Roman river gods, spirits who personified every river in the known world. The father of the Amnis brothers was Oceanus, god of the river that encircled the earth; and their mother was Tethys, goddess of the earth's sources of fresh water. The Amnis had the upper bodies of men, and the lower bodies of huge fish, to swim rapidly through rushing waters. There were many Amnis, including Euphrates, Ganges, Nile, Tigris, and countless more.

Related Names: Amnes, Flumina, Potamoi.

Amor *(ah-MOR)* The One Who Is Love, Passion, and Desire

Amor, or Cupid was the Roman name for Eros, the Greek god of love. His sole parent was Venus, goddess of love, who, as soon as she arose full-grown from the sea's foam, immediately gave birth to Amor. Amor — often portrayed as a child with wings — delighted in flying invisibly among mortals and immortals, shooting enchanted love-arrows into their hearts. When one of his arrows penetrated someone's heart, that person fell hopelessly in love.

Related Names: Amor, Eros, Cupid.
Modern Example: Amor (Love, in English), a 1940 Spanish-language film directed by Argentine filmmaker Luis Bayón Herrera (1889-1956).

Amphion *(AM-fee-on, am-FEE-un)*

Amphion and his twin brother Zethus were the immortal sons of Antiope, a nymph or nature goddess who personified Mount Kithairon in ancient Greece. Zeus, King of the gods on Mount Olympus, was the twins' divine father. Amphion and Zethus built the massive walls of the Greek city-state of Thebes, the most important settlement in Boeotia Province, Greece. Together, Amphion and Zethus ruled Thebes equally, as co-monarchs.

Anax *(AN-ax)* The One Who Is the Great Ruler

Anax was an enormous, legendary giant, and ruler of the Greek city-state of Anactoria. Anax's father was Uranus, the sky, and his mother was Gaia, the earth. Anax's body was so massive that when he died, his corpse had to be buried in a special tomb, over twelve feet long, on the island of Lade.

Related Names: Asterion (not to be confused with the Minotaur).

Andreas *(an-DRAY-us, AN-dree-us)* The Strong Man

Andreas (Andreas Palaiologos) (1453-1503) was an Emperor of Byzantium, in law and in title, if not in fact. Byzantium, located on the Strait of Bosphorus in the Near East, was a Greek-speaking city-state which became the new seat of the Eastern Roman Empire, the "Nova Roma," after Rome itself was conquered and sacked in 410 A.D. Andreas's father was Thomas Palaiologos, Despot or Supreme Ruler of the Byzantine province of Morea; and when Byzantium was destroyed in 1453 by the Turks under Mehmed II the Conqueror, Andreas inherited the throne, though the Empire had ceased to exist.

Related Names: Andreus, Andrew.
Modern Example: Andreas Goldberger (1972-), an Austrian champion ski jumper.

Andreus *(an-DRAY-us, AN-dree-us)* The Strong Man

Andreus was the son of Peneus, a river god in Thessaly, Greece; Andreus's mother was Creusa, a nymph or nature goddess of the Peneios River, also in Thessaly. Andreus was the first person to settle in Boeotia Province, Greece, where he married Evippe, the daughter of Leucon, a Greek prince. The marriage produced Eteocles, who would eventually become King of Boeotia.

Related Names: Andreas, Andrew.

Antaeus *(an-TAY-us, an-TEE-us)* The One Who Is Hostile

Antaeus was an enormous giant from Libya (meaning the entire region of North Africa, to the ancient Greeks). Antaeus's father was Poseidon, god of the sea; and his mother was Gaia, the earth. Antaeus loved to wrestle, and he lured men to his domain so that he could grapple with them and kill them. The earth herself supplied Antaeus with power, so that as long as he touched the earth, he destroyed every challenger, and used their heads to construct Poseidon's temples. But Antaeus finally met his match when he wrestled with Heracles (Hercules), the mightiest Greek demi-god of them all. Heracles knew the secret of Antaeus's power, and lifted him away from the earth, crushing him to death. Centuries later, the Roman general Sertorius reportedly opened Antaeus's tomb; but when he saw that the skeleton was 120 feet long, he hastily ordered the tomb re-sealed forever.

Related Names: Antaios.
Modern Example: Antaeus Hayes, basketball player with the Icelandic Basketball Association.

Antonio *(an-TOW-nee-oh)* The One Who Is a Flower

Prince Antonio Paleologo (1751-1789) was the rightful Emperor of Byzantium — but in name only, since the Byzantine Empire had already been conquered in 1453. Byzantium, located on the Strait of Bosphorus in the Near East, was a Greek-speaking city-state that became the new seat of the Eastern Roman Empire, the "Nova Roma," after Rome itself was conquered and sacked in 410 A.D.

Related Names: Anthony, Antonius.
Modern Example: José Antonio Domínguez Banderas (1960-), Spanish actor.

Antonius *(AN-tuh-nee)* The One Who Is a Flower

Marcus Antonius (Mark Antony) (83 B.C.-30 B.C.) served as part of the Second Triumvirate of 44 B.C. — that is, he was a dictator of Rome, along with two other dictators, Octavian, and Marcus Aemilius Lepidus. However, the Triumvirate dissolved into civil war in 31 B.C. Marcus Antonius ultimately lost the war, and killed himself. His legendary consort, the Egyptian Queen Cleopatra VII, also took her own life.

Related Names: Anthony, Antonio.

Aphros *(AF-rowss)* The One Who Is from the Sea Foam

Aphros was an Ichthyocentaur — sea-gods with humanlike upper bodies, the lower bodies of horses, and gigantic fish tails. Aphros's father was Cronus, god of time; and his mother was Philyra, a nymph or nature goddess. Ahpros's twin brother was Bythos, god of the mysterious depths of the ocean. Aphros, like all Centaurs, was a respected teacher and moral leader. He helped found the Phoenician colony of Carthage in North Africa, inspiring the Carthaginians, whom the Greeks called the Aphroi (Africans), to make epic voyages across the seas.

Modern Example: Aphros, a character in the manga (Japanese comic book) Cyborg 009, published from 1964-1981, created by Japanese artist Shotaro Ishinomori.

Apollo *(uh-PAH-low)* The Father of Light; The Mighty Destroyer

Apollo was the handsome young god of light, medicine, healing, reason, colonization, dance, music, poetry — and most importantly, prophecy. Pilgrims journeyed to his oracles or divine prophets at Delphi, Clarus, and Branchidae to hear their fortunes told. Apollo sometimes even gave the gift of prophecy to deserving mortals, such as Princess Cassandra of Troy.

Apollo was the son of Zeus, King of the Olympian gods, and Leto, one of the Titans or Elder Deities, who had ruled in heaven until Zeus took control. When Hera, queen of the gods, learned that Leto would bear her husband Zeus's love children, she forbade Leto from giving birth anywhere on earth; but Leto discovered the floating island of Delos, where she had her babies. Afterward, the island grew four pillars, which rooted it to the earth. The gods quickly grew to love Apollo, for his speed — he was the world's first Olympic Games champion — and his beautiful recitals on the lyre or harp. Apollo's courage also became legendary, when he slew the terrifying Python, the giant snake of Mount Parnassus.

Apollo's twin sister was Artemis, goddess of hunting; she protected virtuous females, while Apollo protected males. Apollo was sometimes confused with the sun god Helios, because some poets say Helios's chariot and divine steeds pulled the sun across the sky each day, while other poets credit Apollo. Apollo had many facets, and although he could be ruthless, he was still the subject of more Greek art than any other god — holding his lyre or his bow, and wearing his laurel victory-crown.

Related Names: Akesios, Alexikakos, Aphetoros, Apotropaeus, Archegetes, Argurotoxos, Delian Apollo, Delphinios, Horus, Iatros, Klarios, Kynthios, Loxias, Lyceios, Lykegenes, Musagetes, Nomios, Nymphegetes, Parnopius, Phevos, Phoebus, Phoebus Apollo, Phoibos Apollon, Pythian Apollo, Pythios, Smintheus.

Modern Example: Apollo Dukakis, American actor, and brother of actress Olympia Dukakis.

Aquarius (uh-KWAIR-ee-us) The Bringer of Rainwater

Aquarius was the Greek god of annual rainstorms, which watered crops and brought life after the dry season. Aquarius's mother was Pleione, a nymph or nature goddess; and his father was the Titan god Atlas, who held up the earth on his shoulders. Aquarius married the goddess Boeotia and fathered the Hyades, five beautiful goddesses of the stars: Clea, Coronis, Eudora, Phaio, and Phaisyle. Eventually, Aquarius — though immortal, and not prone to natural aging — was

Names for Babies Destined to Become Loyal and Devoted Friends

Girls

Annia • Castalia • Helene • Macaria • Morea
Phaedra • Pherusa

Boys

Aron • Damon • Evenus • Faunus • Gleneus • Hector
Mentor • Nestor • Pythias

killed while hunting lions. In pity, the gods placed Aquarius in heaven, as the constellation Aquarius.

Related Names: Hyas.

Modern Example: Aquarius, the name of the Command Module (CM) for the Apollo 13 manned mission to the Moon; launched on April 11, 1970.

Arcas *(AR-kus)* The Curved One; The Arc

King Arcas was a demi-god, half human and half divine. He became the ruler of Arcadia, a kingdom in the Peloponnesus region of ancient Greece. Arcas's father was Zeus, King of the immortal gods of Mount Olympus, in Greece; and his mother was Callisto, a mortal who gained immortality after Zeus seduced her, then placed her in the night sky as the constellation Ursa Major. After Arcas's mother was deified, Zeus sent the young Arcas to live in Arcadia, a region named in Arcas's honor; there, Arcas became King. He married Chrysopelia, a nymph or nature goddess who personified Arcadia, and had several offspring, including Aphidas, Autolaus, Azan, Diomenia, Elatus, Erymanthus, Hyperippe, and Triphylus.

Ares *(AIR-eez)* War; The Warrior

Ares was the Greek god of war. His father was Zeus, King of the gods on Mount Olympus; and his mother was Hera, Queen of the gods.

The Greeks saw Ares as bloodthirsty, cruel, and savage — the embodiment of war. Some scholars believe the Greeks may have worshipped Ares out of fear rather than devotion. Ares's icons were the sword, spear, helmet, and shield.

Ares was hated by the gods and he cared nothing for them — except for his mistress, Aphrodite, goddess of love and beauty. Aphrodite often slept with Ares, the brother of her husband Hephaestus, the hideous god of volcanoes and blacksmiths. Once, after Ares and Aphrodite had made love, Ares told a boy named Alectryon to guard the doorway, and waken the god at daybreak. But Alectryon fell asleep, allowing Helios, the sun god, to discover Ares and Aphrodite. Helios told Hephaestus of Aphrodite's betrayal. The furious Hephaestus caught the sleeping lovers in a magic net and put them on display, for all the gods to mock. Later, Ares changed Alectryon into a rooster, and to this day, Alectryon's descendants never forget to crow at sunrise.

Ares's own mother, Hera, felt little love for him, as the Greek poet Homer recorded in the 8th Century B.C. He wrote that during the Trojan War, fought between the Greeks and the Trojans in the 12th Century B.C., Hera spied Ares fighting on the Trojan side, against her beloved Greeks. Furious, Hera encouraged King Diomedes of Argos to attack Ares. Diomedes threw his spear, and Athena guided it into Ares's body, wounding him terribly. Ares retreated to Mount Olympus, allowing Hera's champions, the Greeks, to win the battle.

Ares's divine battle-squires were Deimos, or Fear, and Phobos, or Destruction.

Related Names: Ares Enyalius, Enyalios, Gradivus, Mars.

Argus *(AR-gus)* The One Who Is All Eyes

Argus was the Roman name for the enormous giant of Greek mythology whose body was covered with a hundred all-seeing eyes, many of which never slept. Argus's mother was Ismene, a nymph or nature goddess of the Ismenian Spring, in Boeotia, Greece; and his father was Inachus, a river god. One day, when Jupiter, King of the gods, made love to Io, a beautiful nymph, Jupiter's wife Juno learned of her husband's treachery and tried to kill Io. Jupiter changed Io into a white cow, to save her life. Enraged, Juno ordered Argus to keep Jupiter away from the cow at all costs. Jupiter sent the messenger of the gods, Mercury, to kill Argus. After Mercury killed Argus, Juno recognized Argus's valiant sacrifice by transferring his many eyes onto the tails of peacocks.

Related Names: Argos, Argos Panoptes.
Modern Example: Argus Filch, character in the Harry Potter series of novels by British author J.K. Rowling.

Aries *(AIR-eez)* The One Who Is a Ram

Aries was the Roman name for Chrysomallus, a magnificent immortal ram in Greek mythology, with a fleece made of pure gold. Aries's father was Neptune, the Greek god of the seas; and his mother was Theophane, a princess of Thrace. Because Aries could fly, the goddess Nebula begged him to rush to her children, Helle and Phrixus, and save them from being sacrificed to Jupiter. Aries swooped down, gathered up the youngsters, and took them to the city of Colchis. There, Aries ordered Phrixus to sacrifice him to the gods, in the children's place.

Tearfully, Phrixus killed and flayed the noble ram, hanging-up its golden fleece in the sacred forests of Ares, god of war. The fleece became a time-honored symbol of wealth and power; and the gods were so impressed with Aries's sacrifice, that they placed him in heaven, as the constellation Aries.

Related Names: Chrysomallus, Crius, Krios, Khrysomallos.
Modern Example: Aries Merritt (1985-), American champion track and field star.

Arion *(AIR-ee-on, AIR-ee-un)* The Better One; The Braver One

The "black-maned" Arion was the noble, divine horse that Demeter, goddess of spring, gave birth to after being seduced by Poseidon, god of the sea. Arion was trained by Herakles, the mightiest demi-god hero in Greek history. In any chariot race, no team of horses or mortal charioteer, no matter how skilled or determined, could ever defeat Arion. Arion was so fast he could gallop across wheat fields and not damage the crops. And — according to the Roman poet Propertius, in his books of elegies or funerary poems — Arion could even speak aloud.

Related Names: Areion.
Modern Example: Arion, 1986 Japanese anime film, directed by Japanese writer-director Yoshikazu Yasuhiko.

Ariston *(AIR-is-stahn)* The One Who Is the Best

King Ariston (6th Century B.C.), the son of King Agesicles, was the ruler of Sparta, an ancient Greek city-state. Ariston's subjects dedicated many respectful prayers in his honor, during the half-century he ruled Sparta.

Arno *(AR-no)* The One Who Is the Arno River

Arno was the Roman name for the Greek river god Arnos, who personified the Arno River near the Italian city-state of Pisa, in Italy. Arno's father was Oceanus, god of the river that encircled the earth; and his mother was Tethys, goddess of the earth's sources of fresh water. Arno was considered trustworthy and honorable, because he kept his promise to the citizens of Pisa, never to flood their city.

Related Names: Arnos.
Modern Example: Arno Hintjens (1949-), Belgian artist and musician based in Ostend, Belgium.

Aron *(AIR-un, uh-RON)* The High and Exalted Mountain

According to the 1st Century Roman poet Valerius Flavius, Aron was a Greek warrior-hero, and a companion of Prince Jason of Iolchus and his Argonauts — the heroes who stole the magical Golden Fleece, a legendary symbol of wealth and power.

Related Names: Aaron.
Modern Example: Aron Kincaid (1940-), American film-actor and voice-actor.

Asclepius *(es-KLAY-pee-us, es-kuh-LAY-pee-us)* The One Who Opens; The Surgeon

The "soft-fingered" Asclepius was the Greek god of healing and surgery. Asclepius's father was Apollo, god of healing; and his mother was Coronis, a star in heaven. Asclepius was usually shown holding a long stick, with wings at the top, and with two snakes encircling it; or, holding a stick with no wings, and single snake. Ascelpius became the greatest physician in the world, guiding other Greek physicians so that they would respect their patients, particularly women. It was reported that Asclepius even had the power to resurrect patients who had died. When Zeus — King of the immortal gods on Mount Olympus, Greece — learned of Asclepius's incredible power, he hurled a thunderbolt and vaporized the poor doctor. In pity, the other gods placed Asclepius in heaven, as the Ophiuchus constellation.

Related Names: Asklepios.

Asterion *(as-STAIR-ree-ahn)* The Starry One

Asterion the Minotaur was a half-bull, half-human monstrosity with incredible strength and ferocity. Asterion's mother was Queen Pasiphae of Crete, but she disowned him. Asterion lived on the Greek island of Crete, trapped inside the Labyrinth, a great stone maze built by King Minos of Crete. Minos regularly sacrificed victims from rival Athens to the hungry Asterion. One day, while Princess Ariadne, Minos's daughter, watched a group of Athenian victims being hauled to the Labyrinth, she spotted the handsome demi-god Theseus and fell in love with him. She offered to rescue him in exchange for a promise that he would take her to Athens and marry her. He agreed, and she gave him a mystic sword to kill Asterion, and a ball of red wool to use in finding his way back through the Labyrinth. After Theseus slew Asterion and found his way out of the maze, he and Ariadne fled by sea. However, when their ship put-in at the island of Naxos, Theseus and his crew abandoned Ariadne there — but not before she cursed Theseus. The curse worked, because Theseus had promised his father Aegeas that his ship would display a white sail for triumph, or a black sail for death; and Theseus forgot to raise the white sail as he returned. Aegeas spotted the black sail and leapt from a hill into the ocean, forever after known as the Aegean Sea.

Related Names: Minotaur, Minotauros.

Modern Example: The USS Asterion (1912-1944), a United States Navy attack vessel used during World War I and World War II.

Astraeus *(uh-STRAY-us, ASS-tree-us)* The Starry One

Astraeus was the Roman name for one of the Titans, the original deities who ruled in heaven before being overthrown by Jupiter and his Olympian gods. Astraeus's father was Krios, the Titan god of the stars; and his mother was Eurybia, a sea goddess. Astraeus was the god of constellations and astrology. He married Aurora, the "rosy-fingered" goddess of the dawn, and produced Aquilo, god of the north wind; Luciferus, god of the "wandering star," the planet Venus; Notus, god of the south wind; and Zephyrus, god of the west wind; as well as every constellation in heaven.

Related Names: Astraios.

Athos *(ATH-ohs)* The One Who Is Mount Athos

Athos was the god of Mount Athos, in the ancient nation of Thrace (present-day Bulgaria). Athos's sole parent was Gaia, the earth. One day, the Greek architect and engineer Kheirokrates suggested to Alexander the Great, the conqueror, that Mount Athos should be sculpted into a statue of Alexander. Instead, a Christian monastery stands there today.

Modern Example: Athos, one of the characters in the novel, The Three Musketeers, *by Haitian-French author Alexandre Dumas père.*

Atlas *(AT-lus)* The One Who Upholds; The One Who Supports

The enormous giant Atlas was perhaps the greatest of the Titans — the original deities who had ruled in heaven before being overthrown by Zeus and his Olympian gods. Atlas's father was Iapetus, the Titan god of the human life-span; and his mother was Clymene, the Titan goddess of fame. Because Atlas led the Titans in an unsuccessful revolt against Zeus, he was sentenced to hold up the weight of the earth and the sky on his powerful shoulders, forever.

Modern Example: Atlas (Lloyd Hopkins) (1981-), rap music artist

Augustus *(uh-GUS-tus)* The Magnificent One

Augustus (Gaius Julius Caesar Octavianus) (63 B.C.-A.D. 14) was the first Emperor of Rome, ruling as a powerful monarch while still keeping in place the Roman Senate, the elected legislature of the people. Augustus crafted the Pax Romana or Roman Peace, by conquering all nations opposed to Rome's domination, thereby creating the Roman Empire. The Pax Romana, also called the Pax Augusta, lasted for two centuries. Also, Augustus instituted a series of public-works projects in Rome, famously proclaiming that he "found Rome brick and left it marble."

Modern Example: Augustus Hawkins (Augustus Freeman Hawkins) (1907-), civil rights leader, and the oldest surviving former Congressman of the United States House Of Representatives, 1963-1991.

Axion *(AX-ee-on, AX-ee-un)* The One Who Is an Accepted Truth

Axion was a Prince of the Greek city-state of Phegia. His father was King Phegeus. Axion's complicated story begins with Callirhoe, a nymph or nature goddess of the fresh-water sources of Acarnania, a town in ancient Greece. Callirhoe married the Greek prophet and hero Alcmaeon. Callirhoe persuaded Alcmeon to go to Phegia and steal an enchanted necklace from Harmonia, goddess of happy marriages. Axion and his brother Temenus killed Alcmaeon for his crime, and took the necklace for themselves. The enraged Callirhoe pleaded with Zeus, King of the Olympian gods, to transform her two boys, Acarnan and Amphoteros, into grown men, so that they could immediately avenge their father. Zeus agreed, and the two men killed Axion, Temenus, and their father Phegeus.

Related Names: Agenor.

Axius *(AX-ee-us)* The Center, Around Which Everything Rotates

Axius was the Roman name for the Greek god of the Axios River in ancient Macedonia, a Greek-influenced kingdom near Greece. Axius's father was Oceanus,
god of the river that encircled the earth; and his mother was Tethys, the Titan
goddess of earth's fresh-water sources. In describing the Axios River, the Greek
poet Homer, in his epic poem *The Iliad*, wrote, "Axios, whose stream on all Earth
is the loveliest."

Related Names: Axios.

Bacchus *(BOK-kus)* The One Who Shouts; The Riotous One; The One Who Is Twice Born

Bacchus was the Roman name for the devoutly-worshipped, handsome young
Greek god of drunkenness and wine. Bacchus's father was Jupiter, the King of
the immortal gods who lived on Mount Olympus, in Greece; and his mother was
Jupiter's lover Stimula, goddess of the Mainades, the female worshippers of Bacchus. Jupiter's wife Juno, queen of the gods, furious at her husband's cheating,
told him to appear to Stimula in all his godly glory. Jupiter reluctantly obeyed,
and surrounded himself with dazzling lightning. Petrified, Stimula instantly gave
birth to Bacchus. Jupiter stitched-up the infant Bacchus in his thigh, until he
could be born again. Another version of Bacchs being twice-born is also told:
Jupiter seduced Stimula, and Juno angrily sent Titans to slay the infant Bacchus.
They consumed his body but left his heart, fleeing as Jupiter scattered them
with his thunderbolts. Minerva saved Bacchus's heart, and Jupiter placed it in
Stimula's womb, where Bacchus grew and was born a second time. Bacchus
traveled the world, establishing his divinity and inspiring worshippers in countless nations.

Related Names: Bakchos, Bromios, Dendrites, Dionysos, Dionysus, Dionysus Dendrites,
Dithyrambos, Eleutherios, Iacchus, Liber, Liknites, Lyaeus, Zagreus.

Names for Babies Destined to Become Nature-Lovers

Girls

Ambrosia • Anna • Aurora • Carmenta • Carya • Chloe • Cynthia
Daphne • Demeter • Diana • Iris • Penelope • Sylvia

Boys

Acmon • Adonis • Aether • Africus • Alpheus • Amnis
Aquarius • Athos • Axius • Boreas • Elisson • Faunus • Pan • Silvanus

Balius *(BAY-lee-us)* The One Dotted with Color

Balius and Xanthus were the Roman names for two noble, immortal horses owned by Neptune, god of the sea. The father of the two horses was Favonius, god of the west wind; and their mother was Podarge, one of the monstrous winged Harpies. Neptune gave Balius and Xanthos as a wedding gift to the Greek hero Peleus, when he married Thetis, goddess of the sea. The marriage produced Achilles, perhaps the greatest warrior of the Trojan War, fought between the Greeks and Trojans in the 12th Century B.C. Balius and Xanthus pulled Achilles's chariot in battle.

Related Names: Balios.

Basil *(BAY-zul)* The One Who Is King

Basil (Basil I, The Macedonian) (c. A.D. 811-A.D. 886) was an Emperor of Byzantium. Byzantium, located on the Strait of Bosphorus in the Near East, was a Greek-speaking city-state which became the new seat of the Eastern Roman Empire, the "Nova Roma," after Rome itself was conquered and sacked in 410 A.D. Basil's parents are unknown; but he claimed to have been born in Armenia, a nation bordering modern-day Turkey. Basil first became a servant in the royal Byzantine household, then the Emperor's bodyguard, then Emperor. Basil's subjects considered him to be an exemplary monarch, a patron of great artists, and a warrior who enlarged the Empire.

Modern Example: Basil Valdez, Philippine singer and entertainer.

Boreas *(BOR-ee-us, bor-RAY-us)* The North Wind

Boreas was the god of the freezing north wind, and god of winter. He was one of the brother-gods called the Anemoi, spirits who personified the winds that blew from the north, south, east, and west. Boreas's father was Astraeus, god of the stars; and his mother was Eos, the "rosy-fingered" goddess of the dawn. Boreas was often depicted with purple wings, to help him blow across the earth. Boreas raged in from the mountains of Thrace, in Northern Greece, freezing the world. But farther north, on the other side of the mountains, the nation of Hyperborea basked in endless sunshine. One day, Boreas grew tired of his frozen isolation, and swept away the fair Oreithyia, goddess of mountain storms. The marriage produced Chione, goddess of snow.

Modern Example: Boreas Pass, a mountain pass in the Rocky Mountains, between Park County and Summit County, Colorado.

Borus *(BOR-us)* The One Who Is Hard Black Crystal

Borus was a King of Messinia, a nation in the Peloponnesus region of ancient Greece. Borus's father was Penthilus, the illegitimate son of the Greek hero Orestes. King Borus, along with the other Kings of the Peloponnesus, was eventually defeated and expelled by the Heraclides, the sons of the demi-god Heracles (Hercules), after nearly a century of warfare.

Modern Example: Borus Bugdoll, character in the novel, Kingsblood Royal, *by American author Sinclair Lewis.*

Bromios *(BRO-mee-ohs)* The One Who Shouts; The Riotous One

Bromios, also known as Dionysus, was the devoutly-worshipped, handsome young Greek god of drunkenness and wine. Bromios's father was Zeus, the king of the immortal gods who lived on Mount Olympus, in Greece; and his mother was Zeus's lover Semele, goddess of the Mainades, the female worshippers of

Bromios. Zeus's wife Hera, queen of the gods, furious at her husband's cheating, told him to appear to Semele in all his godly glory. Zeus reluctantly obeyed, and surrounded himself with dazzling lightning. Petrified, Semele instantly gave birth to Br omios. Zeus stitched-up the infant Bromios in his thigh, until he could be born again.

Another version of Bromios being born twice is also told. Zeus seduced Semele and Hera angrily sent Titans to murder the infant Bromios. They ate his body but left his heart, fleeing as Zeus scattered them with thunderbolts. Athena saved the heart and Zeus placed it in Semele's womb, where Bromios grew and was born a second time.

Bromios traveled the world, establishing his divinity and inspiring worshippers in countless nations.

Related Names: Bacchus, Bakchos, Dendrites, Dionysos, Dionysus, Dionysus Dendrites, Dithyrambos, Eleutherios, Iacchus, Liber, Liknites, Lyaeus, Zagreus.

Modern Example: Mr. Bromios, character in the 1998 novel, Stardust, *by British author Neil Gaiman (1960-).*

Brontes *(BRON-tez, BRON-tayz)* The One Who Is Thunder

Brontes was one of the Cyclopes, the horrid giants — each possessing only one huge eye apiece — who hammered-out the thunderbolts that Zeus, King of the Olympian gods, hurled to earth. The father of the Cyclopes was Uranus, god of the sky; and their mother was Gaia, the earth. Uranus was so horrified when he first saw the newborn Cyclopes, that he imprisoned them underground. And when the Titans — the original deities who ruled in heaven before Zeus — successfully rebelled against Uranus, they pushed the Cyclopes even further down, into Hades, the underworld of the dead. But when Zeus and his Olympian gods overthrew the Titans, they set the Cyclopes free. In gratitude, the Cyclopes forged mighty weapons for their new Olympian masters: The helmet of invisibility for Hades, god of the dead; the trident for Poseidon, god of the sea; and the thunderbolts for Zeus.

Brychon *(BRY-kon)* The One Who Is the Brychon River

The "ox-horned" Brychon was the god of the Brychon River in Thrace (present-day Bulgaria). Brychon's father was Oceanus, god of the river that encircled the earth; and his mother was Thethys, goddess of the earth's fresh water sources.

Related Names: Brykhon.

Bythos *(BYE-those)* The One Who Is the Depths of the Sea

Bythos was an Ichthyocentaur — sea-gods with humanlike upper bodies, the lower bodies of horses, and gigantic fish tails. Bythos's father was Cronus, god of time; and his mother was Philyra, a nymph or nature goddess. Bythos's twin brother was Aphros, god of the mysterious depths of the ocean. Bythos, like all Centaurs, was a respected teacher and moral leader. His brother Aphros was renowned for helping to found the Phoenician colony of Carthage in North Africa, inspiring the Carthaginians, whom the Greeks called the Aphroi (Africans), to make epic voyages across the seas.

Caanthus *(KAN-thus)* The One Who Is the River Caanthus

Caanthus was the Roman name for Greek god Kaanthos, who personified the River Caanthus, in ancient Greece. His father was Oceanus, god of the river that encircled the earth; and his mother was Tehtys, goddess of the earth's sources of fresh water. One day, Apollo, god of prophecy, fell in love with Caanthus's sister, the goddess Malea, and kidnapped her. Caanthus retaliated by burning Apollo's Theban Temple to the ground. Apollo caught him in the act and killed him. As a result, Caanthus's nephew Ismenus took over for Caanthus, and the river's name was changed to the River Ismenus.

Related Names: Kaanthos, Ismenos, Ismenus.
Modern Example: Caanthus, character in the short story, The Fall of Myrtos, *by American author Bitter Irony.*

Cadmus *(KAD-mus)* The One from the East

Cadmus was the Roman name for Prince Cadmus son of King Phoenix of the Phoenician city-state of Tyre (present-day Tunisia). One day, Cadmus's sister Europa was kidnapped by Jupiter, King of the immortal gods of Mount Olympus, in Greece. Cadmus searched for Europa but never found her. A prophetess suggested Cadmus follow a particular cow, and build a city where the cow rested. Cadmus obeyed, and where the cow slept, Cadmus decided to establish the Greek city-state of Thebes. Cadmus sent servants to the nearby Catsalian Spring for drinking water, but the lurking Lernaean Hydra, a dragon, killed them. In retribution, Cadmus killed the dragon and planted its teeth in the soil of the new city, causing soldiers to spring up. They massacred each other until only five were left. These five established the five greatest families of Thebes, and helped the city-state to prosper. Cadmus married the goddess Concordia and produced Agave, Autonoe, Ino, Polydorus, and Semele. Cadmus's descendants ruled in Thebes for centuries.

Related Names: Kadmos.

Castor *(KAS-tur)* The Hard Worker; The Busy Beaver

Castor and Pollux were the two Roman names for Kastor and his twin brother Polydeuces (Pollux), who were called the Dioscuri, the gods of travelers, and of what we now call St. Elmo's Fire (a discharge of electrical plasma during thunderstorms). The father of Castor and Pollux was Jupiter, High King of the immortal gods of Mount Olympus, in Greece; and their mother was Queen Leda of the Greek city-state of Sparta. When the twins died, Jupiter placed them in heaven as the Gemini constellation.

Related Names: Kastor.

Centauri *(sen-TOR-ree)* The Centaurs

In ancient Greek mythology, the Centauri (Centaurs, in English) were noble, magnificent creatures with the upper bodies of human beings and the lower bodies of horses. The Centauri were renowned as wise teachers and fierce warriors.

The three legendary groups of Centauri were the Centauri Cypreii, Centauri Peloponese, and Centauri Thessalioi. The Centauri Cyprii lived on the island of Cyrus, according to the ancient Greek poet Nonnus (c. 4th Century A.D.), in his poem *Dionysiaca*. Their father was Zeus, High King of the Olympian gods; and their mother was Gaia, the earth. The Centauri Peloponese lived in the Peloponnesus Peninsula region of Greece, according to the anonmyous Greek writer called Pseudo-Apollodorus (c. 2nd Century A.D.), in his book *Bibliotheca*. Their father was Silenus, god of drunkenness; and their mother was Melia, a nymph or nature goddess. Finally, the Centauri Thessalioi lived in the Greek province of Thessaly, according to the ancient Roman poet Ovid (Publius Ovidius Naso) (43 B.C.-A.D. 17), in his poem *Metamorphoses*. Their father was Ixion, ruler of the Lapiths; and their mother was Nephele, a spirit whom Zeus had created from clouds.

Related Names: Centaurus, Kentauroi.

Modern Example: Centauri Prime, the homeworld of the alien Centauri race, in the American television series, Babylon 5, *created by Joseph Michael Straczynski (1954-).*

Cerberus *(SUR-bur-us)* The Death-Demon of the Underworld; The Hound of Hades

The "jagged-toothed" Cerberus was the monstrous three-headed canine with the tail of a snake and the claws of a lion, that safeguarded the gates of Hades, the underworld of the dead. Cerberus made certain that any souls who entered Hades never came out again; he welcomed the souls that came in, but savagely devoured those that tried to escape. Cerberus's father was Typhon, the winged giant; and his mother was Echidna, the female dragon.

Related Names: Kerberos.

Modern Example: Cerberus, character in the Japanese manga series of books, Cardcaptor sakura, *published by Kodansha Limited.*

Charles *(CHAR-ulz)* The One Who Is a Warrior

King Charles VIII (1470-1498) was France's monarch from 1483-1498; and he was also — at least on paper — the Emperor of Byzantium. Byzantium, located on the Strait of Bosphorus in the Near East, was a Greek-speaking city-state which became the new seat of the Eastern Roman Empire, the "Nova Roma," after Rome itself was conquered and sacked in 410 A.D. King Charles could legitimately claim the right to sit on the Byzantine throne because in 1494 he had purchased the title of Emperor from the cash-strapped Andreas Palaiologos, the rightful Byzantine Emperor. Unfortunately for Charles, the Turkish Sultan Mehmed II had already conquered Byzantium in 1453, leaving the exiled Andreas without an empire to transfer; and, Charles died in 1498, while Andreas died in 1503, outliving Charles by 5 years.

Related Names: Carlos.

Chromius *(KRO-mee-us)* The One Who Is Hard, Gleaming Metal

Prince Chromius was the son of Pterelaus, who was the King of the Taphian Islands, in ancient Greece. Chromius's brothers were the heroes Antiochus, Chersidamas, Everes, Mestor, and Tyrannus; and his sister was the beautiful Comaetho.

Modern Example: Chromius, an alien world featured in the 2002 audio book, Anne Manx and the Trouble on Chromius, *by American writer and director Larry Weiner.*

Cladius *(KLAD-ee-us)* The One Who Is the Cladius River

Cladius was the Roman name for Kladeos, a Greek river god who personified the Kladeos River near the town of Elis in ancient Greece. Cladius's father was Oceanus, god of the river that encircled the earth; and his mother was Tethys, goddess of the earth's sources of fresh water. The Greeks honored Cladius by carving his image on one of the columns of the famed Temple of Jupiter at Olympia.

Related Names: Cladeus, Kladeos.

Claudius *(KLAW-dee-us)* The One Who Limps

Claudius (Tiberius Claudius Caesar Augustus Germanicus) (10 B.C.-A.D. 54) was an Emperor of Rome, from A.D 41-A.D. 54. Claudius's father was Drusus, a quaestor or high government official; and his mother was Antonia Minor, the niece of the Roman Emperor Augustus. Claudius's accession was unforeseen because, although a member of the royal family, he limped and was considered inferior. But these handicaps may have insulated Claudius from the bloody rampages carried out by Emperor Caligula and Emperor Tiberius, against other more formidable royal family-members. Claudius's rule was marked by grand building projects and many new laws.

Cleon *(KLEE-on)* The Glorious One

In the ancient Greek city-state of Athens, Cleon (?-422 B.C.) was a Strategos — a high elected official whom some might call a military dictator, though he worked within a democratic framework. He was acknowledged to be Athens's most powerful citizen, gaining the trust of ordinary Athenians, and the enmity of the aristocracy. After a long political career, Cleon was killed in battle in 422 B.C.

Clytius *(KLY-tee-us)* The Renowned and Glorious One

Clytius was one of the Gigantes, the hundred giants whose mother was Gaia, the earth, and whose father was Uranus, the sky. The armored Gigantes, whose legs were huge snakes, rebelled against Zeus, High King of the immortal gods who lived on Mount Olympus, Greece. But when the demi-god Heracles entered the war on his father Zeus's side, the Gigantes were annihilated. However, the Gigantes' blood magically transformed into the people of the nation of Thrace (present-day Bulgaria).

Related Names: Klytios.
Modern Example: Clytius, a Tauren Warrior of the online universe of World of Warcraft, *a multi-player role-playing game created by Blizzard Entertainment.*

Commodus *(KOM-uh-dus)* The One Who Is Pleasant and Agreeable

Commodus (Marcus Aurelius Commodus Antoninus) (A.D. 161-A.D. 192) was an Emperor of Rome. His father was Marcus Aurelius, the philosopher-Emperor; and his mother was the Empress Faustina. Commodus married the noblewoman Bruttia Crispina in an arranged marriage, but there were no children. When Marcus Aurelius died in A.D. 180, Commodus became Emperor. He identified with the Greek demi-god Hercules, whom the ancient Greeks called Heracles. Commodus even fought in the Colosseum to demonstrate his godlike fighting skills. He was killed in A.D. 192, and was deified as a Roman god some years later.

Constantine *(KON-stun-teen)* The Steady, Persistent One

Constantine I (Flavius Valerius Aurelius Constantinus) (c. A.D. 280-A.D. 337) was an Emperor of Rome, and an Emperor of Byzantium. Byzantium, located on the Strait of Bosphorus in the Near East, was a Greek-speaking city-state which became the new seat of the Eastern Roman Empire, the "Nova Roma," after Rome itself was conquered and sacked in 410 A.D. In fact, Constantine himself proclaimed the existence of Nova Roma, and changed the name of Byzantium to

Constantinople. The Eastern Orthodox Church has recognized Constantine the Great as a saint.

Cronus *(KRONE-us)* The One Who is Time

Cronus was the King of the Titans — the original deities who ruled in heaven, before being overthrown by Zeus and his Olympian gods. Cronus was the god of the steady movement of time, as well as the decay caused by the time's passage. Cronus had gained heaven's throne by murdering his father Acmonor Uranus, god of the sky. But Cronus secretly lived in terror of a well-known prediction, that one of his offspring would eventually depose him. So, he ate each god and goddess as he or she was born. But his wife Rhea, goddess of motherhood, gave Cronus a huge stone wrapped in a diaper to eat, instead of her son Zeus, tricking Cronus. When Zeus came of age, he got Cronus to vomit out his brother and sister gods, then led them against Cronus and the Titans, defeating them, and imprisoning them in Hades, the underworld of the dead. However, centuries later, Zeus mercifully granted the Titans their freedom, and made Cronus King of the Islands of the Blessed, a heavenly afterlife.

Related Names: Aeon, Chronos, Kronos, Saturn, Saturnus.
Modern Example: Cronus, a powerful character in the Stargate *television series, which is a product of the 1994 film,* Stargate, *directed by Roland Emmerich.*

Cupid *(KYOO-pid)* The One Who is Love, Passion, and Desire

Cupid was the Roman name for Eros, the ancient Greek god of love. Cupid's sole parent was Venus, goddess of love, who gave birth to Cupid almost as soon as she had arisen full-grown from the foam of the sea. Cupid — often portrayed as a child with wings — delighted in flying invisibly among mortals and immortals, shooting enchanted love-arrows into their hearts. When one of his arrows penetrated someone's heart, he or she fell hopelessly in love.

Related Names: Amor, Eros.
Modern Example: Cupid, one of Santa Claus's eight magical flying reindeer, the other seven being Blitzen, Comet, Dancer, Dasher, Donner, Prancer, and Vixen; from an 1823 poem, A Visit from St. Nicholas, *by American educator and author Clement Clarke Moore (1779-1863).*

Daedalus *(DED-uh-lus, DEED-uh-lus)*

Daedalus was the father of a young Icarus, as well as being a renowned and brilliant engineer from the Greek island of Crete. King Minos of Crete hired Daedalus to build a prison which could hold the Minotaur — the hideous half-bull, half-man monstrosity. Daedalus created the Labyrinth, a stone maze from which the Minotaur would never escape. To show his "gratitude," King Minos imprisoned Daedalus and Icarus in a castle, so that they would never reveal the Labyrinth's secrets. But the clever Daedalus crafted wings from feathers and wax, so that he and Icarus could fly away from their prison. However, Daedalus warned Icarus not to fly too close to the sun, or his wax wings would melt, and he would plummet to his death in the Aegean Sea. Icarus promised to obey, but when he found himself soaring like a bird, he had to fly higher. His wings melted, and he hurtled down to a watery death.

Modern Example: Daedalus (1977-), the stage name of musician and composer Alfred Darlington.

Daemon *(DEE-mun)* The One Who Is a Demon

The wrathful Smaragos (The Smasher) was a Daemon or evil spirit who destroyed the fragile ceramics created by potters. The Daemon could punish dishonest potters by smashing their pots, kilns, and homes.

Modern Example: Daemon, title of a 2006 novel written by American author Leinad Zeraus.

Dameon *(DAY-mee-un)* The One Who Tames

The warrior Dameon was the son of the Greek hero Phlius. He helped the demigod Heracles (Hercules) kill King Augeas of Elis. Augeas had refused to pay Heracles, as agreed, for accomplishing an impossible task — cleaning out the sprawling Augean stables in only one day. Heracles managed to kill Augeas, but Dameon was killed by Prince Cteatus of Hyrmina.

Damon *(DAY-mun)* The One Who Tames

Damon (4th Century B.C.) and his companion Pythias were students of the Greek mathematician and philosopher Pythagoras of Samos. The two men went to the city-state of Syracuse, on the island of Sicily, to further their education. But once there, King Dionysius I imprisoned Pythias on trumped-up charges, and set a date for his execution. Pythias requested a reprieve, that he might sail home, say his good-byes, then return for punishment. When Dionysius denied the request, Damon offered to take his place until Pythias returned. Dionysius relented — if Damon agreed to die if Pythias fled. The bargain was struck. But on the day of execution, Pythias was still absent. As Damon was about to be killed, Pythias appeared and told how he had to battle pirates, and swim the oceans, to return in time to save Damon. King Dionysius was deeply moved, and kept Damon and Pythias for many years as trusted advisors, eventually allowing them to marry into the royal family.

Modern Example: Damon Rivers Headden (1926-1958), an American majority-party leader of the Tennessee House of Representatives, 1955-1957.

Dardanus *(DAR-duh-nus)* The One Who Is From Troy

King Dardanus established the city of Dardania, on Mount Ida (in present-day Turkey). Dardanus's father was Zeus, High King of the immortal gods on Mount Olympus, in Greece; and his mother was Electra, a star-goddess. Dardanus's people had sailed away from a terrible deluge in their homeland of Aracdia, a Greek province, desperately searching for a new home. Dardanus rejected several landing-sites before selecting Mount Ida and founding Dardania. Dardanus married Princess Batea of Samothrace and fathered Idaea, Ilius, Erichthonius, and Zacynthus.

Deion *(DEE-on)* The One Who Comes from God

Deion was the King of Phocis, an ancient Greek province on the Gulf of Corinth. Deion's father was Aeolus, god of the winds; and his mother was the noble-woman Enarete. Deion married the Greek matriarch Diomede, and fathered six illustrious offspring: Actor, later to become King of Phthia, a Greek province; Aenetus, the athlete; beautiful Asterodia; Cephalus, who fathered King Odysseus of Ithaca; Nisus, who would become King of the city-state of Megara; and Phylacus, founder of the city-state of Phylace.

Modern Example: Deion Sanders (Deion Luwynn Sanders) (1967-), professional football player for several championship teams in the National Football League (NFL).

Demetrius *(duh-MEET-tree-us)* From Demeter the Earth Mother

Demetrius II (276 B.C-229 B.C.) was the King Of Macedon, an ancient Greek-influenced kingdom. His father was King Antigonus Gonatas of Macedon. Although Demetrius's legendary ancestor, Alexander the Great, had conquered the known world, Macedonian military power had faded significantly by the time Demetrius was born; and when the armies of Dardania (modern-day Serbia) invaded, Philip was defeated.

Modern Example: Demetrius Terrell Williams (1983-), professional football player currently with the Baltimore Ravens, of the National Football League (NFL).

Dion *(DEE-ahn)* The One Who Comes from God

Dion (Dion I of Syracuse) (403 B.C.-354 B.C.), the son of King Hipparinus, was a King of Syracuse, an ancient Greek city-state on the island of Sicily. Dion studied with the legendary Greek philosopher Plato, but had difficulty putting Platonic precepts into practice, because as a ruler he was an insufferable tyrant. He was deposed and killed in 354 B.C.

Modern Example: Dion Joseph Ignacio (1986-), Philippine actor and musician.

Names for Babies Destined to Become Noble and Virtuous Visionaries

Girls
Alexandra • Asteria • Cassandra • Dione • Lucretia
Paula • Phoebe • Thea

Boys
Apollo • Augustus • Claudius • Cleon
Constantine • Horus • Leo • Proteus • Zeus

Dionysus *(di-uh-NICE-us, di-uh-NEE-sus, dee-uh-NEE-sus)* The One Who Shouts; The Riotous One; The God from the Thigh; The One Who Is Twice Born

Dionysus was the devoutly-worshipped, handsome young Greek god of drunkenness and wine. Dionysus's father was Zeus, the king of the immortal gods who lived on Mount Olympus, in Greece; and his mother was Zeus's lover Semele, goddess of the Mainades, the female worshippers of Dionysus. Zeus's wife Hera, queen of the gods, furious at her husband's cheating, told him to appear to Semele in all his godly glory. Zeus reluctantly obeyed, and surrounded himself with dazzling lightning. Petrified, Semele instantly gave birth to Dionysus. Zeus stitched-up the infant Dionysus in his thigh, until he could be born again.

Another version of Dionysys being twice born is also told. Zeus seduced Semele, and Hera angrily sent Titans to slay the infant Dionysus. They consumed his body but left his heart, fleeing as Zeus scattered them with his thunderbolts. Athena saved Dionysus's heart and Zeus placed it in Semele's womb, where Dionysus grew and was a born a second time.

Dionysus traveled the world, establishing his divinity and inspiring worshippers in countless nations.

Related Names: Bacchus, Bakchos, Bromios, Dendrites, Dionysos, Dionysus Dendrites, Dithyrambos, Eleutherios, Iacchus, Liber, Liknites, Lyaeus, Osiris, and Zagreus.

Draco *(DRAY-ko)* The Dragon

Typhon was an immortal fire-breathing Draco — a Dragon. The Draco's father was Tartarus, the underworld; and his mother was Gaia, the earth. The Draco had a humanlike upper body, except for his hundred heads — one man's head, surrounded by ninety-nine heads of beasts such as lions, bulls, and snakes. The Draco also had huge scaly wings, enormous snakes as legs, and a hundred venomous snakes for fingers. The Draco could produce terrible storms, or shoot brilliant firestorms at heaven.

Related Names: Typhoeus, Typhon.

Modern Example: Draco Malfoy, a character in the Harry Potter series of books, written by British author J.K. Rowling (Joanne Rowling) (1965-).

Drakon *(dra-KON)* The One Who Is a Dragon

Of the many Drakons in Greek mythology, the Drakon Maionios was one of the most deadly. He was depicted as a gigantic snakelike beast who terrorized and killed the people of Lydia (modern-day Turkey). But the monster was eventually killed by the Greek demi-god Heracles (Hercules). As a reward, Queen Omphale of Lydia gave Heracles treasure fit for a king.

Modern Example: Drakon, *the title of a 1944 play by Russian writer Evgeny L'vovich Shvarts (1896-1958).*

Elisson *(EL-uh-sun)* The One Who Is the Elisson River

Elisson was a Greek river god, who personified the Elisson River in the ancient town of Akhaia, Greece. Elissons's father was Oceanus, god of the river that encircled the earth; and his mother was Tethys, goddess of the earth's sources of fresh water. Elisson had the honor of regularly providing water for the Erinyes, the goddesses of vengeance.

Modern Example: Elisson "Tarzan" Brown (1914-1975), world-class marathon runner.

Enamerion *(en-uh-MAIR-ee-on)* The One Who Is a Great Cure

Enamerion was a demi-god, half human and half divine. His father was Ascelpius, the Greek god of healing; however, his mother's name is lost to history. Enamerion, a child-god wearing a hooded cloak, was the god of healing and recovery from ill health.

Related Names: Akesis, Enamerion, Eumerion, Telesphorus.

Erebus *(AIR-uh-bus)* The One Who Is Darkness

Erebus was one of the most ancient of the Greek gods — the lord of total blackness. Erebus's sole parent was Chaos, the first god of all, the elemental nothingness at the beginning of time. Erebus's wife was Nyx, goddess of the night; and the marriage produced many gods, including Aether, god of the earth's atmosphere, and Hemera, goddess of morning.

Related Names: Erebos, Scotus.

Eros *(AIR-ose)* The One Who is Love, Passion, and Desire

Eros — also called Cupid, or Amor — was the ancient Greek god of love. His sole parent was Aphrodite, goddess of love, who gave birth to Eros almost as soon as she had arisen full-grown from the foam of the sea. Eros, often portrayed as a child with wings, delighted in flying invisibly among mortals and immortals, shooting enchanted love-arrows into their hearts. When one of his arrows penetrated someone's heart, he or she fell hopelessly in love.

Related Names: Amor, Cupid.
Modern Example: Eros Luciano Walter Ramazzotti (1963-), Italian songwriter and singer.

Eugenius *(yoo-JEEN-yus)* The One Who Is High-Born

Eugenius (Flavius Eugenius) (?-A.D. 394) was a usurper, a person who became Emperor of Rome even though he was not part of the royal family, and had no legal right to the throne. Eugenius was a respected language teacher, as well as a close personal advisor to General Flavius Arbogastes, a top-level military commander. Eugenius used his position to effectively function as the Emperor. After Valentinian II, the true Emperor, died in A.D. 392, Arbogastes made certain that the Roman Senate installed Eugenius on the throne. After a series of political and military successes, Eugenius's armies were defeated by those of Thodosius I, another Roman Emperor.

Euphrates *(yoo-FRAY-teez)* The One Who Is the Euphrates River

Euphrates was a Greek river god, who personified the Euphrates River in ancient Assyria (present-day Iraq). Euphrates's father was Oceanus, god of the river that encircled the earth; and his mother was Tethys, goddess of the earth's sources of fresh water. The Greeks revered the Euphrates because it brought valuable trade goods to Greece, particularly silk.

Europus *(yur-RO-pus)* The One Who Is the Europus River

The "bright" Europus was a Greek river god, who personified the Europus River in ancient Thessalia (present-day Thessaly, Greece). Europus's father was Oceanus, god of the river that encircled the earth; and his mother was Tethys, goddess of the earth's sources of fresh water. The Europus River was the ancient boundary between Macedonia, a Greek-influenced kingdom, and Greece.

Related Names: Titaressus.

Evander *(ee-VAN-dur)* The One Who Is a Good Man

King Evander ruled the Italian nation of Latium, where the horrible giant Cacus regularly emerged from his cave to cut off men's heads. The Greek demi-god Heracles (Hercules) killed the monster, bringing joy back to King Evander's country. Evander was so grateful he built a beautiful temple in Heracles's honor.

Modern Example: Evander Bradley McGilvary (1864-1953), American educator, philosopher, and theologian.

Evenus *(EV-un-us, EEV-un-us)* The One Who Is the River Euenos

Evenus was a river god who personified the Euenos River in Aitolia, Greece. Evenus's father was Oceanus, god of the river that encircled the earth; and his mother was Tethys, goddess of earth's fresh water sources. Evenus's beautiful daughter was Marpessa, whom the god Idas unexpectedly kidnapped in his flying chariot. Evenus also had a flying chariot, but was never able to catch Idas. In despair, he drowned himself in the Lykormas River, renamed the Euenos River in his honor.

Related Names: Euenos.

Everes *(EV-ur-us)* The One Who Is Very Pleasing and Good

Prince Everes was the son of Pterelaus, who was the King of the Taphian Islands, in ancient Greece. Everes's brothers were the heroes Antiochus, Chersidamas, Chromius, Mestor, and Tyrannus; and his sister was the beautiful Comaetho.

Faunus *(FAWN-us)* The One Who Is a Friend

Faunus was the ancient Roman god of wild forests, goats, sheep, and sheep-herders. He was depicted with a human upper-half, although with goat-horns, and the lower-half of a goat. Faunus's father was Mercury, the messenger of the gods; and his mother was Penelope, a nymph or nature goddess. Faunus made his home in the wooded Greek province of Arcadia, where he roamed joyfully, making sweet music on his pan-pipes (a flute with multiple tubes). Faunus also loved to seduce woodland nymphs, but his appearance often caused them to panic, then flee in terror. Faunus's own mother Penelope fled in disgust when she saw her newborn baby; but Hermes, Faunus's father, took him to Mount Olympus, where all the gods adored the furry creature.

Related Names: Inuus, Phaunos, Pan.
Modern Example: Faunus Swart, South African plant pathologist for the QMS Agri-Science Corporation, based in Letsitele, South Africa.

Galerius *(guh-LAIR-ee-us)* The One Who Is from Gaul

Galerius (Gaius Galerius Valerius Maximianus) (A.D. 305-A.D. 311) was an Emperor of Rome. His father was a goatherd of Serdica (in present-day Bulgaria), with the family name of Armentarius; and his mother was the noblewoman Romula. Galerius joined the Roman Army and rose through the ranks, becoming Emperor in A.D. 293. He married Valeria, daughter of an earlier Roman Emperor, Diocletian; and he was the father to the legendary Emperor Constantine I.

Giacomo *(JOK-uh-mo)* The One Whom God Will Protect

Giacomo Ciantar, an Italian descendant of Dr. Giovanni Chapelle Paleologo (1906-1981), was a member of the Palaiologos family, the dynasty that had ruled the Byzantine Empire from 1259-1453. Byzantium, located on the Strait of Bosphorus in the Near East, was a Greek-speaking city-state that became the new seat of the Eastern Roman Empire, the "Nova Roma," after Rome itself was conquered and sacked in A.D. 410.

Related Names: Jacob, James.
Modern Example: Giacomo Manzù (1908-1991), Italian sculptor.

Giovanni *(jee-oh-VON-ee)* God Is Gracious

Prince Giovanni Giorgio Paleologo (1599-71) was the rightful Emperor of Byzantium — but in name only, since the Byzantine Empire had already been conquered in 1453. Byzantium, located on the Strait of Bosphorus in the Near East, was a Greek-speaking city-state that became the new seat of the Eastern Roman Empire, the "Nova Roma," after Rome itself was conquered and sacked in 410 A.D.

Modern Example: Giovanni Silva de Oliveira (1972-), Brazilian soccer player.

Giuseppe *(joo-SEP-ay)* The One Who Will Add Even More

Prince Giuseppe Paleologo (1790-1860) of Italy was a member of the Palaiologos family, the dynasty that had ruled the Byzantine Empire from 1259-1453. Byzantium, located on the Strait of Bosphorus in the Near East, was a Greek-speaking city-state which became the new seat of the Eastern Roman Empire, the "Nova Roma," after Rome itself was conquered and sacked in A.D. 410.

Related Names: José, Joseph.

Gleneus *(GLEN-yus, GLEN-noos)* The Playful, Dancing One

Gleneus was one of the Pheres Lamioi, the Greek gods of the Lamos River, in Anatolia (modern-day Turkey). The parents of the Pheres Lamioi were the Lamides Nymphs, the nature goddesses who followed Dionysus, god of wine. The Pheres Lamioi were Centaurs — half man, half horse — and they shielded Dionysus from Hera, Queen of the Olympian gods. She hated Dionysus because he was the illegitimate son of her husband, Zeus, High King of the gods. The Pheres Lamioi also assisted Dionysus in his epic war against King Orontes of India.

Granicus *(GRAN-uh-kus)* The One Who Is the River Granicus

Granicus was a god of the River Granicus in ancient Anatolia (present-day Turkey). Granicus's father was Oceanus, god of the river that encircled the earth; and his mother was Tethys, goddess of earth's fresh water sources. Granicus joined with his brother rivers to punish the Greek armies, after their victory over Troy in the bloody Trojan War (12th Century B.C.). The Greeks built a wall to hold back seasonal floodwaters, but Granicus and the other rivers unleashed a terrible flood and completely destroyed the wall.

Related Names: Grenikos.

Modern Example: Granicus, a Cleveland, Ohio, heavy-metal rock band that recorded an album in 1973 and then retired.

Griffin *(GRIFF-un)* The One Who Is a Prince

The "sharp-beaked" Griffin was a noble creature with an eagle's upper body — including red wings and razor-sharp talons — and a lion's lower body. Griffins were eagerly sought because they safeguarded rich veins of gold in the Rhipaean Mountains of Hyperborea (the Far North). But the mortal enemies of the Griffins, the Arismaspia — the one-eyed men — warred eternally with the Griffins for the gold.

Related Names: Gryphis, Gryphon.

Modern Example: Griffin, a character who discovers the secret of invisibility in the 1896 novel, The Invisible Man, *By British author H.G. Wells (Herbert George Wells) (1866-1946).*

Hades *(HAY-deez)* The One Who Is Unseen

The "pitiless" Hades was the ruler of the realm that bore his name — Hades, or Tartarus, the hidden underworld of the dead. Hades's father was Cronos, the Titan ruler of the gods, before Zeus and his Olympian gods took power; and his mother was Rhea, the Titan queen of the gods. Hades was the god of funerals, death, and the minerals in the earth — gold, jewels, and other buried treasure.

When Hades was born, he was actually killed by his father Cronus. Cronus was the King of the Titans — the original deities who ruled in heaven, before being overthrown by Zeus and his Olympian gods. Cronus lived in terror of a prediction that one of his offspring would eventually depose him. So, he ate each god and goddess as he or she was born, including Hades. But Cronus's wife Rhea, goddess of motherhood, gave Cronus a huge stone wrapped in a diaper to eat, instead of her son Zeus, tricking Cronus. When Zeus came of age, he got Cronus to vomit out Hades and the other gods, then led them against Cronus and the

Titans, defeating them. Zeus gave Hades dominion over the underworld, and imprisoned the Titans in Tartarus, Hades's realm.

Eventually, Hades desired a bride. One day, as the goddess Persephone — the lovely daughter of Demeter, goddess of grain — gathered flowers, Hades, emerged from the underworld. Filled with lust for Persephone, he seized her and dragged her below. Demeter searched the earth for kidnapped Persephone, then retreated to her temple in Eleusis, grief-stricken. She laid waste to the earth. No crops grew, and humanity starved.

In desperation, Zeus sent his gods to Demeter, pleading with her to spare humanity. But Demeter vowed that no crops would grow until she could see Persephone again. Finally, Zeus sent Hermes, messenger of the gods, to Hades with a royal command: Let Persephone go. Hades obeyed, but convinced Persephone to eat a few pomegranate seeds. Once she ate the food of the dead, she was condemned to return to Hades for part of each year. Now, when Persephone rejoins Demeter, flowers bloom. When Persephone returns to Hades, winter covers the earth.

Related Names: Aides, Aidoneus Haides, Dis, Dis Pater, Haides, Orcus, Pluton, Pluto, Rex Infernum.

Hadrian *(HAY-dree-un)* From the Province of Hadria

Hadrian (Publius Aelius Traianus Hadrianus) (A.D. 76-A.D. 138) was an Emperor of Rome, known as one of the "Five Good Emperors." Hadrian's father was Publius Aelius Hadrianus Afer, a Praetor or judge; and his mother was the noblewoman Domitia Paulina. Hadrian reigned as Emperor from A.D. 117-A.D. 138, and was a writer and philosopher. He is best-known for constructing the Vallum Hadriani or Hadrian's Wall in Great Britain, a stone barrier about 75 miles long, intended to regulate commerce and keep peace between Rome and the savage tribes of Caledonia (Scotland).

Halimedes *(hal-uh-MEE-deez, huh-LIM-uh-deez)* Master of the Sea

Halimedes was one of the Cyclopes, the horrid giants — each possessing only one huge eye apiece — who hammered-out the thunderbolts that King Zeus of the Olympian gods hurled to earth. The father of the Cyclopes was Uranus, god of the sky; and their mother was Gaia, the earth. Uranus was so horrified when he first saw the newborn Cyclopes, that he imprisoned them underground. And when the Titans — the original deities who ruled in heaven before Zeus — successfully rebelled against Uranus, they pushed the Cyclopes even further down, into Hades, the underworld of the dead. But when Zeus and his Olympian gods overthrew the Titans, they set the Cyclopes free. In gratitude, the Cyclopes forged mighty weapons for their new Olympian masters: The helmet of invisibility for Hades, god of the dead; the trident for Poseidon, god of the sea; and the thunderbolts for Zeus.

Modern Example: Halimedes, a character in the real-time strategy computer game Age of Mythology, *created by Ensemble Studios and released in 2000 by Microsoft Game Studios.*

Hebros *(HEEB-rose)* The One Who Is the Hebros River

Hebros was a river god who personified the Hebros River, "the most beautiful of rivers," that flowed from Thrace (present-day Bulgaria) to the Aegean Sea. Hebros's father was Oceanus, god of the river that encircled the earth; and his mother was Tethys, goddess of the earth's fresh water sources. The Hebros River was known for the many beautiful maidens who bathed in it.

Related Names: Hebrus.

Names for Babies Destined to Become Pacifists and Mediators

Girls

Alethea • Clementia • Concordia • Eirene • Galene • Harmonia
Irene • Libra • Pandora • Paulina • Serena

Boys

Aphros • Hadrian • Letus • Morpheus • Nile • Thanatos

Hector *(HEK-tur)* The One Who Stands Fast

The "glorious" and "goodly" Hector was a Prince of the legendary city-state of Troy, located in modern-day Turkey. Hector's father was Priam, King of Troy; and his mother was Queen Hecuba, a Phrygian. Hector was hailed by the Trojans as their finest warrior, a reputation he reinforced during the Trojan War, a bloody conflict fought in the 12th Century B.C. against the armies of ancient Greece.

According to the Greek poet Homer, in his epic poem, The Iliad, the Trojan War began when Prince Paris, Hector's brother, ran off with the beautiful Queen Helen, wife of King Menelaus of Sparta. Menelaus allied with other Greek kings and their armies, and the Greeks sailed to Troy in a thousand ships, to wage war for ten years. During the war, Hector killed many Greeks, including Patrocles, the dearest friend of Achilles, Greece's greatest warrior. In retribution, Achilles killed Hector, tied the body to his chariot, and dragged it around Troy's walls for nine days.

In the end, the Greeks won the war because of King Odysseus of Ithaca. He convinced the Greeks to build an immense wooden horse, the symbol of Troy, and leave it hollow inside. Greek soldiers hid in the horse, and the other Greek armies sailed away — but only to hide, out of sight of the Trojans. The Trojans thought they had won the war, but Cassandra, a Trojan prophetess, begged the Trojans not to pull the statue into the city. Everyone thought she was insane and wheeled the statue through the gates. That night, the Greeks exited the Trojan Horse, opened the gates of Troy for their waiting armies, and destroyed the city. Nonetheless, even though Troy lost the war, Hector is remembered as one of the greatest warriors of the Trojan War.

Helios *(HEE-lee-ose)* The Sun

Helios was the sun. His father was Hyperion, god of light; and his mother was Thea, goddess of light and vision. Helios's shining temple was located in the East, far beyond the boundaries of mortal kingdoms. Apollo, god of prophecy, escorted Helios across the sky each day in a gleaming chariot, pulled by several immortal horses. But one day, Apollo foolishly granted his demi-god son, Phaëthon, a chance to drive the horses of Helios. Phaëthon, being half mortal, could not control the magnificent steeds, and he brought Helios close to earth, burning cities to ashes. Zeus, king of the gods, witnessed this disaster and swiftly killed Phaëthon with a thunderbolt.

Related Names: Helius, Sol.

Henry *(HEN-ree)* The Powerful Ruler of the Homeland

Henry Herbert Chapelle Paleologo (1914-) is a member of the Palaiologos family, the dynasty that ruled the Byzantine Empire from 1259-1453. Byzantium, located on the Strait of Bosphorus in the Near East, was a Greek-speaking city-state which became the new seat of the Eastern Roman Empire, the "Nova Roma," after Rome itself was conquered and sacked in A.D. 410.

Modern Example: Henry Benjamin Greenberg (1911-1986), professional baseball player for the Detroit Tigers and others.

Hephaestus *(huh-FESS-tus)* The One Who Shines in Daylight

Hephaestus, or Vulcan, was the lame, hideous god of volcanoes, fire, and black-smiths. While forging weapons for the gods, he grew deformed — exactly like many human blacksmiths, because they breathed poisonous arsenic vapors from their forges.

Hephaestus's mother was Hera, Queen of the gods. His father was Zeus, King of the gods, though some legends say Hera created Hephaestus by herself, due to her jealousy over Zeus's solo creation of Athena, goddess of wisdom. But after Hephaestus was born, Hera was repulsed by his ugliness and threw him from Mount Olympus, where he fell many days until he hit Ocean, the river circling the earth. Raised by the nymphs Thetis and Eurynome, Hephaestus punished Hera by making a golden throne which magically seized her and held her prisoner. Later, the lonely Hephaestus decided to rape Athena, but she escaped, causing Hephaestus's semen to impregnate Gaia (earth) and produce the future King Erichthonius of Athens.

Eventually, Hephaestus released Hera after the gods gave him fair Aphrodite, goddess of love, for his wife. But Aphrodite quickly cheated on Hephaestus with his brother, Ares, god of war. Helios, the sun god, told Hephaestus of Aphrodite's betrayal, and Hephaestus caught the lovers in his magic net and put them on display. But this gave Hephaestus no comfort, for he learned that a god as ugly as he could never possess such a beautiful goddess as Aphrodite. He sought other lovers, such as the mortal Anticleia, who bore him Periphetes, a future thief; and Thalia, muse of comedy, who produced the Palici, the twin gods.

Hephaestus's brother Ares, the god of war, wielded the weapons Hephaestus forged — as did Athena, when she assumed her role as warrior-goddess. In fact, Hephaestus — with his assistants, the robot-like Automatons, and the one-eyed Cyclopes — is credited with forging nearly all the weapons and equipment of the gods. These included the shield of Achilles, hero of the Trojan War; the girdle of Aphrodite, goddess of love; the bow and arrows of Eros, god of love; the invisibility-helmet of Hades, god of the underworld; the golden chariot of Helios, the sun god; the winged helmet and sandals of Hermes, messenger of the gods; and the Aegis or breastplate of Zeus, King of the gods.

Hephaestus was worshipped in most Greek manufacturing areas, including Athens, Attica, Phrygia, Thrace, and the Greek colony in Sicily. Hephaestus's forges were thought to rest inside the volcanoes on Lemnos island, and Mount Etna in Sicily.

Related Names: Hephaistos, Vulcan.

Heracles *(HAIR-uh-kleez)* The Glory of Hera

Heracles, or Hercules, was an ancient Greek demi-god, half human and half divine — perhaps the strongest and most beloved Greek hero of all time. Heracles's father was Zeus, High King of the immortal gods of Mount Olympus; and his mother was Zeus's lover, the mortal Alcmene. Zeus's wife despised the illegitimate child Heracles and conspired to kill him. She sent venomous snakes to bite the newborn, but Heracles choked the snakes and played with their bodies. This incident foreshadowed the incredible deeds Heracles would eventually accomplish, striding the earth wielding his war-club, and wearing the lion-head of the giant Antaeus as his war helmet.

But Hera's burning hatred for Heracles never wavered. She put Heracles under an evil spell, causing him to kill his many children, and his wife Megara. Heracles's friend, the hero Theseus took the grieving Heracles to the Oracle (prophetess) at Delphi, who ordered him to perform twelve labors for King Eurystheus of Tiryns, as a punishment. Heracles then proceeded to (1) kill either the Nemean Lion or the lion-headed giant Antaeus, and return with the head as a trophy; (2) kill the Hydra (dragon) of Lake Lerna; (3) hunt the Cerneian Elk, sacred to Artemis, goddess of hunting; (4) kill the Boar of Mount Erymanthos; (5) sweep-out the Augean stables in one day; (6) kill the monstrous Stymphalian Birds; (7) kill the enormous Bull of Crete; (8) rustle the Horses of Diomedes; (9) bring back the magic belt of Hippolyta; (10) rustle the Cattle of Geryon; (11) take the Apples of the Hesperides; and (12) bring back Cerberus, the three-headed dog guarding the gates of Hades, the underworld of the dead. When Heracles had accomplished these labors and more, he was acknowledged by the world to be the greatest hero alive. He received immortality. He then reconciled with Hera and married her daughter Hebe.

Heracles, as well as being a beloved Greek demi-god, was also the name of a young man born to King Alexander III of Macedon (a Greek-influenced nation). But Heracles would never become the Prince of Macedon, because his mother was Alexander's lover, Barsine, a peasant from the nation of Phrygia.

Related Names: Alcides, Herakles, Hercules.
Modern Example: Heracles Almelo (1903-), a championship soccer team based in Almelo, The Netherlands.

Heros *(HE-rows)* The One Who is from the Underworld

Heros was originally a god of Thrace (present-day Bulgaria). However, when the Romans conquered Thrace, they embraced the god as one of their own. Heros was the god of the underworld of the dead, and did not hesitate to kill man or beast.

Related Names: Karabazmos, Pirmeroula.
Modern Example: Heros Severum, a rock band based in Athens, Georgia.

Heraeus *(hair-RAY-us, her-REE-us)* The One Who Honors Hera

Prince Heraeus was the founder of the ancient Greek city-state of Heraea. Heraeus's father was Lycaon, King of Arcadia, another city-state in Greece.

Related Names: Heraeeus.

Hercules *(HER-kyoo-leez)* The Glory of Hera

Hercules was the Roman name for Heracles, an ancient Greek demi-god, half human and half divine — perhaps the strongest and most beloved Greek hero of all time. Hercules's father was Jupiter, High King of the immortal gods of Mount Olympus; and his mother was Jupiter's lover, the mortal Alcmene. Jupiter's wife despised the illegitimate child Hercules and conspired to kill him. She sent venomous snakes to bite the newborn, but Hercules choked the snakes and played with their bodies. This incident foreshadowed the incredible deeds Hercules would eventually accomplish, striding the earth wielding his war-club, and wearing the lion-head of the giant Antaeus as his war helmet.

But Juno's burning hatred for Hercules never wavered. She put Hercules under an evil spell, causing him to kill his many children, and his wife Magera. Hercules's friend, the hero Theseus, took the grieving Hercules to the Oracle (prophetess) at Delphi, who ordered him to perform twelve labors for King Eurystheus of Tiryns, as a punishment. Hercules then proceeded to (1) kill either the Nemean Lion or the lion-headed giant Antaeus, and return with the head as a trophy; (2) kill the Hydra (dragon) of Lake Lerna; (3) hunt the Cerneian Elk, sacred to Diana, goddess of hunting; (4) kill the Boar of Mount Erymanthos; (5) sweep-out the Augean stables in one day; (6) kill the monstrous Stymphalian Birds; (7) kill the enormous Bull of Crete; (8) rustle the Horses of Diomedes; (9) bring back the magic belt of Hippolyta; (10) rustle the Cattle of Geryon; (11) take the Apples of the Hesperides; and (12) bring back Cerberus, the three-headed dog guarding the gates of Tartarus, the underworld of the dead. When Hercules had accomplished these labors and more, he was acknowledged by the world to be the greatest hero alive. He received immortality. He then reconciled with Juno and married her daughter Juventas.

Related Names: Alcides, Heracles, Herakles.
Modern Example: Hercules Brabazon (1821-1906), British Victorian artist.

Hermes *(HER-meez)* The One Who Is a Pile of Marker-Stones

Hermes was the messenger of the gods, as well as the god of travel, commerce, and "crossing over," including crossing to Tartarus or Hades, the underworld of the dead. Hermes was often shown wearing his winged sandals, called the

Talaria; a winged helmet, called the Petasus, forged by Hephaestus, god of blacksmiths; and in his hand, a sceptre with two snakes wrapped around it, the Caduceus. Hermes's name comes from the Greek word *herma*, meaning piles of stones along highways that measured distances and boundaries. Travelers made these markers by tossing stones as they passed. Later, many of these markers were replaced with monuments to Hermes, god of travel.

Hermes was one of the youngest of the Olympian gods — those newer gods who, along with their king, mighty Zeus, overthrew the old Titans or Elder Deities and took control of heaven. Hermes's parents were Zeus and the nymph Maia, a mountain-goddess. Hermes's birthplace was a cave on Mount Cyllene in Southern Greece. The day he was born, Hermes invented the lyre or harp, then rustled the immortal cattle of Apollo, god of the arts. Hermes also invented numerous sports, including boxing, as well as fortune-telling and divination.

Hermes later gained fame by killing the hundred-eyed giant Argos. The story began when Zeus, High King of the immortal gods on Mount Olympus, had tried to hide his lover, fair Io, by changing her into a white cow. But Zeus's wife Hera saw through the ruse and demanded the cow as a gift. Hera then turned the cow over to Argos, ordering him to keep it from Zeus. Furious, Zeus sent Hermes to kill Argos. Hermes put Argos to sleep, and when the monster closed its hundred eyes, Hermes slew it with a sling and a stone.

Some time later, Hermes married the nymph Dryope, and together they produced the half-goat Pan, god of shepherds. Dryope fled from her hideous son, but Hermes took Pan to Olympus, where the gods welcomed him. Hermes also fathered Abderus, who was eventually eaten by the four carnivorous mares of the Greek king Diomedes. Another of Hermes's sons was Hermaphroditus, whose mother was Aphrodite, goddess of love. The gods changed Hermaphroditus into a hermaphrodite — half-male, half-female.

Related Names: Argeiphontes, Enagonios, Hermes Cylleneius, Hermes Psychopompos, Hermes Trismegistus, Mercury.
Modern Example: Hermes Pan (Hermes Pangiotopolous) (1909-1990), Greek-American choreographer and dancer.

Hermus *(HUR-mus)* The One Who Is the Hermus River

The "whirling" Hermus was a Greek river god, who personified the Hermus River in ancient Anatolia (currently the Gediz River, in modern-day Turkey). Hermus's father was Oceanus, god of the river that encircled the earth; and his mother was Tethys, goddess of the earth's sources of fresh water. Hermus was known as compassionate, especially towards Dionysus, the Greek god of wine.

Related Names: Hermos.
Modern Example: The Hermus Vallis, a large canyon on the planet Mars, the fourth planet from the Sun.

Hesperus *(HESS-per-us)* Venus Who Is The Evening Star

The god Hesperus, "the fairest star in the heavens," was the twin brother of the god Eosphorus, "who surpassed many in beauty." Together, these deities were the two aspects of Venus, which the ancient Greeks believed was a star. The father of the twins was Astraeus, the Titan god of constellations; and their mother was Eos, the "rosy-fingered" goddess of the dawn. Hesperus was called the Morning Star, and Eosphorus was called the Evening Star, because Venus shines so brightly at dawn and at dusk.

Related Names: Hesperos, Vesper, Vesperus.
Modern Example: Hesperus, a traditional folk-music ensemble founded in 1979 by American musicians Tina Chancey and Scott Reiss.

Horus *(HOR-us)* The Hawk; The Falcon

Horus, or Apollo, was the handsome young god of light, medicine, healing, reason, colonization, dance, music, poetry — and most importantly, prophecy. Pilgrims journeyed to his oracles or divine prophets at Delphi, Clarus, and Branchidae to hear their fortunes told. Horus sometimes even gave the gift of prophecy to deserving mortals, such as Princess Cassandra of Troy.

Horus was the son of Zeus, the king of the Olympian gods; and Leto, one of the Titans or original deities who had ruled in heaven until Zeus took control. When Hera, queen of the gods, learned that Leto would bear her husband Zeus's love-children, she forbade Leto from giving birth anywhere on earth; but Leto discovered the floating island of Delos, where she had her babies. Afterwards, the island grew four pillars which rooted it to the earth. The gods quickly grew to love Horus, for his speed — he was the world's first Olympic Games champion — and his beautiful recitals on the lyre or harp. Horus's courage also became legendary, when he slew the terrifying Python, the giant snake of Mount Parnassus.

Horus's twin sister was Artemis, goddess of hunting; she protected virtuous females, while Horus protected males. Horus was sometimes confused with the sun god Helios, because some poets say Helios's chariot and divine steeds pulled the sun across the sky each day, while other poets credit Horus. Horus had many facets, and although he could be ruthless, he was still the subject of more Greek art than any other god — holding his lyre or his bow, and wearing his laurel victory-crown.

Related Names: Akesios, Alexikakos, Aphetoros, Apollo, Apotropaeus, Archegetes, Arguro-toxos, Delian Apollo, Delphinios, Iatros, Klarios, Kynthios, Loxias, Lyceios, Lykegenes, Mus-agetes, Nomios, Nymphegetes, Parnopius, Phevos, Phoebus, Phoebus Apollo, Phoibos Apollon, Pythian Apollo, Pythios, Smintheus.

Hyperbius *(hy-PUR-bee-us)* The One With Overwhelming Strength

Hyperbius was one of the Gigantes, the hundred giants whose mother was Gaia, the earth, and whose father was Uranus, the sky. The armored Gigantes, whose legs were huge snakes, rebelled against Zeus, High King of the immortal gods who lived on Mount Olympus, Greece. But when the demi-god Heracles entered the war on his father Zeus's side, the Gigantes were annihilated. However, the Gigantes' blood magically transformed into the people of the nation of Thrace (present-day Bulgaria).

Related Names: Hyperbios.
Modern Example: Hyperbius, character portrayed by actor Riccardo Garrone, in the 1960 Italian film, The Warrior Empress, *directed by Petro Francisci.*

Hyperion *(hy-PEER-ee-un)* The One Who Watches from Above

Hyperion was the god of light. He was also one of the four columns that sup-ported the dome of heaven. Finally, he was a Titan, one of the original deities who ruled in heaven before being overthrown by Zeus and his Olympian gods. Hyperion's father was Uranus, the sky; and his mother was Gaia, the earth. Hyperion married the beautiful Thea, goddess of the radiant light of heaven, and fathered three children: Eos, the "rosy-fingered: goddess of the dawn; Helios, the sun; and Selene, goddess of the moon. A time came when Hyperion helped overthrow Cronus, the Titan king; but Hyperion and the others were themselves defeated, by Zeus, King of the new gods from Mount Olympus, in Greece. Zeus confined the Titans to Hades, but eventually sent them to the Islands of the Blessed, the heavenly afterlife.

Modern Example: The Hyperion-class heavy cruiser, a starship featured in the 1993-1998 science fiction television program, Babylon 5, created by American writer Joseph Michael Straczynski.

Icarus *(IK-uh-rus)* The Follower

Icarus was the young son of Daedalus, the brilliant architect and engineer from the Greek island of Crete. King Minos of Crete hired Daedalus to build a prison which could hold the Minotaur — the hideous half-bull, half-man monstrosity. Daedalus created the Labyrinth, a stone maze from which the Minotaur would never escape. To show his "gratitude," King Minos imprisoned Daedalus and his son Icarus in a castle, so that they would never reveal the Labyrinth's secrets. But the clever Daedalus crafted wings from feathers and wax, so that he and Icarus could fly away from their prison. However, Daedalus warned Icarus not to fly too close to the sun, or his wax wings would melt, and he would plummet to his death in the Aegean Sea. Icarus promised to obey, but when he found himself soaring like a bird, he had to fly higher. His wings melted, and he hurtled down to a watery death.

Ilissus *(il-ISS-us)* The One Who is the Ilissus River

Ilissus was a Greek river god, who personified the Ilissus River of the Greek city-state of Attika. Ilissus's father was Oceanus, god of the river that encircled the earth; and his mother was Tethys, goddess of the earth's sources of fresh water. Boreas, god of the north wind, carried off the goddess Oreithyia from the banks of the Ilissus River.

Related Names: Ilissos.

Names for Babies Destined to Become Powerful, Swift Racers and Climbers

Girls

Arce • Aura • Bia • Camilla • Gymnastica • Iris
Olympias • Pallas • Valeria • Victoria

Boys

Andreas • Antaeus • Arion • Balius • Centauri
Heracles • Hercules • Hermes • Horus • Icarus • Mercury • Xanthes

Inachus *(IN-uh-kus)* The One who is the Inachus River

Inachus was a Greek river god, who personified the Inachus River of the Greek city-state of Argolis; and he was also King of Argos. Inachus's father was Oceanus, god of the river that encircled the earth; and his mother was Tethys, goddess of the earth's sources of fresh water.

Related Names: Inakhos.

Indicus *(IN-duh-kus)* The Ones from India

The Myrmex Indicus were the dog-sized ants of India, creatures which guarded secret hoards of gold in their monstrous ant-hills. Indians would ride teams of camels to the huge ant-hills and grab as much gold as possible, then flee for their lives, trying to outrace the swift Myrmex Indicus.

Related Names: Myrmekes Indikoi.

Indus *(IN-dus)* The One Who Is the Indus River

Indus was a Greek river god, who personified the Indus River in ancient Anatolia (present-day Turkey). Indus's father was Oceanus, god of the river that encircled the earth; and his mother was Tethys, goddess of the earth's sources of fresh water.

Related Names: Indos.

Isaac *(EYE-zik)* The One Who Laughs

Isaac (Isaac II Angelos) (1156-1204) was an Emperor of Byzantium. Byzantium, located on the Strait of Bosphorus in the Near East, was a Greek-speaking city-state which became the new seat of the Eastern Roman Empire, the "Nova Roma," after Rome itself was conquered and sacked in 410 A.D. Isaac's father was Andronikos Angelos; and his mother was the noblewoman Euphrosyne. Isaac ruled as Emperor from 1185-1195, and 1203-1204.

Modern Example: Isaac Asimov (1920-1992), scientist and science-fiction writer.

Jason *(JAY-sun)* The One Who Heals

Jason was the rightful Prince of Iolcus, an ancient Greek city-state; but his throne had been stolen by his uncle, King Pelias. To win back his birthright, Jason journeyed to Colchis, a kingdom near the Black Sea, to seize the Golden Fleece — the hide of the immortal ram Chrysomallos, a prize known throughout the ancient world as a symbol of wealth and power. Jason's companions were the Argonauts, noble warriors who sailed with him on the ship Argo. King Aeëtes of Colchis safeguarded the Golden Fleece and refused to surrender it. Knowing beforehand that Jason would fail, Aeëtes offered the Fleece if Jason could perform a mighty task. Princess Medea, Aeëtes's daughter, secretly pledged to aid Jason with her sorcery, if he would take her back to Iolcus and marry her. Jason agreed, and Medea gave him invulnerability potions to rub on himself and his weapons. Then Jason set out to accomplish his impossible tasks. He yoked the Tuari Chalcei — the living, fire-breathing bronze bulls of the god Hephaestus — and forced them to plow a field, where he planted dragon's teeth. Warriors sprang up from the ground, yet Jason used shield and spear to kill them all. Jason then stole the Golden Fleece, and he and the Argonauts sailed back to Iolcus with Medea.

Modern Example: Jason Lau (1951-), a Chinese-American Grandmaster of the martial art of Wing Chun Kung Fu.

John *(JON)* God is Gracious

John (John I Tzimisces) (c. A.D. 925-A.D. 976) was an Emperor of Byzantium. Byzantium, located on the Strait of Bosphorus in the Near East, was a Greek-speaking city-state which became the new seat of the Eastern Roman Empire, the "Nova Roma," after Rome itself was conquered and sacked in 410 A.D. John distinguished himself as a military strategist, then reigned as the Byzantine Emperor from A.D. 969-A.D. 976.

Related Names: Ian, Jonathan, Nathan.

Modern Example: John Chiang (John Hsiao-yen Chiang) (1941-), Chinese statesman and politician in Taipei, Taiwan.

Julian *(JOO-lee-un)* The One Who Is Related to Julius Caesar

Julian II (Flavius Claudius Iulianus) (A.D. 331-A.D. 363) was an Emperor of Rome. His father was Julius Constantinus, brother of Emperor Constantine I; and his mother was the noblewoman Basilina. Julian was called Julian the Apostate because he rejected the Christian religion sweeping Rome at that time, and guided his subjects back to traditional pagan beliefs — an effort that ultimately proved unsuccessful.

Modern Example: Julian Lennon (born John Charles Julian Lennon, 1963-), English singer, songwriter, and musician.

Julius *(JOOL-yus, JOO-lee-us)* The Youthful One

Julius Caesar (Gaius Julius Caesar) (100 B.C.-44 B.C.) was the Dictator for Life of the Roman Empire. Julius's father was the Roman Senator Gaius Julius Caesar; and his mother was the Roman noblewoman Aurelia Cotta. Julius replaced the Roman Republic — a form of democratic government — with a dictatorship, and with the Roman Empire. Julius began his rise to power by defeating the Gauls (French) and expanding the size of the Empire; starting a civil war in 49 B.C.; crossing the Rubicon River near Rome; defeating all armies sent against him; and declaring himself Dictator for Life. Julius was assassinated in 44 B.C., but the ruling dynasty he founded lived on.

Jupiter *(JOO-pih-tur)* The Father of the Gods; The One Who Is the Bright Sky; The Divine King; The Heavenly Father

Jupiter was the Roman name for Zeus, the ancient Greek god of heaven, the ruler of the immortal gods and mortal men alike. Being all-powerful, Jupiter answered to no one, and could use his thunderbolts — the flashes of light that streaked from the sky — to kill at his pleasure. Wearing his Aegis or armored breastplate, which had been forged by Vulcan, god of blacksmiths, Jupiter ruled over the palace of the gods. He seized control of Olympus by overthrowing his father, Saturn, the greatest of the original gods called the Titans. Because Saturn had feared that one of his children might someday depose him, he ate them all at birth: Ceres (Demeter), Pluto (Hades), Juno (Hera), Vesta (Hestia), and Neptune (Poseidon). But Jupiter's mother Opis saved him by feeding Saturn a boulder wrapped in blankets, disguised as the infant Jupiter. Then she hid Jupiter in Crete, where he grew strong by drinking the milk of the goat Amalthea. Jupiter returned to Saturn and forced him to vomit out all of Jupiter's siblings, and together they waged war against the Titans. Victorious, Jupiter imprisoned Saturn and the Titans in Tartarus, the underworld. Jupiter then assigned the gods their duties: Ceres became goddess of the harvest; Vesta, goddess of the home and family; Neptune, god of the seas; and Pluto, god of the underworld and the dead. Finally, Jupiter married Juno, who then became goddess of marriage and queen of the gods. Jupiter cheated regularly on Juno, fathering many demigods, or half-human/half-divine children. Jupiter's real-world Roman worshippers built an enormous temple in Rome on Capitoline Hill.

Related Names: Agoraios, Horkios, Jove, Jupiter Optimus Maximus, Kronides Hypatos, Olympios, Panhellenios, Theos, Theos Hyspsistos, Xenios, Zeus, Zeus Astrapaios, Zeus Heraios, Zeus Hypsistos, Zeus Kronion.

Modern Example: Sailor Jupiter, also known as Makoto Kino, in the Japanese anime television series, Sailor Moon, *created by Japanese artist Naoko Takeuchi.*

Justin *(JUST-un)* The One Who Is Just

Justin II (Flavius Iustinus Augustus) (c. A.D. 520-A.D. 578) was an Emperor of Byzantium. Byzantium, located on the Strait of Bosphorus in the Near East, was a Greek-speaking city-state which became the new seat of the Eastern Roman

Empire, the "Nova Roma," after Rome itself was conquered and sacked in 410 A.D. Justin married Sophia, the niece of the Empress Theodora; and after Justinian I, Justin's uncle, died in A.D. 565, Justin was crowned Emperor.

Modern Example: Justin Timberlake (Justin Randall "JT" Timberlake) (1981-), American actor, singer, and songwriter, formerly of the band 'N Sync.

Kairos *(KYE-rose)* The One Who is Opportunity and Profit

Kairos was the god of opportunity and profit. His sole parent was Zeus, High King of the immortal gods on Mount Olympus, Greece. Kairos, who was bald, had one very long lock of hair extending from his forehead, because as the god of opportunity, one had to quickly grab his hair, or one's fortune in life might be lost forever.

Related Names: Caerus, Occasio, Tempus.
Modern Example: The Kairos Document, a 1985 declaration by black South African theologians that challenged the unfairness of apartheid, the government's policy of discrimination.

Kyon *(KYE-on)* The One Who Is the Dog Star; The Glowing One

In the Constellation Canis Major (The Larger Dog) the brightest star in that cluster is called Aster Kyon, or the Dog Star; and the ancient Roman god Aster

---

Names for Babies Destined to Be Romantic

Girls
Acantha • Alexandra • Antheia • Aphrodite • Ariadne
Calypso • Danais • Erato • Helen • Martina • Phyllis • Valeria • Venus

Boys
Adonis • Alexandros • Amor • Apollo • Astraeus
Cupid • Eros • Faunus • Pan • Paris • Theseus • Zeus

Kyon personified the shimmering star. The Romans believed Aster Kyon brought scorching heat and diseases to earth, and that it was mankind's duty to offer sacrifices, to keep the god appeased.

Related Names: Aster Cuon, Aster Sirios, Canicula, Kyon Khryseos, Seirios, Sirios, Sirius, Sothos.
Modern Example: Kyon, a character in the Japanese anime television series, The Melancholy of Haruhi Suzumiya, *which premiered in 2006, directed by Tatsuya Ishihara.*

Khryses *(CRY-seez)* The One Who Is Golden

King Khryses was a demi-god, half human and half divine. He was the ruler of Orkhomenos, an ancient Greek city-state. His father was Poseidon, god of the oceans; and his mother was Queen Khrysogeneia. He was the father of Minyas, who became a rich and powerful King of Orkhomenos in his own right.

Related Names: Chryses.

Labor *(LAY-bur)* The One Who Is Hard Work and Exertion

Labor was the Roman name for Ponus, the Greek god of strenuous, sweaty work. Labor's sole parent was Discordia, goddess of discord. Labor had many immortal siblings, among them the Dolores, the goddesses of pain; the Pugnae, the goddesses of combat; and Pertinacia, goddess of stubbornness.

Related Names: Ponos, Ponus.

Ladon *(luh-DON)* The One Who Is the Ladon River

Ladon was a Greek river god, who personified the Ladon River in the Arcadia region of ancient Greece. Ladon's father was Oceanus, god of the river that encircled the earth; and his mother was Tethys, goddess of the earth's sources of fresh water.

Modern Example: Ladon Radim, a character on the Canadian-American science-fiction television series, Stargate Atlantis, *which premiered in 2004 and was created by writers Brad Wright and Robert C. Cooper.*

Latinus *(LAT-un-us)* The One Who Is a Latin

In ancient Roman legends, Latinus was the King of the Latins, an Italian tribe. Latinus's father was Faunus (Pan), Roman god of shepherds; and his mother was Marica, a nymph or nature goddess. King Latinus married Queen Amata, and the marriage produced one daughter, Princess Lavinia. Latinus welcomed the hero Aeneas, who was fleeing the destruction of his home city-state of Troy, following the Trojan War (12th Century B.C.). But a problem arose: Princess Lavinia was supposed to marry King Turnus of the Rutuli nation, but Latinus felt Aeneas was the better man, and promised Lavinia to him. Turnus's armies soon fought the Trojans, but Turnus was defeated and killed, and Aeneas married Lavinia. Because Queen Amata had backed Turnus, she decided to take her own life.

Related Names: Latinos, Latium, Lavinius.

Leneus *(LEN-ee-us, LEN-oos)* Coming from the Wine-Trough

Leneus was the god of the joyous dance that mortals did, while stomping grapes in the wine-trough to make wine. Leneus's sole parent was Silenus, god of drunkenness. Leneus's children were the Lenai, the gods of wine-pressing, who served the god Dionysus, god of wine.

Leo *(LEE-oh)* The Lion

Leo I (Flavius Valerius Leo) (A.D. 401-A.D. 474) was an Emperor of Byzantium. Byzantium, located on the Strait of Bosphorus in the Near East, was a Greek-speaking city-state which became the new seat of the Eastern Roman Empire, the "Nova Roma," after Rome itself was conquered and sacked in 410 A.D. Leo, a Christian monarch, ruled from A.D. 457 to his death in A.D. 474.

Modern Example: Leó Szilárd (1898-1964), Hungarian-American mathematician and physicist who helped the United States develop the world's first nuclear weapon.

Leon *(LEE-ahn)* The Lion

Leon was one of the Gigantes, the hundred giants whose sole parent was Gaia, the earth. Leon was unique among the Gigantges, because he had the head of a noble lion in place of a human head. Leon was eventually killed by the Greek demi-god Heracles (Hercules), who took Leon's mane and wore it as a trophy.

Related Names: Leo.

Modern Example: León Felipe Camino Galicia (1884-1968), Spanish-Mexican poet and soldier.

Letus *(LEE-tus)* The One Who Is Death

Letus was the Roman name for Thanatos, the winged Greek god of peaceful, natural death. Letus's sole parent was Nox, goddess of night. Letus was known for his compassion, and his gentle embrace that carried mortals to the next world; in this sense he was similar to his twin brother Somnus, god of peaceful slumber.

Related Names: Mors, Thanatos, Thanatus.

Liber *(LEE-bur, LYE-bur)* The One Who is Freedom

Liber was the devoutly-worshipped, handsome young Roman god of drunkenness and wine. Liber's father was Jupiter, ruler of the immortal gods who lived on Mount Olympus, in Greece; and his mother was Jupiter's lover Stimula, goddess of the Mainades, the female worshippers of Liber. Jupiters's wife Juno, queen of the gods, furious at her husband's cheating, told him to appear to Stimula in all his godly glory. Jupiter reluctantly obeyed, and surrounded himself with dazzling lightning. Petrified, Stimula instantly gave birth to Liber. Zeus stitched-up the infant Liber in his thigh, until he could be born again.

Another version of Liber being twice-born is also told: Jupier seduced Stimula, and Juno angrily sent Titans to slay the infant Liber. They consumed his body but left his heart, fleeing as Jupiter scattered them with his thunderbolts. Minerva saved Liber's heart, and Jupiter placed it in Stimula's womb, where Liber grew and was born a second time.

Liber traveled the world, establishing his divinity and inspiring worshippers in countless nations. Liber eventually married the beautiful Princess Ariadne of Crete, whose name was changed to Libera after she married the god.

Related Names: Bacchus, Bakchos, Bromios, Dendrites, Dionysos, Dionysus, Dionysus Dendrites, Dithyrambos, Eleutherios, Iacchus, Liknites, Lyaeus, Zagreus.

Linus *(LYE-nus)* The One Who Is The Flax-Seed Plant

The "doomed" god Linus was one of the greatest poets, singers, and harp-players in ancient Greek history. Linus's mother was Urania, one of the Muses, the goddesses who brought inspiration to humankind; and his father was Amphimarus, a sea god. One year, Linus entered a singing competition against Apollo, god of prophecy and music. When Linus won the contest, Apollo killed him. The entire world mourned Linus; the Egyptians even composed a hymn for Linus, and the citizens of Thebes buried him in their city with honors.

Related Names: Linos, Oetolinus)

Modern Example: Linus van Pelt, a character in the long-running comic strip series, Peanuts, *created by American cartoonist Charles Schultz (1922-2000). Also Linus Pauling (1901-1994), American quantum chemist and biochemist, and winner of two Nobel Prizes.*

Livos *(LEE-vos)* The One Who Is Black

Livos was the god of the warm south-west wind, that blew in from Africa. He was one of the brother-gods called the Anemoi, spirits who personified the winds that blew from the north, south, east, and west. The father of the Anemoi was Astraeus, god of the stars; and his mother was Eos, the "rosy-fingered" goddess of the dawn. The Anemoi were often depicted with wings, to help them waft across the earth.

Related Names: Afer Ventus, Africus, Lips.

Louis *(LOO-iss)* The One Who Is a Famous Warrior

Louis Maria d'Arenberg (1757-1795) was a member of the Palaiologos family, the dynasty that had ruled the Byzantine Empire from 1259-1453. Byzantium, located on the Strait of Bosphorus in the Near East, was a Greek-speaking city-state which became the new seat of the Eastern Roman Empire, the "Nova Roma," after Rome itself was conquered and sacked in A.D. 410.

Related Names: Luis.

Luciferus *(loo-sih-FUR-us)* Bringer of Dawn; Bringer of Light

Luciferus was the Roman name for Eosphorus, the Greek god "who surpassed many in beauty," and was the personification of the "morning star," or the brilliant planet Venus as it appears at dawn. Luciferus's twin brother was Vesperus, the personification of the "evening star," or Venus as it appears at dusk. The father of the twins was Astraeus, the Titan god of constellations; and their mother was Aurora, the "rosy-fingered" goddess of the dawn.

Related Names: Eosphoros, Eosphorus, Phosphorus, Lucifer.

Modern Example: Luciferus, a character within the universe of the online role-playing game, Evolution.

Lucius *(LOO-shuss, LOO-see-us)* The One Who is the Light

Lucius Antonius (20 B.C.-A.D. 25) was the grandson of Mark Antony (Marcus Antonius), co-ruler of the Roman Empire along with Octavian, and Marcus Aemilius Lepidus. Lucius's father was Iullus Antonius, Mark Antony's son; and his mother was Claudia Marcella, niece to the Roman Emperor Augustus. When Lucius's father killed himself after an adulterous affair, Lucius asked the Emperor Augustus to banish him to Gaul. While in Gaul, Lucius was appointed a Praetor (judge), and served with honor.

Modern Example: Lucius J. Henderson (1861-1947), American silent-film director, with more than 70 films to his credit.

Luctus *(LUK-tus)* The One Who Is Sorrow and Mourning

Luctus was the Greek god of sadness and mourning. He was sometimes included in the group of gods called the Algea, the Sorrows, the deities of unbearable grieving. Luctus's father was Aether, god of the skies; and his mother was Gaia, the earth. Luctus would emerge from Hades, the underworld of the dead, to stand among mourners at funerals and increase the lamentations of humankind.

Related Names: Luctus, Penthos, Penthus.

Lycus *(LIKE-us)* The One Who Is a Wolf

Lycus eventually became a King of Thebes, an ancient Greek city-state founded by the legendary hero Cadmus. Lycus's father was Chthonius, founder of one of the five greatest families of Thebes; and his mother was Alcyone, a star-goddess.

Modern Example: Lycus (Marcus Lycus), a character in the 1966 film, A Funny Thing Happened on the Way to the Forum, *a comedy set in ancient Rome, directed by American filmmaker Richard Lester.*

Magnes *(MAG-nus)* The Greatest One

Magnes and his brother Macedon were demi-gods, half-human and half-divine. Their father was Zeus, High King of the immortal gods on Mount Olympus, Greece; and their mother was the fair mortal, Thyia. Magnes married the nymph of the Greek island of Seriphos, and had four noble sons: Dictys, Eioneus, Pierus, and Polydectes.

Mantus *(MAN-tus)* The One Who Waits

In ancient Roman mythology, as adopted from the earlier Etruscan culture, Mantus was the god of the underworld of the dead. His wife was Mania, Queen of the dead. The present-day Italian city of Mantua is named after Mantus.

Modern Example: Little Mantus Creek, a town in Gloucester County, New Jersey.

Manuel *(MAN-yool, MAN-yoo-el, MON-well)* God Is With Us

Manuel (Manuel I Komnenos) (1118-1180) was an Emperor of Byzantium. Byzantium, located on the Strait of Bosphorus in the Near East, was a Greek-speaking city-state which became the new seat of the Eastern Roman Empire, the "Nova Roma," after Rome itself was conquered and sacked in 410 A.D. Manuel allied the Byzantine Empire with numerous kingdoms, to expand Byzantium's territory and power, but eventually his armies were vanquished at Myriokephalon, Phrygia (modern-day Turkey).

Modern Example: Manuel Luis Quezon y Molina (1878-1944), first President of the Philippines while it was under American control; and the second President after Emilio Aguinaldo (whom the American government never recognized).

Marcus *(MARK-us)* The Warlike One

The Roman aristocrat Marcus Atius Balbus (105 B.C.-51 B.C.) became part of the royal family of the Roman Emperor Gaius Julius Caesar, by marrying Caesar's youngest sister Julia. Julia produced three daughters: Atia Balba Prima, Atia

Balba Caesonia, and Atia Balba Tertia. Balbus eventually earned the post of Praetor, a military commander in the Roman Army.

Modern Example: Marcus Garvey (Marcus Mosiah Garvey, Jr.) (1887-1940), American businessman and civil rights leader.

Maris *(MAIR-us)* The One Who Is from the Sea

In ancient Roman mythology, as adopted from the earlier Etruscan culture, Maris was the god of farming and crops.

Related Names: Maris Halna, Maris Isminthians.
Modern Example: Maris Riekstins (1963-), Latvian Secretary of State and Minster of Foreign Affairs.

Mark *(MARK)* The Warlike One

Mark Antony (Marcus Antonius) (83 B.C.-30 B.C.) served as part of the Second Triumvirate of 44 B.C. — that is, he was a dictator of Rome, along with two other dictators, Octavian, and Marcus Aemilius Lepidus. However, the Triumvirate dissolved into civil war in 31 B.C. Mark Antony ultimately lost the war, and killed himself. His legendary consort, the Egyptian Queen Cleopatra VII, also took her own life.

Names for Babies Destined to Become Scholars and Teachers

Girls
Cassandra • Clio • Daria • Moneta • Mystis
Nona • Phoebe • Sophia • Xenia

Boys
Aphros • Damon • Eugenius • Hadrian • Mentor • Myson • Odysseus
Periander • Proteus • Pythias • Solon • Thales • Ulysses

Mars *(MARZ)* War; The Warrior

Mars, or Ares, was the Roman god of war. His father was Jupiter, rule of the gods on Mount Olympus; and his mother was Juno, Queen of the gods.

The Romans saw Mars as fierce and pitiless — the embodiment of war. Some scholars believe the Romans may have worshipped Mars out of fear rather than devotion. Mars's icons were the sword, spear, helmet, and shield.

Mars was feared by the gods and he cared little for them — except for his cherished mistress, Venus, goddess of love and beauty. Venus often slept with Mars, the brother of her husband Vulcan, the hideous god of volcanoes and blacksmiths. Once, after Mars and Venus had made love, Mars told a boy named Alectryon to guard the doorway, and waken the god at daybreak. But Alectryon fell asleep, allowing Sol, the sun-god, to discover Mars and Venus. Sol told Vulcan of Venus's betrayal. The furious Vulcan caught the sleeping lovers in a magic net and put them on display, for all the gods to mock. Later, Mars changed Alectryon into a rooster, and to this day, Alectryon's descendants never forget to crow at sunrise.

Mars had many other amorous conquests, including the fair Silvia, a Vestal Virgin, or priestess of Vesta, Roman goddess of the hearth. Mars seduced Silvia against her will as she lay sleeping beside a riverbank. Later, Silvia bore the demi-god twins, Romulus and Remus; but Silvia's vengeful father Amulius abandoned the infants in a forest. Miraculously, they were suckled by the she-wolf Lupa, then later discovered by the shepherd Faustulus, who took them home to his wife Larenta. Under Larenta's care, the twins grew to young manhood and later founded the "Eternal City" of Rome, whose armies would one day conquer much of the world.

Mars pursued many women, but his own mother, Juno, felt little love for her fearsome son, as the Greek poet Homer recorded in the 7th Century B.C. He wrote that during the Trojan War, fought between the Greeks and the Trojans in the 12th Century B.C., Juno spied Mars fighting on the Trojan side, against her beloved Greeks. Furious, Juno encouraged King Diomedes of Argos to attack Mars. Diomedes threw his spear, and the goddess Minerva guided it into Mars's body, wounding him terribly. Mars retreated to Mount Olympus, allowing Juno's champions, the Greeks, to win the battle.

Related Names: Ares, Ares Enyalius, Enyalios.

Modern Example: Mars Blackman, character in the 1986 film, She's Gotta Have It, *directed by American filmmaker Spike Lee (Shelton Jackson Lee) (1957-).*

Matthew *(MATH-thyoo)* The Gift of God

Matthew (Matthew Cantacuzenus) (c. 1325-1391) was crowned a co-Emperor of Byzantium in 1353. Byzantium, located on the Strait of Bosphorus in the Near East, was a Greek-speaking city-state which became the new seat of the Eastern Roman Empire, the "Nova Roma," after Rome itself was conquered and sacked in A.D. 410. Matthew's father was Emperor John VI Cantacuzenus, and his mother was the Empress Eirene Asanina. Matthew ruled Thrace (present-day Bulgaria) until 1357, when his armies were defeated and he was forced to abdicate.

Modern Example: Matthew Tawo Mbu (1929-), Nigerian statesman and former Foreign Minister.

Matton *(MAT-un)* The One Who Kneads Bread Dough

Matton and his brother Ceraon were demi-gods, half human and half divine, although the names of their parents have been lost to history. They were the gods of baking, and they served Demeter, goddess of grain. As household gods, Matton would help mortals knead their bread dough, after Ceraon had helped them mix together the ingredients. In gratitude, the citizens of the Greek city-state of Sparta erected statues to honor Matton and Ceraon.

Modern Example: Prince Matton, a character in the 1982 French-Hungarian animated film, Les Maîtres du Temps, *directed by Rene Laloux.*

Maurice *(mor-REES)* The Moor with a Dark Complexion

Maurice (Flavius Mauricius Tiberius Augustus) (A.D. 359-A.D. 602) was an Emperor of Byzantium. Byzantium, located on the Strait of Bosphorus in the Near East, was a Greek-speaking city-state which became the new seat of the Eastern Roman Empire, the "Nova Roma," after Rome itself was conquered and sacked in A.D. 410. Maurice was born in Cappadocia (modern-day Turkey) and rose through the ranks of the Roman Army to become a top-level military commander. The Byzantine Emperor Tiberius II adopted him, and when Tiberius died in A.D. 582, Maurice became Emperor. Through a series of military successes, Maurice revived the previously bankrupt Byzantine Empire.

Modern Example: Maurice Fréchet (1878-1973), French professor and mathematician.

Maximilian *(max-uh-MILL-yun)* The One Who Is the Greatest

Maximilian Joseph, Duke of Bavaria (1808-1888) was a member of the Palaiolo-gos family, the dynasty that had ruled the Byzantine Empire from 1259-1453. Byzantium, located on the Strait of Bosphorus in the Near East, was a Greek-speaking city-state which became the new seat of the Eastern Roman Empire, the "Nova Roma," after Rome itself was conquered and sacked in A.D. 410.

Modern Example: Maximilian Kolbe (1894-1941), Polish priest who offered to die in another's place at the Auschwitz death camp in Poland, during World War II; Kolbe was canonized as a Catholic Saint in 1982.

Maximus *(MAX-uh-mus)* The One Who Is the Greatest

Maximus (Magnus Maximus) (c. A.D. 335-A.D. 388) took the throne of the Roman Empire by force. After a series of military victories in Hispania (Spain), Gaul (France), and Rome itself, Maximus ruled as Emperor from his new capital of Augusta Treverorum, Gaul. But fresh Roman armies defeated Maximus and killed him in A.D. 335.

Memnon *(MEM-non)* The One Who is Steadfast and Resolute

Memnon was a legendary demi-god Prince of Ethiopia, in Africa. His father was Tithonus, a Prince of the city-state of Troy (modern-day Turkey); and his mother was Eos, the "rosy-fingered" goddess of the dawn. Memnon was hailed by the Tro-jans as a noble warrior, a reputation he reinforced during the Trojan War, a bloody conflict fought in the 12th Century B.C. against the armies of ancient Greece.

According to the Greek poet Homer, in his epic poem, *The Iliad*, the Trojan War began when Prince Paris of Troy, brother of Hector, ran off with the beautiful Queen Helen, wife of King Menelaus of Sparta. Menelaus allied with other Greek kings and their armies, and the Greeks sailed to Troy in a thousand ships, to wage war for ten years. During the war, Memnon killed many Greeks, including Antilochus, son of King Nestor of Pylos.

In the end, the Greeks won the war because of King Odysseus of Ithaca. He convinced the Greeks to build an immense wooden horse, the symbol of Troy, and leave it hollow inside. Greek soldiers hid in the horse, and the other Greek armies sailed away — but only to hide, out of sight of the Trojans. The Trojans thought they had won the war, but Cassandra, a Trojan prophetess, begged the Trojans not to pull the statue into the city. Everyone thought she was insane and wheeled the statue through the gates. That night, the Greeks exited the Trojan Horse, opened the gates of Troy for their waiting armies, and destroyed the city. Nonetheless, even though Troy lost the war, Memmon was made into a god by Zeus, High King of the Olympian gods of Greece.

Mentor *(MEN-tur, MEN-tor)* The Spirited One

Mentor was the trusted companion of King Odysseus, ruler of the Greek city-state of Ithaca. When Odysseus sailed off to fight in the Trojan War (12th Century B.C.), he asked Mentor to take care of his wife Penelope, and his young son Telemachus. Odysseus did not return for twenty years — ten years fighting in the war, and another ten years battling the seas and the gods to return to Ithaca. Once home, Odysseus found his palace overrun with drunken, disrespectful princes wishing to marry Penelope. The goddess Athena disguised herself as Mentor and helped Odysseus to kill every suitor, restoring honor to Odysseus's house. The word "mentor" now means a worthy teacher and friend.

Modern Example: Mentor Huebner (1917-2001), American production illustrator and storyboard artist for over 250 films.

Mercury *(MUR-kyur-ree)* The Merchant; The Traveler

Mercury, or Hermes, was the messenger of the gods, as well as the god of travel, commerce, financial prosperity, and feasting. Most importantly, Mercury was the god of "crossing over," including helping newly deceased souls cross over to Tartarus, or Hades, the underworld of the dead. Mercury was often shown wearing his winged sandals, called the Talaria; a winged helmet, called the Petasus, forged by Vulcan, god of blacksmiths; and in his hand, a staff with two snakes wrapped around it, the Caduceus. Mercury's name comes from the Latin word for merchant; and merchants sought out the familiar piles of stones along highways that measured distances and boundaries. Travelers made these markers by tossing stones as they passed. Later, many of these markers were replaced with monuments to Mercury, god of travel.

Mercury was one of the youngest of the Olympian gods — the newer gods who, along with their king, mighty Jupiter, overthrew the old Titans or elder deities and took control of heaven. Mercury's parents were Jupiter and the nymph Maia, a mountain-goddess. Mercury's birthplace was a cave on Mount Cyllene in Greece. The day he was born, Mercury invented the lyre or harp, then rustled the immortal cattle of Apollo, god of the arts. Mercury also invented numerous sports, including boxing, as well as fortune-telling and divination.

Mercury later gained fame by killing the hundred-eyed giant Argus. The story began this way: Jupiter, king of the gods, tried to hide his lover Io by changing her into a white cow. But Jupiter's wife Juno saw through the ruse and demanded the cow as a gift. Juno then turned the cow over to Argus, ordering him to keep it from Jupiter. Furious, Jupiter sent Mercury to kill Argus. Mercury put Argus to sleep, and when the monster closed its hundred eyes, Mercury killed it with a sling and a stone.

Mercury's achievements included fathering the half-goat Pan, the merry god of shepherds. Mercury took his beloved son Pan to Olympus, where the gods welcomed him. Mercury also fathered Abderus, who was eventually eaten by the four carnivorous Mares of Greek King Diomedes. Another of Mercury's sons was Hermaphroditus, whose mother was Venus, goddess of love. The gods changed Hermaphroditus into a hermaphrodite — half-male, half-female.

Related Names: Argeiphontes, Enagonios, Hermes, Hermes Cylleneius, Hermes Psychopompos, Hermes Trismegistus, Mercury.

Modern Example: Mercury, a town in Nye County, Nevada, near the infamous "Area 51" Nellis Air Force Range, where extraterrestrials have been reported to reside.

Mestor *(MES-tur)* The One Who Comes Home

Prince Mestor was the son of Pterelaus, who was the King of the Taphian Islands, in ancient Greece. Mestor's brothers were the heroes Antiochus, Chersidamas, Chromius, Everes, and Tyrannus; and his sister was the beautiful Comaetho.

Michael *(MIKE-ul)* The One Who Is Like God

Michael (Michael I Rangabe) (?-A.D. 844) was an Emperor of Byzantium. Byzantium, located on the Strait of Bosphorus in the Near East, was a Greek-speaking city-state which became the new seat of the Eastern Roman Empire, the "Nova Roma," after Rome itself was conquered and sacked in A.D. 410. Michael's father was the nobleman Theophylaktos Rangabe, a naval commander. Michael was crowned Emperor in A.D. 811 and ruled until A.D. 813.

Related Names: Miguel.
Modern Example: Michael Buble (1975-), Grammy nominated musician and big band singer.

Minotaur *(MIN-uh-tor)* The Bull Belonging to Minos

The Minotaur was a half-bull, half-human monstrosity with incredible strength and ferocity. The Minotaur's mother was Queen Pasiphae of Crete, but she disowned him. He lived on the Greek island of Crete, trapped inside the Labyrinth, a great stone maze built by King Minos of Crete. Minos regularly sacrificed victims from rival Athens to the hungry Minotaur. One day, while Princess Ariadne, Minos's daughter, watched a group of Athenian victims being hauled to the Labyrinth, she spotted the handsome demi-god Theseus and fell in love with him. She offered to rescue him in exchange for a promise that he would take her to Athens and marry her. He agreed, and she gave him a mystic sword to kill the Minotaur, and a ball of red wool to use in finding his way back through the Labyrinth. After Theseus slew the Minotaur and found his way out of the maze, he and Ariadne fled by sea. However, when their ship put-in at the island of Naxos, Theseus and his crew abandoned Ariadne there — but not before she cursed Theseus. The curse worked, because Theseus had promised his father Aegeas that his ship would display a white sail for triumph, or a black sail for death; and Theseus forgot to raise the white sail as he returned. Aegeas spotted the black sail and leapt from a hill into the ocean, forever after known as the Agean Sea.

Related Names: Asterion, Minotauros.

Minyas *(MIN-yus)* The One Who Is Many

King Minyas was the rich and powerful ruler of Orkhomenos, an ancient Greek city-state; in time, his subjects came to be known as the Minyans. Minyas's father was the demi-god King Khryses of Orkhomenos, half human and half divine, whose father was Poseidon, god of the oceans. Minya's offspring include Clymene, mother of the demi-god Phaëthon; and the Minyades, the princesses who insulted the god Dionysus and were turned into bats for their insolence.

Montanus *(mon-TAN-us)* The Ones Who Are Mountains

The ancient Romans used the name Montanus for the Greek gods originally called the Oros, the elderly, white-bearded men, who personified all the mountains of the known world. The sole parent of the Montanus was Terra, the earth; and her children were numerous: Aetna, Athos, Helicon, Nysus, and Olympus, to name a few. The Greeks believed that the mountains were alive and often prayed to them for good fortune.

Related Names: Mons, Ourea, Oros, Numina Montanum.

Morpheus *(MOR-fee-us)* The One Who Is the Shape of Dreams

Morpheus was the Greek god of dreams, and the ruler of the Oneiroi — the dreams of humankind. Morpheus's sole parent was Hypnos, god of sleep. Morpheus came to mortals and immortals alike, sometimes appearing in dreams with important news from Zeus, High King of the immortal gods on Mount Olympus.

Modern Example: King "Morphy" Morpheus, a character in the comic strip, Little Nemo in Slumberland, *created by American cartoonist Winsor McCay (1871-1934), which ran in newspapers from 1905-1911.*

Morus *(MOR-rus)* The One Who is Death and Destruction

The "all-destroying" Morus was the ancient Greek god of sadness, hopelessness, and damnation. Morus's sole parent was Nyx, goddess of night. Morus was responsible for guiding human beings towards their own destruction. His sister

Ker dragged people towards painful, tragic death; while his brother Thanatos eased people towards natural, painless death.

Related Names: Moros.

Myles *(MILES, MY-leez)* The One Who Is Powerful

Myles was a Prince of Laconia, or Lacedaemonia, a province of ancient Greece. His father was King Lelex of Laconia; and his mother was the noblewoman Cleocharia. After Lelex's death, Myles became King, and married Taygete, the nymph (nature goddess) of Mount Taygete in Laconia. They produced a son, Eurotas, who fathered his own son, Sparta, founder of the city-state of Sparta. Myles gained lasting fame for having invented the grain mill, which grinds wheat into bread-flour.

Myson *(MYE-sun)* The One Who has Great Strength

Myson (c. 600 B.C.), who lived in the ancient Greek town of Chenae, was one of the Seven Sages — the wisest men of the ancient world, according to the Greek philosopher Plato. Myson's father was Strymon, an absolute monarch (tyrannos in Greek, or tyrant) of the country near Chenae, yet Myson chose to live a simple life, as a farmer and a philosopher. When Solon, another one of the Seven Sages, saw Myson getting his plow ready long before the planting season, he said, "Now is not the season for the plow, Myson." Myson answered, "Not to use it, but to make ready."

Neilos *(NYE-los, NEE-los)* The One Who Is the Nile River

Neilos, or Nile, was the river god who personified the Nile River in the ancient nation of Egypt, in North Africa. Neilos's father was Oceanus, god of the river that encircled the earth; and his mother was Tehtys, goddess of earth's fresh water sources. Neilos was very kind to the Pygmaioi (Pygmies), the small black-skinned African folk whom the Greeks knew of, and cherished as gentle, intelligent dwarves.

Related Names: Neilos, Nile, Nilus.

Nephalion *(nuh-FAIL-yun)* The One Who Is the Clouds

Prince Nephalion was one of the heirs to the throne of Crete, a Greek island. Nephalion's father was King Minos, who had succeeded in imprisoning the Minotaur, a fierce beast who was half-man, half-bull. Nephalion's mother was Pareia, a nymph or nature goddess of the fresh water sources of Paros Island. Nephalion's three brothers were Eurymedon, Khryses, and Philolaus. These four princes were infamous for having made war on the demi-god Heracles (Hercules), son of Zeus, High King of the Olympian gods.

Modern Example: Nephalion Cattleheart, a large butterfly of the genus Parides, species anchises, subspecies nepahlion, found primarily in tropical climates.

Neptune *(NEP-tyoon, NEP-toon)* The King of the Sea

Neptune, or Poseidon, was the god of the sea, earthquakes, and horses. To the ocean-going Greeks, he may have been equal in importance to his brother Jupiter, ruler of the gods on Mount Olympus.

Neptune's moods could change quickly, and when he was angry, he sent epilepsy and other diseases to afflict mankind. Worse, he could strike the earth with his trident and trigger deadly earthquakes and storms at sea.

Neptune traveled his watery kingdom in a chariot pulled by giant seahorses. His royal palace lay hidden on the sea-bottom, constructed of rare jewels and coral. Neptune was a descendant of kings: His father was Saturn, King of the Titans; and his mother was Opis, the Titan queen. Saturn, Opis, and the other Titans had once ruled in heaven, but had been defeated by Jupiter and his Olympian gods. Saturn had always feared his children would depose him, so he swallowed each one, including Neptune. But Opis managed to save young Jupiter, the future god-king, by swaddling a boulder in blankets and tricking Saturn into eating it. Opis hid Jupiter until he grew strong enough to return and force Saturn to vomit out the gods. Then Jupiter and his new gods warred with the Titans, defeating them. Jupiter gained dominion over heaven and earth, and gave his brother Pluto control of the underworld, and his brother Neptune dominion over the seas.

Neptune's beautiful wife was Amphitrite, one of the fifty Nereid sea-nymphs who lived under the Mediterranean. Amphitrite's parents were Doris, goddess of river deltas, and gentle Nereus, the fish-tailed "Old Man of the Sea," god of fishing. Amphitrite is often depicted sitting in a chariot beside Neptune, pulled by sea-gods called Tritones.

Neptune was especially honored by the Romans as Neptune Equester, the god and patron of horse racing and horses. Romans celebrated the festival of the Neptunalia in his honor.

Related Names: Enosichthon, Neptune, Poseidon, Seischthon.
Modern Example: Sailor Neptune, also known as Michiru Kaioh, in the Japanese anime television series, Sailor Moon, *created by Japanese artist Naoko Takeuchi.*

Nereus *(NAIR-roos, NAIR-ee-us)* The Old Man of the Sea

The gentle Nereus was known affectionately by the ancient Greeks as, "The Old Man of the Sea." He was the fish-tailed god of fish and fishing, who lived with his wife Doris, goddess of river deltas, and his fifty beautiful daughters, the Nereids, at the bottom of the Mediterranean Sea. The Nereids often rode dolphins up to the water's surface, to help sea-farers. Nereus's father was Pontuns, a god of the seas; and his mother was Gaia, the earth.

Related Names: Nereos, Geron Halios, and Geron Halius.
Modern Example: Nereus Acosta (Juan Romero Nereus Olaivar Acosta) (1996-), Philippine educator, statesman, and member of the Philippine House of Representatives.

Nero *(NEE-ro)* The One Who Is Powerful

Nero (Nero Claudius Caesar Augustus Germanicus) (A.D. 37-A.D. 68) was an Emperor of Rome. His adoptive father was the Emperor Claudius, and when Claudius died in A.D. 54, Nero ascended to the throne. Although his reign was marked by military, political, and economic successes, he was also known as a tyrant. He was deposed by the Roman Army in A.D. 68, and took his own life.

Modern Example: Nero Bellum, vocalist for the band Psyclon Nine (2000-).

Nestor *(NESS-tur)* The One Who Comes Home

Nestor, a legendary hero, was the ruler of the ancient Greek city-state of Pylos. Nestor's father was King Neleus, son of Posedion, the sea god; and his mother was Chloris, goddess of flowers. When the demi-god Heracles (Hercules) killed Neleus, Nestor ascended to the throne. He married the goddess Eurydice and fathered nine children, including the demi-god hero Perseus, Antilochus, and Thrasymedes, who would become renowned as warriors. Nestor lived to be over 100, and during his lifetime he sailed on the Argo and helped the hero Jason win the Golden Fleece, a symbol of power; and he fought in the Trojan War, side-by-side with Antilochus and Thrasymedes.

Modern Example: Nestor Khergiani (1975-), native of the Eastern European nation of Georgia, and a champion judoka or practitioner of the Japanese martial art of judo.

Niccolo *(nih-KO-lo)* The Victory of the People

Duke Niccolo Pignatelli (1658-1719) of Bisaccia was a member of the Palaiologos family, the dynasty that had ruled the Byzantine Empire from 1259-1453. Byzantium, located on the Strait of Bosphorus in the Near East, was a Greek-speaking city-state which became the new seat of the Eastern Roman Empire, the "Nova Roma," after Rome itself was conquered and sacked in A.D. 410.

Related Names: Dominic, Nicholas.

Names for Babies Destined to Become Sea-Farers

Girls

Actaea • Agave • Amphitrite • Callisto • Calypso • Ceto
Eunice • Galene • Halie • Melia • Melita • Nasaea • Proto • Thetis

Boys

Aphros • Bythos • Maris • Neptune • Poseidon • Nereus
Periander • Perseus • Pontus • Portunus • Proteus • Thaumas

Nikolaos *(nik-uh-LAY-ohs)* The Victory of the People

Nikolaos Kanabos (13th Century A.D.) was an Emperor of Byzantium. Byzantium, located on the Strait of Bosphorus in the Near East, was a Greek-speaking city-state which became the new seat of the Eastern Roman Empire, the "Nova Roma," after Rome itself was conquered and sacked in A.D. 410. In 1204, the Chrtisian clergy and the Senate lawfully elected Nikolaos the Byzantine Emperor. However, Nikolaos eventually chose to decline the honor.

Related Names: Dominic, Nicholas.
Modern Example: Nikolaos Sifounakis (1949-), Greek politician and Chairman of the Committee on Culture and Education for the European Parliament.

Nile *(NILE)* The One Who is the Nile River

Nile, or Neilos, was the river god who personified the Nile River in the ancient nation of Egypt, in North Africa. Nile's father was Oceanus, god of the river that encircled the earth; and his mother was Tehtys, goddess of earth's fresh water sources. Nile was very kind to the Pygmaioi (Pygmies), the small black-skinned African folk whom the Greeks knew of, and cherished as gentle, intelligent dwarves.

Related Names: Neilos, Nilus.
Modern Example: Nile Rodgers (1952-), American composer, producer, musician, and co-founder of the band, Chic.

Notus *(NO-tus)* The One Who Is the South Wind

The "benevolent, swift-whirling" Notus was the god of the moist, stormy south wind, that blew in during the summer season. He was one of the brother-gods called the Anemoi, spirits who personified the winds that blew from the north, south, east, and west. The father of the Anemoi was Astraeus, god of the stars; and his mother was Eos, the "rosy-fingered" goddess of the dawn. The Anemoi were often depicted with wings, to help them waft across the earth. Notus liked to make his home in the nation of Ethiopia, in Africa.

Related Names: Notos.
Modern Example: Notus, a town in Canyon County, Idaho.

Nysus *(NYE-sus)* The One from Mount Nysus

Nysus was the Roman name for Nysos, a god of the ancient woodlands of Greece who lived on the legendary Mount Nysos. Nysus's sole parent was Silenus, the elderly god of drunkenness; and his children were the Nysiades, the nymphs or nature goddesses of Mount Nysos. Nysus's greatest achievement was helping to raise the infant Bacchus, god of wine. When Bacchus was grown, he decided to invade India, leaving his kingdom of Thebes in Nysus's trust-worthy hands. When Bacchus returned in triumph, Nysus would not give back the throne of Thebes to the god. Bacchus loved Nysus so much that he waited patiently for three years, persuaded Nysus to relent, and recovered his kingdom.

Related Names: Nysos.

Odysseus *(oh-DIS-soos)* The One Who Is Hatred Itself

Odysseus, or Ulysses, was a legendary King of Ithaca, a Greek city-state. His grandfather was Arcesius, another King of Ithaca. Odysseus was hailed by the Greeks as a noble warrior, a reputation he reinforced during the Trojan War, a bloody conflict fought in the 12th Century B.C. against the armies of the ancient city-state of Troy (modern-day Turkey).

According to the Greek poet Homer, in his epic poem, The Iliad, the Trojan War began when Prince Paris of Troy, brother of Hector, ran off with the beauti-ful Queen Helen, wife of King Menelaus of Sparta. Menelaus allied with other Greek kings and their armies, and the Greeks sailed to Troy in a thousand ships, to wage war for ten years. In the end, the Greeks won the war because Odysseus convinced the Greeks to build an immense wooden horse, the symbol of Troy, and leave it hollow inside. Greek soldiers hid in the horse, and the other Greek armies sailed away — but only to hide, out of sight of the Trojans. The Trojans thought they had won the war, but Cassandra, a Trojan prophetess, begged the Trojans not to pull the statue into the city. Everyone thought she was insane and wheeled the statue through the gates. That night, the Greeks exited the Trojan Horse, opened the gates of Troy for their waiting armies, and destroyed the city. However, Odysseus could not enjoy his triumph, because it took him another ten years to return home, a story told by Homer in, The Odyssey. Odysseus battled monsters, contended with the immortal gods, and traveled to Hades itself, before he rejoined his beloved wife Penelope and son Telemachus.

Related Names: Ulysses.

Olympios *(oh-LIM-pee-ohs)* From Mount Olympus

Olympios, or Zeus, was the god of heaven, the ruler of the immortal gods and mortal men alike. Being all-powerful, Olympios answered to no one, and could use his thunderbolts — the flashes of light that streaked from the sky — to kill at his pleasure. Wearing his Aegis or armored breastplate, which had been forged by Hephaestus, god of blacksmiths, Olympios ruled over the palace of the gods on Mount Olympus, in Thessaly, Greece. He seized control of Olympus by overthrowing his father, Cronus, the greatest of the Titans or Elder Deities. Because Cronus had feared that one of his children might someday depose him, he ate them all at birth: Demeter, Hades, Hera, Hestia, and Poseidon. But Olympios's mother Rhea saved him by feeding Cronus a boulder wrapped in blankets, disguised as the infant Olympios. Then she hid Olympios in Crete, where he grew strong by drinking the milk of the goat Amalthea. Olympios returned to Cronus and forced him to vomit out all of Olympios's siblings, and together they waged war against the Titans. Victorious, Olympios imprisoned Cronus and the Titans in Tartarus, the underworld. Olympios then assigned the gods their duties: Demeter became goddess of the harvest; Hestia, goddess of the home and family; Poseidon, god of the seas; and Hades, god of the underworld and the dead. Finally, Olympios married Hera, who then became goddess of marriage and queen of the gods. Olympios cheated regularly on Hera, fathering many demigods, or half-human/half-divine children. Olympios's real-world Greek worshippers built an enormous gold-and-ivory statue to Olympios in the Temple of Zeus (Olympios) at Olympia; and this vanished monument is now called one of the Seven Wonders of the Ancient World.

Related Names: Agoraios, Horkios, Jove, Jupiter, Jupiter Optimus Maximus, Kronides Hypatos, Panhellenios, Theos, Theos Hyspsistos, Xenios, Zeus, Zeus Astrapaios, Zeus Heraios, Zeus Hypsistos, Zeus Kronion.

Orion *(or-RYE-un)* The Water of a Human Being

Orion was one of the Gigantes, the hundred giants whose sole parent was Gaia. Orion was known for his masculine beauty and for his incredible power to walk on water. Orion sought out the lovely Merope, a star goddess, and seduced her against her will. Merope's father, King Oinopion of the Greek island of Chios, gouged out Orion's eyes for his crimes, but Orion traveled to Helios, the sun, and got his eyesight back. Orion then became the lover of Artemis, goddess of hunting; but he eventually died while fighting Scorpio, the gigantic scorpion sent against him by Gaia, the earth. Zeus, King of the Olympian gods, placed Orion in heaven, as the Orion constellation. The three stars on Orion's belt are the brightest and most visible.

Orontes *(or-RON-tez)* The One Who is the Orontes River

Orontes was a Greek river god, who personified the Ladon River near the ancient Greek city-state of Antioch. Orontes's father was Oceanus, god of the river that encircled the earth; and his mother was Tethys, goddess of the earth's sources of fresh water. Orontes was wild and uncontrollable until the Greek god Heracles (Hercules) tamed the river by moving mountains out of its path.

Orpheus *(OR-fee-us)* The One Who is the Blackness of Night

Orpheus was a demi-god, half human and half divine. His father was King Oiagros, ruler of the Greek city-state of Pieria; and his mother was Calliope, one of the Muses, the goddess-daughters of Zeus, High King of the gods, and of Mnemosyne, goddess of memory. Orpheus sang so beautifully that history would have remembered him just for his voice and his stirring poetry; but he was even more renowned for descending into Hades, the underworld of the dead, while still alive. He pleaded with Hades, god of death, and Persephone, goddess of death, to let his deceased wife Eurydice return to earth. Hades and Persephone were deeply touched by Orpheus's pleas, and agreed to release Eurydice. But they warned him that he must not look back at Eurydice, as they climbed back to the world of the living. While accompanying Eurydice out of Hades, Orpheus glanced back at her, and she fell back into the underworld forever.

Modern Example: Orpheus Roye (1973-), football player currently playing for the Cleveland Browns, in the National Football League (NFL).

Osiris *(oh-SY-rus)* The Prophet Who Sits on the Throne

Osiris was the devoutly-worshipped, handsome young Greek god of drunkenness and wine. Osiris's father was Zeus, the king of the immortal gods who lived on Mount Olympus, in Greece; and his mother was Zeus's lover Semele, goddess of the Mainades, the female worshippers of Osiris. Zeus's wife Hera, queen of the gods, furious at her husband's cheating, told him to appear to Semele in all his godly glory. Zeus reluctantly obeyed, and surrounded himself with dazzling lightning. Petrified, Semele instantly gave birth to Osiris. Zeus stitched-up the infant Osiris in his thigh, until he grew to adulthood. Osiris traveled the world, establishing his divinity and inspiring worshippers in countless nations.

Related Names: Bachhus, Bakchos, Bromios, Dendrites, Dionysos, Dionysus, Dionysus Dendrites, Dithyrambos, Eleutherios, Iacchus, Liber, Liknites, Lyaeus, Zagreus.

Otus *(OH-tus)* The One Who Is Doom

Otus was one of the Gigantes, the hundred giants whose mother was Gaia, the earth, and whose father was Uranus, the sky. The armored Gigantes, whose legs were huge snakes, rebelled against Zeus, High King of the immortal gods who lived on Mount Olympus, Greece. But when the demi-god Heracles entered the war on his father Zeus's side, the Gigantes were annihilated. However, the Gigantes' blood magically transformed into the people of the nation of Thrace (present-day Bulgaria).

Pallas *(PAL-us)* The One Who Wields a Spear

In ancient Greek mythology, Pallas was a Titan, one of the original deities who ruled in heaven before being overthrown by Zeus and his Olympian gods. Pallas's father was Crius, the Titan god of the stars; and his mother was Eurybia, a sea goddess. Pallas was the god of war — and when he married Styx, goddess of hatred, he fathered many gods and goddesses related to war. These included Bia, goddess of power; Cratus, god of strength; Nike, goddess of triumph; and Zelos, god of jealousy.

Pan *(PAN)* The One Who Is All; The Rustic One

Pan was the ancient Greek god of wild forests, goats, sheep, and sheep-herders. He was depicted with a human upper-half, although with goat-horns, and the lower-half of a goat. Pan's father was Hermes, the messenger of the gods; and his mother was Penelope, a nymph or nature goddess. Pan made his home in the wooded Greek province of Arcadia, where he roamed joyfully, making sweet music on his pan-pipes (a flute with multiple tubes). Pan also loved to seduce woodland nymphs, but his appearance often caused them to panic, then flee in terror. Pan's own mother Penelope fled in disgust when she saw her newborn baby; but Hermes, Pan's father, took Pan to Mount Olympus, where all the gods adored the furry creature.

Related Names: Faunus, Inuus.

Modern Example: Pan Bouyoucas (1946-), Greek-Canadian film critic, playwright, and author.

Paris *(PAIR-us)* The One Who Is Like a Wall

Paris was a Prince of Troy, the legendary walled city-state also known as Ilium (located in present-day Turkey). Paris's father was King Priam of Troy; and his mother was Queen Hecuba.

Paris bore much of the responsibility for starting the Trojan War, the ten-year-long conflict between the Trojans and the Greeks, during the 12th Century B.C. The Trojan War was chronicled in *The Iliad*, an epic poem written by the Greek poet Homer (c. 8th Century B.C.-?).

According to Homer, Paris ran off with Queen Helen of Sparta, wife of King Menelaus. Menelaus allied with other Greek kings and their armies, and the Greeks sailed to Troy in a thousand ships, to wage bloody warfare for ten years

In the end, the Greeks won the war because of King Odysseus of Ithaca. He convinced the Greeks to build an immense wooden horse, the symbol of Troy, and leave it hollow inside. Greek soldiers hid in the horse, and the other Greek armies sailed away — but only to hide, out of sight of the Trojans. The Trojans thought they had won the war, but Cassandra, a Trojan prophetess, begged the Trojans not to pull the statue into the city. Everyone thought she was insane, and wheeled the statue through the gates. That night, the Greeks exited the Trojan Horse, opened the gates of Troy for their waiting armies, and destroyed the city.

Nonetheless, Paris, although not noted as a skillful warrior, shot a poisoned arrow through the heel of Achilles, Greece's greatest warrior, and killed him.

Related Names: Alexander, Alexandros.
Modern Example: Paris, the historic capital city of the European nation of France.

Peloreus *(puh-LOR-ee-us)* The Huge, Monstrous One

Peloreus was one of the Gigantes, the hundred giants whose mother was Gaia, the earth, and whose father was Uranus, the sky. The armored Gigantes, whose legs were huge snakes, rebelled against Zeus, High King of the immortal gods who lived on Mount Olympus, Greece. But when the demi-god Heracles entered the war on his father Zeus's side, the Gigantes were annihilated. However, the Gigantes' blood magically transformed into the people of the nation of Thrace (present-day Bulgaria).

Modern Example: Peloreus Sound, an ocean inlet popular with sailboat enthusiasts, located in Ottawa, Ontario, Canada.

Penthos *(PEN-thos)* The One Who Is Sorrow and Mourning

Penthos was the Greek god of sadness and mourning. He was sometimes included in the group of gods called the Algea, the Sorrows, the deities of unbearable grieving. Penthos's father was Aether, god of the skies; and his mother was Gaia, the earth. Penthos would emerge from Hades, the underworld of the dead, to stand among mourners at funerals and increase the lamentations of humankind.

Related Names: Luctus, Penthus.
Modern Example: Penthos, guest character on an episode of, Far Out Space Nuts, *an American television series from producers Sid and Marty Krofft, that aired from 1975-1976.*

Periander *(pair-ee-AN-dur)* The Traveler of the Aegean Islands

King Periander (6th Century B.C.) was the absolute monarch (tyrannos in Greek, or tyrant) of the ancient Greek city-state of Corinth. His father was King Cypselus, another Corinthian tyrant. Periander was renowned for having built the Diolkos, the wooden bridge across the Isthmus of Corinth that was used to haul ships overland.

However, Periander had a darker side, as well; he killed his wife Melissa for unknown reasons, then buried all her clothing instead of burning the garments as required by local tradition. Years later, when Periander sent emissaries to the Corinthian Oracle of the Dead, inquiring about some buried treasure, Melissa's spirit suddenly appeared — but swore she would reveal nothing, due to Periander's mistreatment of her. Periander ordered his servants to immediately burn mounds of clothes in the Corinthian Temple of Hera, while he humbly prayed to Melissa's spirit. Melissa relented, and told Periander the treasure' location. Periander, as well as being a despot, was also known as one of the Seven Sages, the wisest men of the ancient world, according to the Greek philosopher Plato. His favorite saying, according to Hyginus, a Roman writer of the 1st Century A.D., was, "Everything should be carefully studied."

Modern Example: Periander A. Esplana, Philippine writer and theologian.

Perses *(PURR-seez)* The One Who Destroys; The One Who Sacks

Perses was one of the Titans, the original deities who ruled in heaven before being overthrown by Zeus and his Olympian gods. Perses was the god of plunder and destruction. His father was Crius, the Titan god of the stars; and his mother was Euribya, goddess of ocean navigation. Perses's daughter was Hecate, goddess of childbirth, wild places, crossroads, and witchcraft.

Related Names: Peraeus, Persaios.

Perseus *(PER-see-us)* The Destroyer

Perseus was one of the greatest warrior-heroes of ancient Greece. His father was Zeus, High King of the immortal gods of Mount Olympus; and his mother was the demi-goddess Danae. Zeus seduced Danae against her will, by changing himself into shimmering rain, and surrounding her. Danae's father, King Akrisios of Argos, placed Danae and the infant Perseus in a strongbox, and pushed them out to sea. They came to Seriphos Island, where Perseus grew to manhood.

One day, Seriphos's scheming ruler, King Polydectes, told Perseus to kill Medusa — a female demon so hideous that anyone seeing her face would turn to stone — then return with her head. The gods gave Perseus an enchanted sword, levitating sandals, an invisibility helmet, and a polished shield. Next, Perseus visited the Graiai — witches who shared one eyeball — and hid the eye until they revealed where Medusa lived. Perseus found Medusa and cut off her head, using his shield as a mirror so as not to look at her face.

As Perseus sailed home, he discovered the Ethiopian Princess Andromeda bound to a sea-cliff, where a sea-monster was supposed to eat her, and thus spare Ethiopia. Perseus killed the dragon and took Andromeda as his wife. Back in Seriphos, Perseus revealed the head to Polydectes, turned him to stone, then sailed to Argos, to regain his kingdom. When King Akrisios ran away in terror, Perseus assumed his rightful place as King of Argos.

Phaunos *(FAWN-ohs)*

Phaunos was the ancient Roman god of wild forests, goats, sheep, and sheep-herders. He was depicted with a human upper-half, although with goat-horns, and the lower-half of a goat. Phaunos's father was Mercury, the messenger of the gods; and his mother was Penelope, a nymph or nature goddess. Phaunos made his home in the wooded Greek province of Arcadia, where he roamed joyfully, making sweet music on his pan-pipes (a flute with multiple tubes). Phaunos also loved to seduce woodland nymphs, but his appearance often caused them to panic, then flee in terror. Phaunos's own mother Penelope fled in disgust when she saw her newborn baby; but Hermes, Phaunos's father, took him to Mount Olympus, where all the gods adored the furry creature.

Related Names: Inuus, Faunus, Pan.
Modern Example: Phaunos, a character in the online role-playing game, Yohoho!Puzzle Pirates, released in 2003 by Three Rings Design, of San Francisco, California.

Philemon *(FILL-uh-mahn)* The One Who Is Affectionate and Loving

Philemon and his wife Baucis were an elderly couple who lived in a simple peasant home in Phrygia (present-day Turkey). Although they were poor, they were very much in love, and had helped one another bear the burdens of life. Zeus, the High King of the Olympian gods, and Hermes, messenger of the gods, traveled the land in disguise, asking for food and rest; but at a thousand homes they were rudely turned away. However, at the little cottage of Philemon and Baucis, the gods were cheerfully welcomed. Although the couple had little, they gave all the food they had, not knowing that they were feeding immortal gods. But when their wine-cups magically refilled every time the gods took a drink, Philemon and Baucis realized the truth. The gods asked the couple to follow them up a nearby hill, and there, Philemon and Baucis saw a terrible flood inundate everything except their house — which transformed into a golden palace, a shrine to Zeus. There, Philemon and Baucis spent their days as priests in the shrine, until they both died at the same moment and were changed into intertwining trees that will live forever. As the great Roman poet Ovid said of Philemon and Baucis, "They now are gods, who served the gods."

Modern Example: Philemon Beecher Van Trump (1839-1916), American author and mountain climber, with several notable sites in Yosemite National Park, California, named after him.

Philip *(FILL-up)* The Friend of Horses

Philip V (221 B.C.-179 B.C.) was the King Of Macedon, an ancient Greek-influenced kingdom. His father was King Demetrius II of Macedon, and his mother was Queen Chryseis of Macedon. Although Philip's legendary ancestor, Alexander the Great, had conquered the known world, Macedonian military power had faded significantly by the time Philip was born; and when Rome invaded, Macedon was defeated, and annexed as a province of the Roman Empire.

Modern Example: Philip Alfred Mickelson (1970-), American championship professional golfer.

Philomelus *(fill-LAHM-uh-lus)* The One Who Loves Leisure-Time

Philomelus was the Roman name for Philomelos, a Greek god of farming. His father was Jasius, a god of grain; and his mother was Ceres, goddess of the harvest. Philomelus made the first chariot and the first plow, and gave both devices to humankind. As a reward, the gods placed him in heaven as the constellation Bootes.

Related Names: Bootes, Eubouleus.

Phineas *(FIN-ee-us)* The One Who Comes from the Serpent's Mouth

King Phineas was the ruler of the ancient land of Thrace (present-day Bulgaria). Phineas could accurately predict the future, infuriating the gods, who liked to

Names for Babies Destined to Be Warriors

Girls

Athena • Dolores • Eris • Harpina • Hecate • Larina
Lyssa • Minerva • Myrina • Victoria • Zoe

Boys

Achilles • Agamemnon • Ajax • Alexander • Ares • Aron • Basil
Dameon • Hector • John • Julius • Marcus • Mars • Memnon
Prax • Odysseus • Ulysses

keep secrets. Zeus, High King of the gods on Mount Olympus, Greece, banished Phineas to a desert island where he could never enjoy his food, because the monstrous winged Harpies snatched the food away. However, when the hero Jason, Prince of Iolchus, and his warriors (the Argonauts) arrived, they defeated the Harpies. In gratitude, Phineas revealed how Jason could safely sail through the Symplegades, the crashing rocks that destroyed passing ships.

Related Names: Phineus.

Pietro *(pee-AY-tro)* The One Who Is a Rock

Prince Pietro Giuseppe Paleologo (1673-1706) of Italy was a member of the Palaiologos family, the dynasty that had ruled the Byzantine Empire from 1259-1453. Byzantium, located on the Strait of Bosphorus in the Near East, was a Greek-speaking city-state which became the new seat of the Eastern Roman Empire, the "Nova Roma," after Rome itself was conquered and sacked in A.D. 410.

Related Names: Peter.

Plato *(PLAY-tow)* The One Who Has Broad Shoulders

King Plato (2nd Century B.C.) was the ruler of Greco-Bactria (in present-day Afghanistan), a Greek-influenced nation whose greatest city was Ai Khanoum, destroyed by invaders in the 2nd Century B.C. Plato was the younger brother of Eucratides I, Greco-Bactria's greatest ruler, who was murdered in 145 B.C., thus enabling Plato to come to power.

Modern Example: Plato, the nickname of Brazilian soccer player Jose Manuel Vargas (1989-).

Polydeuces *(pol-ee-DOO-suz, pol-ee-DOO-seez)* The Sweet One

Polydeuces (Pollux) and his twin brother Castor (Kastor) were the Dioscuri, the gods of travelers, and of what we now call St. Elmo's Fire, a discharge of electrical plasma during thunderstorms. The father of Polydeuces and Castor was Zeus, King of the immortal gods of Mount Olympus, in Greece; and their mother was Queen Leda of the Greek city-state of Sparta. When the twins died, Zeus placed them in heaven as the Gemini Constellation.

Related Names: Pollux, Polydeukes.

Pontus *(PON-tus)* The One Who Is the Ocean

Pontus was the ocean, one of the first and most elemental of the ancient Greek gods. His sole parent was Gaia, the earth. He married Thalassa, a goddess of the sea, and produced the countless fish in the sea, as well as the many sea-divinities worshipped by the Greeks.

Related Names: Pontos.

Modern Example: Pontus Hanson (1894-1962), Swedish swimmer and Olympic champion in the 1908 Olympics in London, Great Britain, and the 1912 Olympics in Stockholm, Sweden.

Porphyrion *(por-FEER-ee-un)* The One Who Surges Forward

Porphyrion was one of the Gigantes, the hundred giants whose mother was Gaia, the earth, and whose father was Uranus, the sky. The armored Gigantes, whose legs were huge snakes, rebelled against Zeus, High King of the immortal gods who lived on Mount Olympus, Greece. But when the demi-god Heracles entered the war on his father Zeus's side, the Gigantes were annihilated. However, the

Gigantes' blood magically transformed into the people of the nation of Thrace (present-day Bulgaria).

Modern Example: The Porphyrion Fire Insurance Company, employer of Mr. Leonardn Bast, a character in the 1910 novel Howards End, *written by British author E. M. Forster (Edward Morgan Forster) (1879-1970).*

Portunus *(POR-chuh-nus, por-TOON-us)* The Good Harbor

Portunus was the Roman name for Palaimon, a child-god of the oceans. Portunus's mother was Ino, also called Leukothea, the mortal princess who became a sea goddess; and his father was Athamas. Portunus began life as Melikertes, a happy boy with loving parents. But when his mortal parents tried to raise the infant Bacchus, god of wine, Queen Juno of the Olympian gods drove Athamas insane. He tried to kill his family, and Ino and Melikertes fled, but fell from a cliff into the ocean. The gods instantly changed them into the sea gods Palaimon and Leukothea, saving their lives. Afterward, Portunus was often seen happily riding on the backs or dolphins, guiding passing ships to safe harbors.

Related names: Palaemon, Palaimon.
Modern Example: The USS Portunus, a United States Navy landing craft built in 1944, and decommissioned in 1952.

Porus *(POR-us)* The One Who Serves His Own Purposes

Porus was the Greek god of serving one's own purposes, of doing whatever was good for oneself. Porus's sole parent was Metis, goddess of wise advice. Porus was always scheming to take advantage of good, fair-minded people, so that he could advance; always seeking advice that could bring profit to him.

Related Names: Poros.

Poseidon *(po-SY-dun)* The One Who Gives Water from the Wooded Mountains; Lord of Giving; The Earth-Shaker

Poseidon, or Neptune, was the god of the sea, earthquakes, and horses. To the ocean-going Greeks, he may have been equal in importance to his brother Zeus, King of the gods. The Greeks of Corinth and other city-states worshipped Poseidon as their primary god, praying to him for calm waters as they colonized new islands. To insure the colonists' safety, Poseidon was thought to work closely with Apollo, god of prophecy, to ensure safe passage for colonists.

But Poseidon's moods could change quickly, and when he was angry, he sent epilepsy and other diseases to afflict mankind. Worse, he could strike the earth with his trident and trigger deadly earthquakes and storms at sea.

Poseidon traveled his watery kingdom in a chariot pulled by giant seahorses or Tritons. His royal palace lay hidden on the sea-bottom, constructed of rare jewels and coral. Poseidon was a descendant of kings: His father was Cronus, King of the Titans; and his mother was Rhea, the Titan Queen. Cronus, Rhea, and the other Titans had once ruled in heaven, but had been defeated by Zeus and his Olympian gods. Cronus had always feared his children would depose him, so he swallowed each one, including Poseidon. But Rhea managed to save young Zeus, the future god-king, by swaddling a boulder in blankets and tricking Cronus into eating it. Rhea hid Zeus until he grew strong enough to return and force Cronus to vomit out the gods. Then Zeus and his new gods warred with the Titans, defeating them. Zeus gained dominion over heaven and earth, and gave his brother Hades control of the underworld, and his brother Poseidon dominion over the seas.

Poseidon's beautiful wife was Amphitrite, one of the fifty Nereid sea-nymphs who lived under the Mediterranean. Amphitrite's parents were Doris, goddess of river deltas, and gentle Nereus, the fish-tailed "Old Man of the Sea," god of fishing. Amphitrite is often depicted sitting in a chariot beside Poseidon, pulled by sea-gods called Tritons.

Related Names: Ennosigaios, Enosichthon, Neptune, Seischthon.
Modern Example: Poseidon "Postie" Paterson, a character in the Selby series of books by Austra-lian author Duncan Ball.

Prax *(PRAX)* The One Who Practices

Prax, a Greek warrior-hero, belonged to a family that included some of the great-est warriors in Greek history, including the legendary Achilles; Neoptolemus; and Pergamus. Pergamus had erected a temple to his ancestor Achilles near the Greek city-state of Sparta, and young Spartan warriors stopped to worship Achil-les there, before going to war.

Modern Example: Prax, a character in an episode of the science fiction television series, Star Trek: Voyager, *a show which premiered in 1995, and was created by Rick Berman, Michael Piller, and Jeri Taylor.*

Prometheus *(pro-MEE-thee-us)* The One Who Thinks Ahead

Prometheus was one of the Titans, the original Greek deities who ruled in heaven before being overthrown by Zeus and his Olympian gods. Prometheus's father was Iapetus, the Titan god of the human lifespan; and his mother was Clymene, the Titan goddess of fame. Prometheus formed men from soil and water, then gave them the god-like gift of fire — against the royal command of Zeus. Zeus retaliated by ordering the gods to create Pandora, the first woman, so that she and her descendants would plague mankind forever. (Note: This was an ancient, baseless, and chauvinist concept.) Prometheus was ordered chained to the Caucasus Mountains dividing Europe from Asia; there, his liver was eaten daily by an eagle, and re-grown nightly, so that his punishment could continue forever. Years later, the Greek hero Heracles shot the eaagle and freed Prometheus.

Related Names: Desmotes.
Modern Example: Prometheus and Bob, an American stop-animated segment of the Nickelodeon Animation Studios television program, KaBlam!, *broadcast from 1996-2000.*

Proteus *(PRO-tee-us)* The First One

Proteus was one of the ancient Greeks' earliest ocean-gods, known as the "old man of the sea," whose wisdom allowed him to predict the future His sole parent was Poseidon, god-king of the oceans. Proteus lived on Lemnos, a Greek island, as well as on Pharos Island in Egypt. Gods and mortals who wanted Proteus to tell their future had to grab him while he sunned himself on the beach. He usually tried to wriggle away by changing himself into a sea creature, but if a questioner was persistent enough, Proteus would answer honestly. He was the one who told Thetis, a sea goddess, that her son, the Greek hero Achilles, would be killed in the Trojan War (waged in the 12th Century B.C.). As Proteus predicted, Achilles never returned.

Related Names: Melikertes.

Pythias *(PITH-ee-us)* The One from Pythia

Pythias (4th Century B.C.) and his companion Damon were students of the Greek mathematician and philosopher Pythagoras of Samos. The two men went to the city-state of Syracuse, on the island of Sicily, to further their education. But once there, King Dionysius I imprisoned Pythias on trumped-up charges, and set a date for his execution. Pythias requested a reprieve, that he might sail home, say his good-byes, then return for punishment. When Dionysius denied the request, Damon offered to take his place until Pythias returned. Dionysius relented — if Damon agreed to die if Pythias fled. The bargain was struck. But on the day of execution, Pythias was still absent. As Damon was about to be killed, Pythias appeared and told how he had to battle pirates, and swim the oceans, to return in time to save Damon. King Dionysius was deeply moved, and kept Pythias and Damon for many years as trusted advisors, eventually allowing them to marry into the royal family.

Quietus *(KWI-uh-tus)* The One Who Is Peaceful

Quietus (Titus Fulvius Iunius Quietus) (?-A.D. 261) was labeled a usurper, a person who tried to become an Emperor of Rome by military conquest. Quietus's father was Fulvius Macrianus, a Roman general; and his mother was the noblewoman Iunia. Quietus was a general like his father, and was proclaimed Emperor by his troops in A.D. 260. However, when Quietus's armies marched against the legal Emperor Gallienus, Quietus was defeated.

Modern Example: Quietus 2, a Canadian band that performed from 1980-1986.

Remus *(REEM-us)* The One Who Is From Rome

Remus (c. 771 B.C.-c.753 B.C.), and his twin brother Romulus (c. 771 B.C.-c. 717 B.C.), were the legendary demi-gods who established the city-state of Rome — and therefore the Roman Empire. Mars, the Roman god of war, was the twins' father; and their mother was Rhea Silvia, a descendant of Anaeas, the hero of ancient Troy. According to legend, a female wolf allowed the infants Remus and Romulus to drink her milk, raising them as wild children until they could be tamed and educated by humans. Romulus went on to serve as Rome's first ruler.

Rex *(REX)* The One Who Is King

Rex is used as an alternate name for several mythological personages:

Title	English Meaning	Roman Name	Greek Name
Oedipus Rex	*Oedipus the King*	*Oedipus*	*Oedipus*
Rex Infernus	*King of Fire*	*Pluto*	*Hades*
Rex Silentum	*King of Silence*	*Pluto*	*Hades*
Rex Superum	*King of Heaven*	*Jupiter*	*Zeus*
Rex Umbrarum	*King of Shadows*	*Pluto*	*Hades*

Modern Example: Rex Lasat Navarrete (1969-), Philippine-American writer and comedian.

Richard *(RICH-urd)* The One Who is Brave and Powerful

Richard Chapelle, descended from Dr. Giovanni Chapelle Paleologo (1835-1901), was a member of the Palaiologos family, the dynasty that had ruled the Byzantine Empire from 1259-1453. Byzantium, located on the Strait of Bosphorus in the Near East, was a Greek-speaking city-state which became the new seat of the Eastern Roman Empire, the "Nova Roma," after Rome itself was conquered and sacked in A.D. 410.

Modern Example: Richard Rodgers (1902-1979), an American composer of more than 900 published songs and 40 Broadway musical.

Risus *(RYE-zuss)* The One Who Is Laughter

Risus was the Roman name for Gelus, the ancient Greek god of cheerfulness and laughter. Greeks would traditionally raise their wine-cups and offer a toast to Risus before drinking. Risus would fill the heart of all true believers with joy.

Related Names: Gelos, Gelus.

Modern Example: Risus, an online role-playing game created by American writer and publisher S. John Ross (Samuel John Ross) (1971-).

Romanos *(ro-MAHN-ohss)* The Roman

Romanos (Romanos I Lekapenos) (c. A.D. 870-A.D. 948) was an Emperor of Byzantium. Byzantium, located on the Strait of Bosphorus in the Near East, was a Greek-speaking city-state which became the new seat of the Eastern Roman Empire, the "Nova Roma," after Rome itself was conquered and sacked in 410 A.D. Romanos's father Theophylaktos had been an Armenian soldier in the Byzantine army, and Romanos followed his father into the military, eventually becoming a general, then Emperor in A.D. 920.

Romulus *(ROM-yoo-lus)* The One Who Is From Rome

Romulus (c. 771 B.C.-c. 717 B.C.), and his twin brother Remus (c. 771 B.C.-c.753 B.C.), were the legendary demi-gods who established the city-state of Rome — and therefore the Roman Empire. Mars, the Roman god of war, was the twins' father; and their mother was Rhea Silvia, a descendant of Anaeas, the hero of ancient Troy. According to legend, a female wolf allowed the infants Romulus and Remus to drink her milk, raising them as wild children until they could be tamed and educated by humans. Romulus went on to serve as Rome's first ruler.

Names for Babies Destined to Be Wealthy

Girls

Agatha • Claire • Cleone • Evarne • Lachesis • Laurine
Leanira • Paula • Prima • Rosmerta

Boys

Aries • Hermes • Kairos • Khryses • Mercury • Minyas
Montanus • Remus • Romulus • Shai • Tempus • Tiberius

Modern Example: Romulus Zachariah Linney (1930-), award-winning American author, educator, and playwright.

Sangarius *(san-GAIR-ee-us)* The One Who Is the Sangarius River

Sangarius was the Roman name for Saggarios, a Greek river god who personified the Sangarius River in ancient Anatolia (modern-day Turkey). Sangarius's father was Oceanus, god of the river that encircled the earth; and his mother was Tethys, goddess of the earth's sources of fresh water. Sangarius got his name from a mortal, Sangas, who insulted Juno, Queen of the Olympian gods, and was transformed into a river. Sangarius was known to completely change course, to honor the dead.

Related Names: Saggarios.

Modern Example: Sangarius, a merman character in the online role-playing game, Achaea, Dreams of Dvine Lands, *released in 1997 by Iron Realms Entertainment.*

Saturn *(SAT-urn)* The One Who is Time

Saturn was the King of the Titans — the original deities who ruled in heaven, before being overthrown by Jupiter and his Olympian gods. Saturn was the god of the steady movement of time, as well as the decay caused by the time's passage. Saturn had gained heaven's throne by murdering his father Uranus, god of the sky. But Saturn secretly lived in terror of a well-known prediction, that one of his offspring would eventually depose him. So, he ate each god and goddess as he or she was born. But his wife Opis, goddess of motherhood, gave Saturn a huge stone wrapped in a diaper to eat, instead of her son Jupiter, tricking Saturn. When Jupiter came of age, he led his Olympian gods against Saturn and the Titans, defeating them, and imprisoning them in Tartarus, the underworld of the dead. However, centuries later, Jupiter granted the Titans their freedom, and made Saturn the ruler of the Islands of the Blessed, a heavenly afterlife. The Romans honored Saturn by naming the week-day Saturday after him and by celebrating his annual festival, the Saturnalia.

Related Names: Aeon, Chronos, Cronus, Kronos, Saturnus.

Modern Example: Sailor Saturn, also known as Hotaru Tomoe, in the Japanese anime television series, Sailor Moon, *created by Japanese artist Naoko Takeuchi.*

Scorpio *(SKOR-pee-oh)* The Scorpion

Scorpio was a fierce scorpion "of very great size." Scorpio's sole parent was Gaia, the earth. Gaia ordered Scorpio to destroy Orion, one of the Gigantes, the huge men who wreaked havoc on earth. After an epic battle, Scorpio stung Orion to death. Jupiter placed Scorpio and Orion in heaven, as companion constellations — the constellation Scorpio, and the constellation Orion.

Related Names: Scorpius, Skorpios.

Severus *(SEV-ur-us)* The One Who Is Severe

Severus (Lucius Septemus Severus) (A.D. 146-A.D. 211) was an Emperor of Rome. A native of the city of Leptis Magna (in modern-day Tunisia, Africa), Severus's father was Publius Septimus Geta, a nobleman of the Moors, an ethnic people of North Africa; and his mother was Fulvia Pia, a Roman. Severus eventually became a Senator, then a successful military commander. When his loyal troops proclaimed him Emperor in A.D. 193, Severus journeyed to Rome, had the Emperor Didius Iulianus killed, and ascended to the throne.

Modern Example: Severus Snape, a character in the Harry Potter series of books, by British author J.K. Rowling (Joanne Rowling) (1965-).

Shai *(SHAY)* The One Who Is Destined and Ordained

In ancient Greek mythology, as adopted from the earlier Egyptian culture, the god Shai — also called Agathodaemon — was the spirit associated with destiny and good fortune. The Greeks regularly toasted the god's health, and he became known as The Good God.

Related Names: Agathodaemon, Agathodaimon, Agathos Deos, Sai.

Silenus *(suh-LEEN-us)* Moving Here and There, Through the Wine

Silenus was the Roman name for Silenos, an ancient Greek satyr or nature god, and the god of intoxication and grape-pressing devices. Silenus's father was Mercury, messenger of the gods; and his mother was Terra, the earth. The fat old Silenus was always drunk, riding a braying jackass, as he accompanied Bacchus, the young god of wine, on his journeys across the earth. When Silenus and

Mercury went to Phrygia (modern-day Bulgaria), Silenus got hopelessly lost; but because the mortal King Midas helped Silenus, Bacchus was quite grateful, and gave Midas the power to turn things to gold, just by touching them.

Related Names: Pyrrhichus, Silenos

Silvanus *(Sil-VAN-us, SIL-vuh-nus)* The One from the Forest

The "goat-footed" Silvanus was an ancient Roman genius loci, or nature guardian-god, who preserved the earth's forests. Silvanus's father was Jupiter, High King of the immortal gods; and his mother was Jupiter's lover, Aex, a nymph or nature goddess. Silvanus was related to the earlier Selvans, a nature god identified with the Etruscans, an Italian culture that predated Rome. Silvanus was a companion of Faunus, the god of shepherds and woodlands. Silvanus became a legendary hero when he changed into a sea-monster and battled Typhon, the hurricane, thus rescuing Jupiter and the gods from injury. Jupiter honored Silvanus's heroism by placing him in heaven as the constellation Capricorn.

Related Names: Aegipan.

Sirius *(SEER-ee-us)* The One Who Is the Dog Star; The Glowing One

Sirius was the Roman name for Seirios, the ancient Greek god who personified the brilliant Dog Star in the constellation Canis Major (The Larger Dog). The Greeks believed Sirius brought scorching heat and diseases to earth, and that it was mankind's duty to offer sacrifices to keep the god appeased.

Related Names: Aster Cuon, Aster Kyon, Aster Sirios, Canicula, Kyon Khryseos, Seirios, Sirios, Sothos.

Modern Example: Sirius Orion Black, a character in the Harry Potter series of books, written by British author J.K. Rowling (pen-name of Joanne Rowling) (1965-).

Sol *(SOUL, SOLL)* The Sun

Sol was the Roman name for Helios, the ancient Greek god who was the sun. Sol's father was Hyperion, god of light; and his mother was Thea, goddess of light and vision. Sol's shining temple was located in the East, far beyond the boundaries of mortal kingdoms. Apollo, god of prophecy, escorted Sol across the sky each day in a gleaming chariot, pulled by four immortal horses. But one day, Apollo foolishly granted his demi-god son, Phaëthon, a chance to drive the horses of Sol. Phaëthon, being half mortal, could not control the magnificent steeds, and he brought Sol close to earth, burning cities to ashes. Jupiter, High King of the gods, witnessed this disaster and swiftly killed Phaëthon with a thunderbolt.

Related Names: Helios, Helius.
Modern Example: Sol LeWitt (1928-2007), American conceptualist and minimalist artist.

Solon *(SOL-un, SO-lon)* The One Who Has Great Wisdom

Solon (c. 638 B.C.-558 B.C.), who lived in the ancient Greek city-state of Athens, was one of the Seven Sages — the wisest men of the ancient world, according to the Greek philosopher Plato.

Solon's father was the noble patrician Execestides, renowned for his compassion. Solon rose through the political ranks and was eventually named Archon Eponymous, one of three ruling monarchs of Athens. Solon helped write Athens's Constitution and its new law codes. One of Solon's favorite quotes was, "I grow old learning something new every day."

Modern Example: Solon Ménos (1859-1918), French-educated Haitian statesman, writer, and ambassador to the United States.

Stephanos *(steh-FAH-nos)* The One Who Is a Crown

Stephanos was the Greek god who personified the heavenly Constellation Corona. The Greeks named several stars in this constellation, including the Crown of Ariadne, the Crown of Dionysis, and the Crown of Theseus.

Related Names: Steven.
Modern Example: Stephanos Dragoumis (1842-1923), a Prime Minister of Greece in 1909.

Strymon *(STRY-mun)* The One Who Is the Strymon River

Strymon was a Greek river god, who personified the Strymon River in ancient Thrace (present-day Bulgaria), as well as being a King of Thrace. Strymon's father was Oceanus, god of the river that encircled the earth; and his mother was

Tethys, goddess of the earth's sources of fresh water. The Strymon River had previously been a useful waterway, but after Strymon insulted the Greek demi-god Heracles (Hercules), Heracles filled it with boulders.

Modern Example: Strymon, a character portrayed by Argentine actor Victor Bo in the 1985 American-Argentinian film, Barbarian Queen, *directed by Argentine filmmaker Héctor Olivera.*

Talos *(TAL-ohs)* The One Who is the Sun

Talos was a huge bronze robot or automaton, created by Hephaestus, the Greek god of volcanoes and blacksmiths. Talos was built to resemble a handsome young Greek hero, except that he was made of shimmering metal. Zeus, High King of the immortal gods on Mount Olympus, was so impressed with Talos that he gave the living machine as a gift to Europa (a nymph or nature goddess), to safeguard her on her island-home of Crete. Talos walked completely around the island each day, repelling and killing bandits. But he met his match when Jason, the Prince of Iolchus, arrived with the sorceress Medea, who destroyed Talos with her spells.

Related Names: Talus.

Tantalus *(TANTLE-us)* The One Who Suspends the Sun in the Air

The Roman poet Ovid (43 B.C.-A.D. 17) said that Tantalus — called Tantalos by the ancient Greeks — was a mortal. But other ancient writers said Tantalus's father was Jupiter, High King of the immortal gods on Mount Olympus, Greece; and his mother was Plouto, a nymph or nature goddess. One day, Tantalus was invited by Jupiter to a feast on Mount Olympus. When he arrived, Tantalus stole ambrosia, the food of the gods, then boiled his son Pelops and offered him to the gods. The gods rejected the foul food, except for Ceres, goddess of grain. She was upset that her daughter Proserpina was missing, and being distracted, ate poor Pelops's shoulder. Jupiter resurrected Pelops and replaced his shoulder with ivory. As a punishment, Tantalus was banished to Hades, the underworld of the dead. His feet were immobilized in a pond, with tree-branches full of luscious fruit hanging just overhead. When he tried to pick the fruit, the branches moved up. When he bent to drink, the water went down. Also, a boulder hung suspended over his head, ready to fall at any moment. This was Tantalus's eternal punishment.

Related Names: Tantalos.

Modern Example: Tantalus Ebony, a character in the Charlie Bone series of books by British author Jenny Nimmo (1944-).

Taurus *(TAR-us, TOR-us)* The One Who Is a Bull

The Taurus Cretan was a magnificent bull, given by Poseidon the sea god to King Minos of the Greek island of Crete. Minos was ordered by Poseidon to sacrifice the bull to the gods, but Minos was so impressed with it that he put it out to pasture. Furious, Poseidon drove the animal insane, and it rampaged through Crete. Fortunately, the demi-god Heracles (Hercules) captured the bull and released it on the Greek seacoast, where it marauded through the kingdom of Marathon before the hero Theseus killed it.

Modern Example: Taurus Jabbar "The Bull" Sykes (1975-), professional heavyweight boxer.

Tempus *(TEMP-us)* The One Who Is Time

Tempus was the Roman god of opportunity and profit. His sole parent was Jupiter, High King of the immortal gods. Tempus, who was bald, had one very long lock of hair extending from his forehead, because as the god of opportunity, one had to quickly grab his hair, or one's fortune in life might be lost forever.

Related Names: Caerus, Kairos, Occasio.

Modern Example: Tempus, a time-traveling villain on the 1990s television series, Lois and Clark: The New Adventures of Superman, *created by American writer Deborah Joy Levine.*

Tereus *(TAIR-ree-us, TAIR-roos)* The Smooth, Polished One

King Tereus was a ruler of Thrace (present-day Bulgaria). His father was Ares, the Greek god of war; and his mother was Cyrene, a nymph or nature goddess. Tereus married Princess Procne of Thebes and produced a son, Itys. However, when Tereus assaulted his sister Philomela, both Procne and Philomela killed poor Itys. Before Tereus could seek revenge, the gods changed Procne and Philomela into immortal songbirds. However, Ares changed Tereus into an immortal hawk, so that Tereus, Procne, and Philomela could battle forever.

Modern Example: Terius "The Dream" Nash, music producer and husband of singer-songwriter Nivea Nash.

Thales *(THAY-leez)* The One Who Blossoms

Thales (c. 624 B.C.-546 B.C.), who lived in the ancient city-state of Miletos (present-day Turkey), was one of the Seven Sages — the wisest men of the ancient world, according to the Greek philosopher Plato. Thales's father was Examyas, an aristocrat from Phoenicia (present-day Tunisia), and a descendant of King Cadmus of Tyre; and his mother was Cleobulina, a Phoenician noblewoman. Thales was one of Greece's earliest scientists, and one of its greatest philosophers. One of Thales's favorite quotes was, "Know thyself."

Modern Example: Thales Leites Lourenco (1981-), a Brazilian middleweight martial-artist.

Thanatos *(THAN-uh-tos)* The One Who Is Death

Thanatos, or Letus, was the winged Greek god of peaceful, natural death. Thanatos's sole parent was Nyx, goddess of night. Thanatos was known for his compassion, and his gentle embrace that carried mortals to the next world; in this sense he was similar to his twin brother Hypnus, god of peaceful slumber.

Related Names: Letus, Mors, Thanatus.
Modern Example: Thanatos, a band that premiered in 1993.

Thaumas *(TAH-muss)* The One Who Is a Miracle

Thaumas was the ancient Greek god of the ocean's breath-taking marvels. Thaumas's father was Pontos, the ocean; and his mother was Gaia, the earth. Thaumas and Electra had many daughters, including the "swift-footed" Iris, goddess of rainbows; and the winged avenging goddesses known as the Harpies.

Theodore *(THEE-uh-dor)* The Gift of God

Theodore (Theodore I Laskaris) (c. 1174-1221) was an Emperor of the Nicaean Empire, a colony established by Byzantium. Byzantium, located on the Strait of Bosphorus in the Near East, was a Greek-speaking city-state which became the new seat of the Eastern Roman Empire, the "Nova Roma," after Rome itself was conquered and sacked in 410 A.D. Theodore's mother was a Byzantine noble-woman, Joanna Karatzaina; and his father was a Byzantine nobleman, Manuel Laskaris. Theodore married the Byzantine Emperor's daughter, Anna Angelina, and soon won fame as a military leader.

Modern Example: Theodore Roosevelt (1858-1919), twenty-sixth president of the United States.

Thermodon *(THURM-uh-don)* The One Who Is the Thermodon River

Thermodon was a Greek river god, who personified the Thermodon River in ancient Anatolia (present-day Turkey), near Thermiskyra, legendary home of the Amazon warrior-women. Thermodon's father was Oceanus, god of the river that encircled the earth; and his mother was Tethys, goddess of the earth's sources of fresh water.

Theseus *(THEE-soos)* The One Who Sets a Foundation

The demi-god hero Theseus rose to become a King of Athens — Athens be-ing perhaps the greatest city-state in ancient Greece. Theseus's mother was Aethra, goddess of light; and his father was Aegeas, an earlier King of Athens.

Theseus's greatest exploit was his destruction of the savage Minotaur of Crete, a half-bull, half-human monstrosity. King Minos of Crete had ordered the construction of the Labyrinth, a great stone maze where victims from Athens and other city-states were sacrificed to the Minotaur. Princess Ariadne was Minos's daughter, and one day, while she watched a group of Athenian victims being hauled to the Labyrinth, she spotted the handsome Theseus and fell in love with him. She offered to rescue him in exchange for a promise that he would take her to Athens and marry her. He agreed, and she gave him a mystic sword to kill the Minotaur, and a ball of red wool to use in finding his way back through the Labyrinth. After Theseus slew the Minotaur and found his way out of the maze, he and Ariadne fled by sea. However, when their ship put-in at the island of Naxos, Theseus and his crew abandoned Ariadne there — but not before she cursed Theseus. The curse worked, because Theseus had promised his father Aegeas that his ship would display a white sail for triumph, or a black sail for death; and Theseus forgot to raise the white sail as he returned. Aegeas spotted the black sail from afar, and leapt from a hill into the ocean, forever after known as the Agean Sea. Meanwhile, back on Naxos, Dionysus, the god of wine, took pity on Ariadne and married her. Theseus returned and founded a great ruling dynasty in Athens, building the Parthenon Temple to Athena which still stands to this day.

Thomas *(TAH-mus)* The Twin

Thomas (Thomas Palaiologos) (1409-1465) was the Despot or supreme ruler of Morea, a swath of Greece belonging to the Byzantine Empire. Byzantium, located on the Strait of Bosphorus in the Near East, was a Greek-speaking city-state which became the new seat of the Eastern Roman Empire, the "Nova Roma," after Rome itself was conquered and sacked in A.D. 410. When Byzantium was finally conquered in 1460 by the Turks under Mehmed II the Conqueror, Thomas became perhaps the only member of the royal family who might still become Emperor of Byzantium. However, Thomas fled with his wife and children to Rome, thus effectively bringing the Byzantine Empire to an end.

Modern Example: Thomas Thomas (1917-1998), Indian physician, cardiac surgeon, and poet.

Thrasus *(THRAY-sus)* The One Who Is a Reckless Daredevil

Thrassus was the Roman name for Thrasos, the Greek god of reckless, daredevil behavior. Thrasus's sole parent was Discordia, goddess of discord and strife. Thrassus visited certain mortals when they were just born, and instilled them with the spirit of arrogance and rashness.

Related Names: Thrasos.

Thrax *(THRAX)* The Gladiator from Thrace

Thrax was a Prince of Edonia, a kingdom in Thrace (modern-day Bulgaria). Thrax's father was Ares, the Greek god of war; and his mother is unknown. Thrax was a conqueror, plundering many Greek islands. However, Thrax met his match when he confronted the god Apollo on the island of Delos. Apollo retaliated by infecting Thrax and his armies with fatal leprosy.

Modern Example: Thrax, an extraterrestrial character who appeared on the science fiction television program, Star Trek: Deep Space Nine, created by American filmmakers Rick Berman and Michael Piller.

Tiberius *(tie-BEER-ee-us)* The One from the Tiber River

Tiberius Caesar Augustus (42 B.C.-A.D. 37) was an Emperor of Rome. Tiberius's father was Tiberius Claudius Nero, a high government official; and his mother was Livia Drusilla. Tiberius married Julia the Elder, daughter of another Roman Emperor, Augustus, creating the Julio-Claudian family, which ruled the Roman Empire from 27 B.C.-A.D. 68. Tiberius has also been called a great military strategist and conqueror.

Tigris *(TYE-grus)* The One Who Is the Tigris River

Tigris was a Greek river god, who personified the Tigris River in ancient Assyria (present-day Iraq). Tigris's father was Oceanus, god of the river that encircled the earth; and his mother was Tethys, goddess of the earth's sources of fresh water.

Timotheus *(tim-uh-THEE-us)* The One Who Honors God

Prince Timotheus was the monarch of the Asian city-state of Heraclea Pontica (modern-day Turkey), named in honor of the Greek warrior-hero Heracles (Hercules). Heraclea Pontica bordered Megara, a Greek city-state. Timotheus's father was King Clearchus, a legendary tyrant.

Related Names: Timothy.

Triton *(TRY-tun)* The Third One

Triton was a one of many Greek gods of the ocean. Triton's mother was Amphitrite, a sea nymph or nature goddess; and his father was Poseidon, god-king of the oceans. Triton was often portrayed as a merman, with one or two fish-tails, and an upper half that was human in appearance. Using his mystic staff and conch shell, Triton controlled sea-creatures and ocean currents. Lake Tritonis, in

Libya (the Greek name for all of North Africa) was named for the god Triton. Once, Triton helped the Greek hero Jason, Prince of Iolcus (a Greek city-state), find the Golden Fleece — an enchanted sheepskin and a symbol of power. Triton lived with Poseidon and Amphitrite in a palace made of gold, at the bottom of the Mediterranean Sea, far from mortal eyes.

There was also a race of sea gods and goddesses called Tritons. These were children of Triton and were compared to mermen/mermaids, or fish-tailed horses, who pulled the chariot of Poseidon, god of the oceans.

Modern Example: King Triton, ruler of the undersea kingdom of Atlantica, in the 1989 Walt Disney Feature Animation film, The Little Mermaid, *directed by American filmmakers Ron Clements and John Musker.*

Tychon *(TY-kon)* The One Who Bears Fruit

Tychon was one of the Daimones, the Greek woodland gods or Satyrs who were always depicted as being very excited, ready for virtually anything. The sole parent of the Daimones was Dionysus, the Greek god of wine and drunkenness.

Related Names: Tykhon.

Typhon *(TY-fonn)* The Hurricane; The Tornado

The monstrous Typhon was an immortal fire-breathing Draco, a dragon. Typhon's father was Tartarus, the underworld; and his mother was Gaia, the earth. Typhon had a humanlike upper body, except for his hundred heads — one man's head, and ninety-nine heads of beasts such as lions, bulls, and snakes. Typhon also had huge scaly wings, enormous snakes as legs, and a hundred venomous snakes for fingers. Typhon could produce terrible storms, or shoot brilliant firestorms at heaven.

Related Names: Typhoeus, Typhon.

Ulysses *(yoo-LISS-eez)* The One Who Is Hatred Itself

Ulysses was the Roman name for Odysseus, a legendary King of Ithaca, an ancient Greek city-state. Ulysses's grandfather was Arcesius, a legendary King of Ithaca. Ulysses was hailed by the Greeks as a noble warrior, a reputation he reinforced during the Trojan War, a bloody conflict fought in the 12th Century B.C. against the armies of the ancient city-state of Troy (modern-day Turkey).

According to the Greek poet Homer (8th Century B.C.), in his epic poem, *The Iliad*, the Trojan War began when Prince Paris of Troy, brother of Hector, ran off with the beautiful Queen Helen, wife of King Menelaus of Sparta. Menelaus allied with other Greek kings and their armies, and the Greeks sailed to Troy in a thousand ships to wage war for ten years. In the end, the Greeks won the war because Ulysses convinced the Greeks to build an immense wooden horse, the symbol of Troy, and leave it hollow inside. Greek soldiers hid in the horse, and the other Greek armies sailed away — but only to hide, out of sight of the Trojans. The Trojans thought they had won the war, but Cassandra, a Trojan prophetess, begged the Trojans not to pull the statue into the city. Everyone thought she was insane and wheeled the statue through the gates. That night, the Greeks exited the Trojan Horse, opened the gates of Troy for their waiting armies, and destroyed the city. However, Ulysses could not enjoy his triumph, because it took him another ten years to return home, a story told by Homer in, *The Odyssey*. Ulysses battled monsters, contended with the immortal gods, and traveled to Hades itself, before he rejoined his beloved wife Penelope and son Telemachus.

Uranus *(YER-uh-nus)* The One Who Never Tires

Uranus was the Roman name for Ouranos, the "ethereal" blue sky, which the ancient Greeks believed was a blue hemisphere covering the earth. Uranus's sole parent was Terra, the earth. Uranus ruled in heaven countless eons and was the father of the Titans, the original deities who governed the universe before being overthrown by Jupiter and his Olympian gods. But long before Jupiter was born, Uranus's son, the Titan god Saturn, overthrew Uranus and ruled the Titans for eons before Jupiter finally wrested control.

Related Names: Acmon, Akmon, Acmonides, Akmonides, Caelum, Caelus, and Ouranos.
Modern Example: Sailor Uranus, also known as Amara or Hakura Tenoh, in the Japanese anime television series, Sailor Moon, *created by Japanese artist Naoko Takeuchi.*

Xanthos *(ZAN-those)* The One Who Is the Zanthos River

Xanthos was a Greek river god, who personified the Xanthos River in ancient Anatolia (present-day Turkey). Xanthos's father was Oceanus, god of the river that encircled the earth; and his mother was Tethys, goddess of the earth's sources of fresh water. Once, when Xanthus felt he had been insulted by the Greek warrior-hero Achilles, he tried to drown Achilles in a flood; but Hera, Queen of the Olympian gods, sent Hephaestus, god of volcanoes and blacksmiths, to dry up the river.

Related Names: Scamander.

Xanthus *(ZAN-thus)* The One Who Is Blond and Bright

Xanthus and Balius were the Roman names for two noble, immortal horses in ancient Greek mythology. Both horses were owned by Neptune, god of the sea. The father of the two horses was Favonius, god of the west wind; and their mother was Podarge, one of the monstrous winged Harpies. Neptune gave Xanthus and Balius as a wedding gift to the Greek hero Peleus, when he married Thetis, goddess of the sea. The marriage produced Achilles, perhaps the greatest warrior of the Trojan War, fought between the Greeks and Trojans in the 12th Century B.C. Xanthus and Balius pulled Achilles's chariot in battle.

Related Names: Xanthos.

Yale *(YALE, YAY-lee)* The One Who is the Fertile Land

Yale was the Roman name for a fantastic creature in ancient Greek mythology. Yales roamed the savannahs of Ethiopia, Africa. It was the color of an African lion, as enormous as a hippopotamus, with the tail of an elephant, the head of a wild boar, and flexible horns about two feet long.

Related Names: Eale.

Modern Example: Yale University, a private academic institution established in 1701; a member of the Ivy League, an athletic association of eight East-coast universities.

Zagreus *(ZAG-ree-us)* The One Who Is Remembered by God

Zagreus was an ancient Greek god of mysterious religious ceremonies. His mother was the goddess Persephone, Queen of Hades, the underworld of the dead. His grandfather, Zeus, High King of the Olympian gods, loved his grandson Zagreus, and gave him some thunderbolts to play with. But jealous Hera, Zeus's wife, got some older gods, the Titans, to kill Zagreus. Zeus succeeded in bringing the child back to life.

Modern Example: Zagreus, a character in the 1930 novel, The Apes of God, *by British author Wyndham Lewis (1882-1957).*

Zelos *(ZELL-us, ZEEL-ohs)* The One Who Is Devoted to a Cause

Zelos was the god of passionate devotion, even rage and jealousy. His father was Pallas, the Titan god of war; and his mother was Styx, the river running through Hades. Zelos, together with his siblings — Bia, goddess of power; Cratus, god of strength; and Nike, goddess of triumph — upheld the divine laws of Zeus, High King of the immortal gods on Mount Olympus, Greece.

Related Names: Invidia, Zelus.
Modern Example: Zelos Wilder, a character in the video game, Tales of Symphonia, *created by the Japanese firm Namco Tales Studio.*

Zephyrus *(ZEFF-ur-us)* The West Wind

The "light-winged" Zephyrus was the god of the west wind, ushering in spring with fresh breezes. He was one of the brother-gods called the Anemoi, spirits who personified the winds that blew from the north, south, east, and west. Zephyrus's father was Astraeus, god of the stars; and his mother was Eos, the "rosy-fingered" goddess of the dawn. Zephyrus was often depicted with purple wings, to help him waft across the earth.

Related Names: Favonius, Zephyros.
Modern Example: Zephyrus, a Coyena — a sentient being, part coyote and part hyena, featured on the Web site Coyena Central.

Zeus *(ZOOS)* The Heavenly Father of the Gods

Zeus, or Jupiter, was the god of heaven, the ruler of the immortal gods and mortal men alike. Being all-powerful, Zeus answered to no one, and could use his thunderbolts — the flashes of light that streaked from the sky — to kill at his pleasure. Wearing his Aegis or armored breastplate, which had been forged by Hephaestus, god of blacksmiths, Zeus ruled over the palace of the gods on Mount Olympus, in Thessaly, Greece. He seized control of Olympus by overthrowing his father, Cronus, the greatest of the Titans or Elder Deities. Because Cronus had feared that one of his children might someday depose him, he ate them all at birth: Demeter, Hades, Hera, Hestia, and Poseidon. But Zeus's mother Rhea saved him by feeding Cronus a boulder wrapped in blankets, disguised as the infant Zeus. Then she hid Zeus in Crete, where he grew strong by drinking the milk of the goat Amalthea. Zeus returned to Cronus and forced him to vomit out all of Zeus's siblings, and together they waged war against the Titans. Victorious, Zeus imprisoned Cronus and the Titans in Tartarus, the underworld. Zeus then assigned the gods their duties: Demeter became goddess of the harvest; Hestia, goddess of the home and family; Poseidon, god of the seas; and Hades, god of the underworld and the dead. Finally, Zeus married Hera, who then became goddess of marriage and queen of the gods. Zeus cheated regularly on Hera, fathering many demigods, or half-human/half-divine children. Zeus's real-world Greek worshippers built an enormous gold-and-ivory statue to Zeus in the Temple of Zeus at Olympia; and this vanished monument is now called one of the Seven Wonders of the Ancient World.

Related Names: Agoraios, Horkios, Jove, Jupiter, Jupiter Optimus Maximus, Kronides Hypatos, Olympios, Panhellenios, Theos, Theos Hyspsistos, Xenios, Zeus Astrapaios, Zeus Heraios, Zeus Hypsistos, and Zeus Kronion.

Our Favorite Names

Girls' Names

_____   _____

_____   _____

_____   _____

_____   _____

_____   _____

_____   _____

Boys' Names

_____   _____

_____   _____

_____   _____

_____   _____

_____   _____

_____   _____